Sustainable Development in Rural China

Sustainable development in marginal areas, especially in those where rural poverty and environmental degradation are interwoven, is a great concern of development agencies worldwide, and much effort is put into development programmes, technology transfer schemes and so on. The problem is particularly acute in China, where increasing regional differences and inequality are eroding governmental poverty-reduction efforts and exacerbating ecological crises.

This book, based on extensive original research, examines the situation in China, especially in the Loess Plateau of Shaanxi province. It explores, in particular, by what means or mechanisms the poor join together to learn and adopt new technologies, and what farmer self-organising innovation means for development professionals improving their extension services in these areas.

Before his academic career, **Bin Wu** spent many years in the diverse environments of China's countryside, army campuses and urban factories. As an interdisciplinary scholar, Dr Wu has a wide range of research interests in the areas of environment, technology and society, with a special focus on the role of ordinary people. His current research at Cardiff University is to create and manage a global labour market database.

Sustainable Development in Rural China

Farmer innovation and self-organisation in marginal areas

Bin Wu

RoutledgeCurzon
Taylor & Francis Group
LONDON AND NEW YORK

First published 2003
by RoutledgeCurzon
11 New Fetter Lane, London EC4P 4EE

Simultaneously published in the USA and Canada
by RoutledgeCurzon
29 West 35th Street, New York, NY 10001

RoutledgeCurzon is an imprint of the Taylor & Francis Group

Typeset in Times New Roman by
Newgen Imaging Systems (P) Ltd, Chennai, India
Printed and bound in Great Britain by
MPG Books Ltd, Bodmin

British Library Cataloguing in Publication Data
A catalogue record for this book is available from the British Library

Library of Congress Cataloging in Publication Data
Wu, Bin, 1957 Nov. 6–
Sustainable development in rural China : farmer innovation and self-organisation in marginal areas / Bin Wu.
p. cm.
Includes bibliographical references and index.
1. Sustainable development – China. 2. Rural development projects – China. 3. China – Economic conditions – 1976–2000. 4. China – Economic conditions – 2000– I. Title.

HC430.E5W8 2003
338.951′07′091734–dc21 2002037180

ISBN 0–415–29719–2

To Huiping, Ruosi and Ruoxing

Contents

Figures

Tables

Boxes

Acknowledgements

Numerous people and institutions have contributed their support and help in the completion of this book. First, this book has resulted from a revision of my PhD dissertation. I would like to express my sincere thanks to the University of Hull in the UK, Shaanxi Academy of Social Sciences (SASS) and Zhidan county government in China for their support of my PhD research and fieldwork during the period of 1995–2000. Special thanks are due to Professor Jules Pretty, Dr Mike Parnwell, Professor Shi Guorui and He Jiang, whose influence has been important in forming and improving the theme of this book.

I would like to thank Professor Tony Lane and my other colleagues in the Seafarers International Research Centre at Cardiff University. Without their encouragement and support, I doubt whether I would have been able to complete this manuscript.

My thanks also to Peter Sowden, the commissioning editor at RoutledgeCurzon, Drs Fulong Wu and Yaping Wang, without their encouragement I might not have revised my dissertation into a book. In addition, Professor Stephen Feuchwang at the London School of Economics and Dr Jason Xiao at Cardiff School of Business have read through this manuscript and made constructive comments.

Finally, I owe a debt of gratitude to my wife, Bai Huiping, and my daughters, Ruosi and Ruoxing. My appreciation of their contribution can never be fully expressed.

Abbreviations

AT	appropriate technology
CCS	collective commune system
CDR	complexity, diversity and risk-prone
FCN	farmer communication networks
FEA	farmland-extensive agriculture
FSI	farmer self-organising innovation
FTA	farmers' technique association
GR	green revolution
HEA	highly efficient agriculture
HIC	household innovative capacity
HRS	household responsibility system
IKS	indigenous knowledge system
LIA	labour-intensive agriculture
LPI	local pillar industry
NBS	National Bureau of Statistics of China
NGO	non-governmental organisation
PR	participatory research
PRP	poverty reduction programme
RCS	rainfall collection system
SAD	Shaanxi Agriculture Development
SARO	Shaanxi Agricultural Regionalisation Office
SBS	Shaanxi Bureau of Statistics
SPRO	Shaanxi Poverty Reduction Office
SRL	sustainable rural livelihoods
SWRD	Shaanxi Water Resource Department
TT	technology transfer
TVE	township and village enterprise
ZARO	Zhidan Agricultural Regionalisation Office
ZCAD	Zhidan County Agricultural Department
ZCEG	Zhidan Chronicle Editor Group
ZPRO	Zhidan Poverty Reduction Office
ZPSO	Zhidan Planning and Statistics Office
ZRST	Zhidan Rural Survey Team

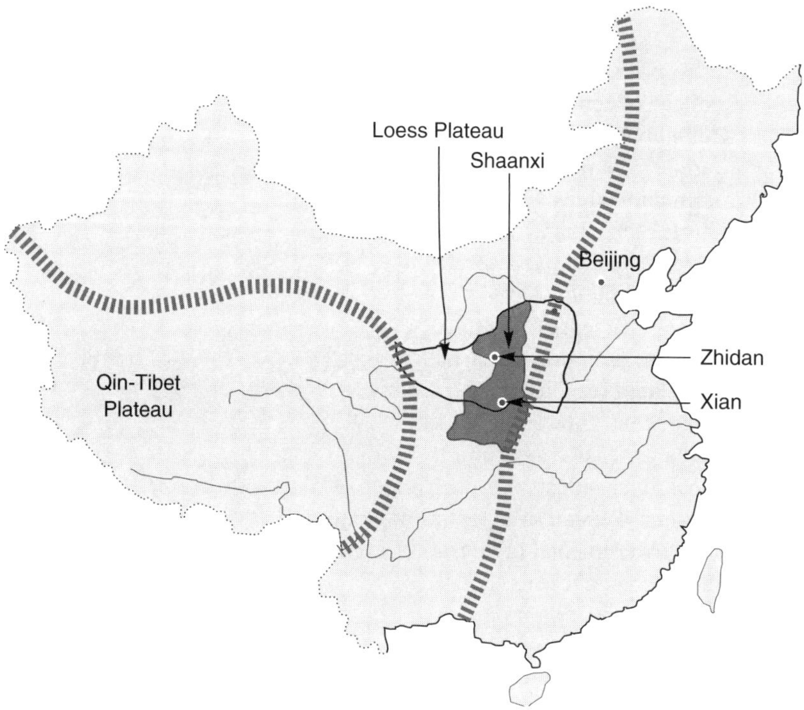

Map 1 Map of fieldwork location.

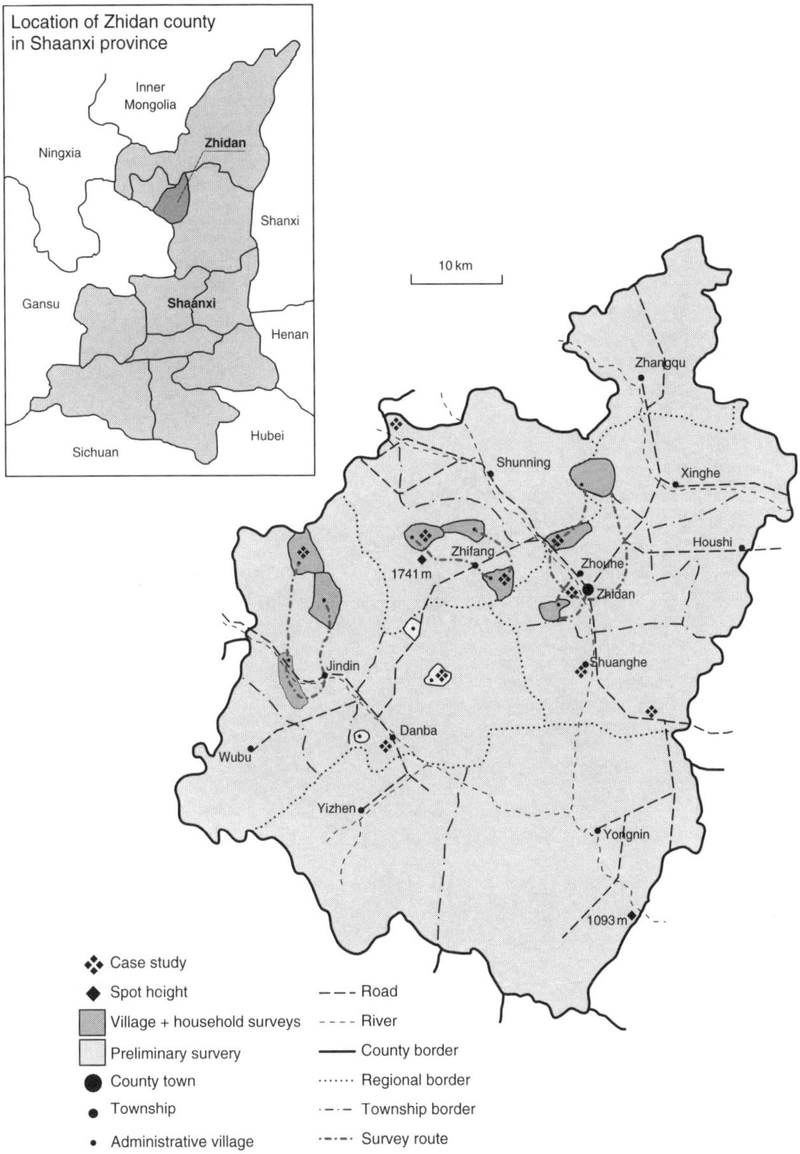

Map 2 Survey map of Zhidan.

1 Introduction

When *Rural Development: Learning from China* was published in the late 1970s (Aziz 1978), nobody could have imagined that Mao's model described in that book could be totally abandoned five years later. At the turn of the century, China's development seems to have approached a new crossroad due to increasing social contradictions, conflicts and ecological crises. Despite extensive literature on rural reform, development and sustainability, few writers have actually considered the role of the rural poor. As a result, rural development and innovation are seen as a process of a 'big push' from government, initiative by 'new professionals' or the growth of local entrepreneurs. Whilst there is no reason to exclude the above elements, the rural poor, the 'first actors' of sustainable development in these poor regions of China, are largely neglected. To fill the gap, this book draws attention to the innovative potential of ordinary farmers and the implications for sustainable development in the marginal areas of China. Accordingly, this chapter begins by outlining the main challenges to rural development and sustainability, followed by a critical review of major theoretical approaches. Section 1.3 clarifies the research questions and framework of analysis, whilst the final section outlines the book's structure and content.

1.1 Challenges of unsustainable development in rural China

Alongside its impressive achievements in rural development, China's ecological crises have attracted increasing attention (Smil 1993, 1997; Xu and Tan 1995; Rivera 1997; Zheng and Qian 1998; Edmonds 1999; Hao 2001; World Bank 2001a; Huang 2002). Unprecedentedly, the lower reaches of the Yellow River, the second largest river in China, have frequently dried up since the 1990s (Chen and Mu 2000). In contrast to the frequent severe drought in the north, there have been terrible floods in south China (1998), which have left over 3,000 people dead and over 200 million people homeless (Chen *et al.* 1999; XNA 2000). If the impacts of these two events have mainly been limited within the border of China's territory, increasingly frequent sandstorms in north China have had impacts on its neighbours such as Korea and Japan, and even North America (Hao 2000; Brown 2001).

Geographically, China's ecological crises are particularly severe in its western region where rural poverty, ecological fragility and economic underdevelopment are probably interwoven. In contrast to the successful 'taking-off' of either rural industrialisation or commercialised agriculture in economically advanced regions or resource-rich zones, these poor areas suffer from 'double pressures' from both unfavourable geographic environments and increasing market competition. Great variation in resource endowment and infrastructure, in addition to various policy biases, have resulted in a widening regional economic gap and income inequality (Shen 1999). Associated with ecological degradation, the marginalisation process has threatened social stability and challenged the capacity of the government to maintain regional harmony (Edmonds 1994; Fan 1997; Jalan and Ravallion 1997; Yao and Liu 1998; Ravllion and Jalan 1999; Benjamin *et al.* 2000; *China Daily* 2001; Glantz *et al.* 2001; Riskin *et al.* 2001; CASN 2002).

Linked with ecological crises and economic marginalisation, rural poverty is still a serious issue against China's rural development. Despite great efforts and remarkable achievements in reduction of absolute poverty, according to recent reports (Khan 1998; Piazza and Liang 1998; Yao 2000; Chen and Wang 2001; World Bank 2001b), China has a long way to go to eliminate rural poverty, because most of the remaining poor are concentrated in resource-poor and geographically remote areas that are not easily accessed by outsiders. In addition, despite the decline in the number of people living in poverty, the severe condition of the remaining poor has not been alleviated, but has even been exacerbated, compared with the early period of the government's poverty-reduction programme (PRP) (World Bank 2001b).

In short, ecological degradation, economic marginalisation and rural poverty are challenging China's rural development and sustainability at the turn of the century. Rather than being separate from each other, they are interconnected and interwoven. This suggests that environmental sustainability cannot be achieved unless these three challenges can be properly addressed.

1.2 Approaches to unsustainable challenges

Not surprisingly, the challenges faced by rural China can be approached from different angles, related to various philosophical roots and methodological perspectives, resulting in different images and solutions. Roughly, four schools of thought can be distinguished.

The *technical approach* views the challenges as technical or engineering issues that can be analysed in terms of individual factors or single dimension (e.g. overpopulation, infrastructure, human capital, backward technology). Accordingly, the coping strategy should concentrate on either improving these factors (e.g. increasing investment on research, education and infrastructure) or enhancing inter-sector and inter-region management (CAS 1992; Cheng 1992; Fan and Pardey 1997; Hossain 1997; Li and Zhang 1998; Yonggong 1998; Zhang and Fan 2000; CPIRC 2001; IFPRI 2001).

From the methodological perspective, the technical approach is actually based upon the following assumptions: the *homogeneous environment* in both natural and social systems, which allow scientists to find a universal solution to all poor regions or locations; *demand similarity* among all farmers, which can, thus, be treated by a standard package; and a *linear process* of knowledge development from research centres to rural users. With its emphasis on external capital accumulation, the technical approach underestimates the complexity of local environments, the diversity of farmer's demands and the high risk attached to application of new technology in the poor regions.

In contrast to the exogenous-push perspective, the *institutional approach* pays more attention to endogenous dynamics, which can be released through adjusting economic institution and resource allocation mechanisms (World Bank 1999). Rejecting the assumption of 'conservative and backward' farmers, it views the incomplete market system and ambiguous property definition as the main barriers to rural development and sustainability. To cope with the challenges, it calls for an 'induced technological and institutional innovation' to fully reflect local resource constraints and comparative advantages (Hanstad and Li 1995; Lin and Li 1995; Lin and Zhang 1997; Yin 1998).

While focusing on the market mechanism, the institutional approach assumes that appropriate technology is available for farmer choice on the one hand, and that there is no constraint on farmers' access to and use of market information on the other. Both assumptions, however, are questionable if the highly uneven distribution of natural and physical capital in rural China is taken into account. With an emphasis on 'individual rationality', it seems to neglect 'social rationality', involving the collective benefits or social profit within a community or region (Hoff *et al.* 1993: 13). Ultimately, we do not know how market mechanisms can overcome the 'biases', which favour those locations and households well endowed with resources.

The *political approach* views rural issues as national or political problems, not limited to specific regions or groups. A good example is the debate about the 'peasant burden' (heavy taxation and fees levied on rural producers) and its impacts on rural income and social development. This approach is not limited within the economic field, but sheds light on interest contradictions and conflicts between rural and urban groups. It suggests that, constrained by the delay in reform of the political system, local governments actually have very limited capacity to meet their responsibilities in public services and environmental protection (Oi 1993; West and Wong 1995; Park *et al.* 1996; Rozelle *et al.* 1997; He 1998; Morduch and Sicuklar 1998; Zheng and Qian 1998; Wang and Hu 1999; Bernstein and Lu 2000; Gao 2001).

Whilst the political approach offers insights into the macro-system and political environment, it seems to pay little attention to the demands and role of the ordinary people. As a result, it gives the impression that the rural poor can do nothing, but wait for 'new professionals' to come. Even if the rural people are taken into account, the focus of this approach is often on the 'rural elite' at the price of neglecting the 'voice of the poor'.

Different from both the economic and political approaches, the *organisational approach* draws attention to the processes and mechanisms of rural reorganisation, which vary greatly since the dissolution of the collective commune system (CCS)

(RCRE 1996; Yao *et al.* 1996). While there has been a mushrooming of township and village enterprises (TVEs) in advanced regions and farmers' technique associations (FTAs) in resource-rich areas (e.g. plains or valleys accessible by transport), only a few collective (*empty-shell villages*) or private enterprises exist in the poor areas, which constrains the poor's access to external resources, and forces their decision-making towards ever-shorter time horizons (Shen *et al.* 1992; Wang 1994, 1995; Muldavin 1996; Cao 2000; Kindopp 2000).

To cope with the challenges, the 'third sector', non-governmental organisations (NGOs) are believed to be the 'new hope to rural China' (He 2001). Since many uncertain factors are involved, it seems too early to predict how much room for manoeuvre the government will allow the NGOs and what role they can play in sustainable development. Even if fully supported by the government, it is still questionable whether they will be able to reach the poorest in rural China.

Needless to say, the above divisions are neither absolute, nor necessarily exclusive of each other. A common deficiency shared by them is perhaps the lack of proper means to reflect the complexity of the local environment and the voices of the poor. As a result, little is known about the intrinsic dynamics and innovation potential among the poor.

1.3 Farmer innovation? Research questions and framework

The gap between the challenges facing rural areas and academic response calls for a methodological development to reveal the roles of the rural poor and their interface with external resources and dynamics. To cope with the interwoven challenges, both technological and organisational innovation are vital for the rural poor to secure their livelihoods. Integrating the two aspects together, a central question of this book is: how can the innovative capacity of the rural poor be enhanced in order to cope with various challenges and to secure their livelihoods?

The core question above can be further divided into three aspects. First, does any innovative capacity or potential exist in the rural poor? If so, how can it be revealed and confirmed? Second, by what kinds of organisation format and mechanisms can these poor learn, share and diffuse new technologies or techniques by themselves? Finally, what lessons should be learned from both government intervention and farmer practice in order to promote the release of intrinsic dynamics and development potential among the poor?

To address the above issues, this book examines the organisational condition and mechanisms of farmer innovation in the marginal areas of China. The term *farmer innovation* here is widely used to refer to all farmer activities related to learning, adopting, spreading and sharing new technologies (processes, methods, seeds, crops, production factors), knowledge (experience, skills, know-how) and production style. In contrast to conventional 'agricultural extension', which is dominated by urban professionals and controlled by government, farmer innovation emphasises the nature of farmer's decision, control and management of technology choice and processes, although the source of new technologies may not necessarily come from the farmers themselves.

Farmer innovation cannot be separated from organisational innovation upon which it depends. The term *self-organisation* used in this book refers to all organisational types, formats, processes or mechanisms that are used by farmers themselves for purposes of technology learning and co-operation in production, as distinct from externally controlled agricultural extension organisations. Whereas formal organisations such as TVEs and FTAs have been popularised in advanced regions, informal organisations such as social networks and personal linkages are the main format used by the poor.

Compared with institutionalised processes, farmer innovation and self-organisation are more localised or personalised, and vary greatly from one village to another. They are particularly important in the marginal areas where the poor stock of natural, physical, financial and human assets constrains the inflow of external capital, technology and information. Although overlaps exist, marginal areas are different from 'poor areas' in many ways. First, in the former, the emphasis is on the complexity of rural environment and development, resulting in a combination of economic and ecological dimensions, whilst in the latter, the concern is with the government's target of poverty reduction, strongly influenced by policy factors and administrative divisions. Second, the marginal areas are viewed as intermediate between core and sterile zones, and reflect economic and environmental change both inside and outside; however, the poor areas are defined in contrast to non-poor areas, without a sub-division system to address economic and environment change. Therefore, as a tool of geographic observation, the core–marginal division can be applied at various levels including the 'poor areas' in which government location biases and increasing regional inequalities can be observed and revealed.

By applying the core–marginal division to rural China, the challenges to unsustainable development can be easily understood. Whilst economic rationale drives the capital transfer from marginal to core areas, leading to marginalisation, the ecological system in the marginal areas is leading towards sterilisation, a process of the decline of carrying capacity and environmental crises. In the absence of a distinction between core and marginal areas, government development assistance has excluded marginal zones in advanced regions on the one hand, and provided funds to central zones and non-poor households within the 'poor areas' on the other. As a result, the government's PRP can neither stop marginalisation nor promote ecological improvement, because these peripheral zones and the poorest in rural China have less chance of access to government aid compared with the central zones.

In the absence of a systematic investigation, we do not know to what extent the marginal areas have suffered from marginalisation? How has marginalisation accelerated ecological degradation and crises? What lessons should development professionals learn from China's development practices? Parallel with conventional agricultural extension, how do the rural poor use their own 'networks', 'organisations' or mechanisms to undertake their own 'innovation projects' in order to cope with the challenges from the marginal environment (both national and market) and secure their livelihoods? The above questions cannot be addressed without an empirical survey, which is the theme of this book.

1.4 Book structure and content

Following the research framework described in the previous section, the argument is presented in seven chapters, besides this introductory chapter. Chapter 2 is a literature review that aims to clarify the theoretical background of rural sustainability and innovation approaches related to the developing world. After examining the role of the rural poor in various innovation schools, it draws attention to the social capital and the impacts on farmer innovation and self-organisation.

Regarding challenges to sustainable development in China, Chapter 3 considers its marginal areas, the marginalisation process and impacts on the government's poverty-reduction efforts. In the light of the geographical complexity of rural China, it begins by examining the limitations of the conventional regional divisions, resulting in an emergence of the core–marginal approach. Applying this approach to its uneven development, Section 3.2 illustrates the marginalisation process, whilst Section 3.3 interprets the limitations of the government poverty-reduction programme.

The challenges and dilemmas facing rural China are shown by an empirical study conducted in Shaanxi province. In Chapter 4, background information is provided on the province with a focus on its environmental and technological change. Shaanxi's resources, environment and development are examined in a broad prospective. Then follows an overview of the environmental challenges, relevant factors and impacts on rural livelihood systems. In relation to challenges from poverty and the environment, Section 4.3 sheds light on the gap between agricultural research and extension, whilst the final section summarises research findings and working hypotheses.

In Chapters 5–7, an in-depth study is presented of Zhidan county in north Shaanxi, with a focus on farmer innovation practice and organisation patterns. Accordingly, Chapter 5 introduces Zhidan's environment and development background. Based upon field observation and household questionnaire surveys, Chapter 6 examines rural livelihood systems and household innovation capacity, while Chapter 7 describes and distinguishes various 'innovation organisation' patterns illustrated by several case studies.

The book is concluded, in Chapter 8, with a review of the argument, and a discussion of the theoretical and policy implications of its findings. It begins by summarising the challenges facing China's environment and development. Section 8.2 emphasises the role of social capital and farmer self-organisation. Section 8.3 generalises the innovative dynamics and potential of the rural poor, along with a discussion on its theoretical implications for innovation studies. This book ends with policy implications regarding the interfaces between farmer self-organisation and professional participation.

2 Sustainability and farmer innovation in the developing world

Despite many differences, China shares with the developing world a common challenge to achieve harmonious development with regards to population, environment, economy and social systems. In this sense, the emergence of the 'sustainable development' (SD) movement worldwide has provided an important motivation for China to join the international community in moving towards 'a common future'. Due to the great variety that exists in philosophical base, value system and academic background, different people view SD in different ways. A good example is the role of the rural poor, which is perceived differently from one school of thought to another. By reviewing the debates on rural development and innovation in the developing world, this chapter attempts to identify an appropriate theoretical basis for farmer innovation studies in China. Among numerous literatures, special attention will be paid to the sustainable livelihood approach. The discussion is presented in four parts. To begin, the principles of sustainable rural livelihoods are briefly introduced, with special consideration of the role of farmer performance. Focusing on the marginal areas, Section 2.2 compares various innovation approaches, with special attention to the relationship between the rural poor and professionals. Section 2.3 considers the role of social capital in farmer innovation and self-organisation. The final section summarises the main findings from the literature review, and raises further questions for empirical studies in China.

2.1 Rural development and sustainability: roles for farmers

Although increasingly popularised in development debates, sustainability can be interpreted in various ways. Focusing on rural poverty elimination in the developing world, this section attempts to identify a theoretical framework for farmer innovation studies. Accordingly, it begins by outlining various understandings on rural development, followed by the principles of sustainable rural livelihoods (SRL). Various roles for farmer participation are indicated in Section 2.3 and the final section highlights theoretical approaches and methodological frameworks for innovation studies.

2.1.1 What is rural development: various approaches

The meaning of rural development varies according to the understanding of development itself. The emphasis on economic growth and 'taking-off' in the 1950s, for instance, left no place for rural development but agricultural economy (Lea and Chaudhri 1983: 1). Realising the limitation of a narrow economic perspective, the modernisation theory sees development as a process of 'social transformation' from a traditional or pre-modern society to a modern or westernised society (Moore 1963). Subordinated to national industrialisation and modernisation, rural development is, thus, involved in two interconnected objectives: 'agricultural modernisation' or 'transforming traditional agriculture' (Schultz 1964), and 'rural modernisation' or 'transforming traditional peasants'. The former refers to the replacement of traditional labour-intensive and low-external-input technology systems, while the latter is related to the removal of 'development barriers' including indigenous knowledge, traditional value systems and conservative attitudes (Brohman 1996: 20).

In contrast to functionalist explanations of development and modernisation, Marxism stresses the structure and conflict of social relationships, which is related to expanding capitalism and technology (Harriss 1982: 22). Rejecting the modernisationists, diagnosis of underdevelopment, for instance, the dependency school argued that rural backwardness and mass poverty in peripheral countries resulted from capitalist world systems (Hettne 1990). Employing the core–satellite model, rural development in the developing world is, thus, referred to two dimensions: *vertically* unequal economic and technological exchange between developed capitalist countries and underdeveloped ones; and *horizontally* exploitative relations between landlords and the landless peasantry. Rural development in peripheral countries, therefore, refers not only to the breakdown of the capitalist world system, but also to eradication of the 'exploitative system' (Friberg and Hettne 1985).

Despite conflict with each other, modernisation and neo-Marxism share a common belief that rural development is connected with 'relatively large-scale units of production' (Harriss 1982: 37). In contrast, 'neo-populists' believe that 'small is beautiful' (Shumacher 1974) because not only do most rural people in the developing world depend on small farms to survive, but also the family farming system is supposed to be more efficient, compared with that of bigger farms (Johnson and Kilby 1975; Lipton 1977). Neo-populist ideas have received particular attention since the mid-1970s, when the approach was adopted by the World Bank and UN agencies. As an important content of the 'new strategy', rural development was defined as:

> a strategy designed to improve the economic and social life of a specific group of people – rural poor. It involves extending the benefit of development to the poorest among those who seek a livelihood in the rural area [sic]. The group includes small-scale farmers, tenants and the landless.
>
> (World Bank 1975)

More than narrow agricultural innovation or economic growth, according to the definition above, rural development is representative of a new development orientation, 'people-centred development' instead of 'thing-centred development' (Chambers 1997: 36–38). Rather than waiting for trickle-down effects, the new approach retargets the priority to satisfaction of basic needs through 'growth with justice' or 'redistribution with growth' (Chenery *et al.* 1974). Compared with the radical approach of neo-Marxism, the neo-populist school seeks to help the rural poor to 'demand and control more of the benefits of development' (Chambers 1983: 168).

Concerning the vast majority of rural poor living in resource-poor and ecologically fragile areas, a crucial question arises: where is the primary source to drive rural development in marginal areas? Generally, two different approaches can be distinguished. The 'exogenous' development approach, which dominated in the past, asserts that fundamental ideas (knowledge, technique and solution) and resources (physical, financial, talent) come from outside, so that the core issue for marginal areas is how to attract and utilise external capital, technologies or professionals more effectively. By contrast, the alternative approach emphasises an 'endogenous' development, which implies 'growing or originating from within'. Typically, the latter would look first at 'what natural, social and human resources are available, and then ask: can anything be done differently that results in more productive use of these available resources?' (Pretty and Hine 1999).

In theory, the endogenous development approach seems more promising than its rival due to its emphasis on the intrinsic dynamics and development potential within the poor. From this perspective, rural development can be viewed as a process of endogenous development based upon farmers' own selection and creation, although their actions are subject to various constraints and external influences. In other words, rural development is a process of farmers' self-selection and determination that aims to meet their needs, under various possibilities, conditions and constraints.

In reality, however, the exogenous approach has dominated development practice for a long time despite many deficiencies and limitations. Many questions arise: why is it necessary to adopt an endogenous development approach instead of a convenient exogenous development for the marginal areas? How can the rural poor select and determine rural development by themselves? What interfaces exist between endogenous and exogenous dynamics? To address these questions, a good base is the SRL approach, which is the topic of the next section.

2.1.2 Sustainable rural livelihoods: principles and analysis frame

The co-existence of rural poverty and environmental degradation has been an important factor stimulating debates on SD world-wide, since the late 1980s. According to the World Commission on Environment and Development (WCED 1987: 43), SD is a development that 'meets the needs of the present, without compromising the ability of future generations to meet their own needs'. The definition, however, leaves a good deal of room for manoeuvre, because 'it does not specify whose model of development should be followed, nor who will determine the economic, social or biological needs of the present or of future generations' (Vivian 1992).

It seems over simplistic to assume, for instance, that SD is 'a form of societal change that, in addition to traditional development objectives (e.g. satisfaction of basic needs), has the objective or constraint of ecological sustainability' (Lele 1991). A minimal revision or repair of the traditional development path, however, according to Chambers and Conway (1992), is not enough. They argued that the eradication of rural poverty cannot be achieved by conventional 'production thinking' (e.g. producing enough food), 'employment thinking' (e.g. needing large numbers of new 'workplaces') or 'poverty-line thinking' (simplified understanding and measuring of poverty issues) because they do not capture 'the complex and diverse realities of most rural life. Instead of a single dimension, what is needed is an integrated approach, sustainable rural livelihoods (SRL):

> A livelihood comprises the capabilities, assets (including material and social resources) and activities required for a means of living. A livelihood is sustainable when it can cope with and recover from stresses and shocks and maintain or enhance its assets and capabilities, whilst not undermining the natural resource base.
>
> (Carney 1998: 4)

It is widely recognised that livelihoods comprise five basic capital assets that serve different functions in satisfying basic needs (Carney 1998; Pretty and Ward 2001). They are:

- *Natural capital*: various natural resources or processes that can be used for food, wood, clean water, recreation and leisure.
- *Social capital*: trust, reciprocity and obligation, norms and sanctions that encourage people working together.
- *Human capital*: related to individual capability, health, nutrition, education, skills and knowledge.
- *Physical capital*: for example, local infrastructure, road and irrigation systems, farm machines.
- *Financial capital*: for example, savings, credit and subsidies.

Integrating the five capitals together, Pretty and Hine (2001) establish an asset-based model. Figure 2.1 shows that these five assets are transformed by policies, processes and institutions to give desirable outcomes such as food, job, welfare, economic growth, a clean environment, etc.

Figure 2.1 illustrates how the SRL concept provides a methodological basis to define and measure rural sustainability on the one hand, and to learn lessons from development practice in the past on the other. First, the SRL is dependent on a balance of the five inputs. It seems to suggest that rural poverty cannot be alleviated merely through one or two measures; what is needed is a balanced or harmonious approach to all five capitals.

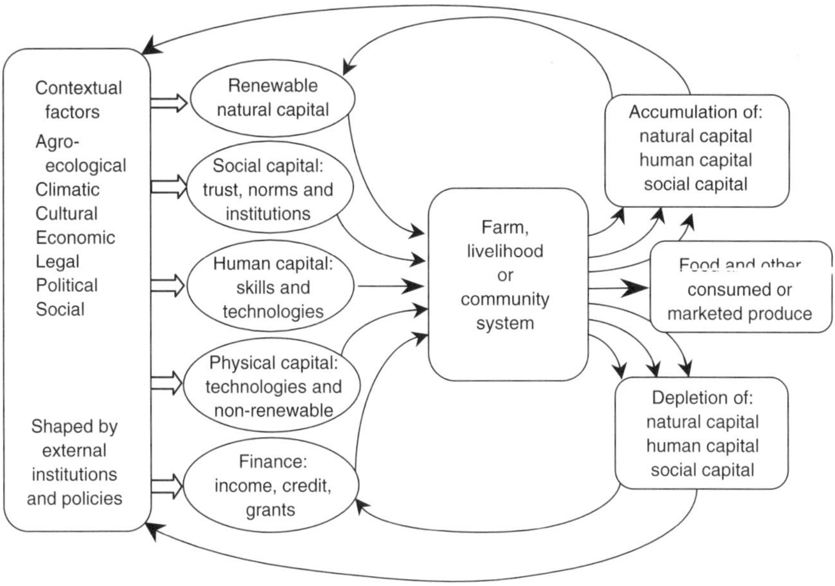

Figure 2.1 Asset-based model of livelihood systems.

Source: Pretty and Hine 2001.

Second, the SRL as a desired output concerned with more than food production and consumption. In the face of challenges and uncertainty from both natural and market environments, the diversification of production and income is, thus, crucial for the rural poor to secure their livelihoods (Ellis 1998).

Third, the SRL is not a static system but a dynamic process, which has at least three kinds of statuses, trends or consequences: downward or negative feedback to depletion of natural, human, social or other capitals; upward or positive feedback to accumulation of five capitals; and balance between positive and passive feedback resulting in no reduction of capital assets in the total. A fundamental principle of sustainable systems is that they do not deplete capital assets. To achieve sustainable rural livelihoods and poverty alleviation, it is crucial to adopt a balanced strategy of capital inputs in general, and pay more attention to improving natural, social and human capitals in particular (Pretty and Hine 2001).

Finally, regarding balance and harmony among the five assets, it is very important to reveal their interconnection and interaction, which involves complex interfaces between exogenous (universal, scientific) and endogenous (local, indigenous) knowledge and dynamics. In view of the reality of overwhelming attention to the former, it is crucial for the SRL model to recognise and promote the latter, that is, full use and release of the intrinsic dynamics and development potential of the rural poor.

Maintenance and enhancement of the five assets is not the end of the SRL, but a means to strengthen the adaptive and creative capacity of the poor to cope with various challenges, shocks and uncertainty from unfavourable natural and social environments. In this sense, the SRL cannot be achieved without technical and organisational changes, both of which can be decomposed and analysed by endogenous and exogenous dimensions. The various components that have been described lead to different approaches to the role of the rural poor even under the umbrella of the SRL. Reflecting the above framework, the next section concerns exogenous organisational change and its impacts on the rural poor, which is followed by an examination of exogenous technological change. Endogenous technological and organisational change will be the focus of the section that follows next.

2.1.3 Exogenous organisation for farmer participation

One of the important distinctions between conventional development and the SRL approach is in the relationship between farmers and the state. Emphasising 'nation-building', both modernisation and neo-Marxist perspectives view rural development as a top-down process through elite initiatives, political mobilisation and government intervention (Hettne 1990: 29). In contrast, the SRL approach stresses bottom-up, farmer participation and empowerment (Blackburn and Holland 1998; Holland and Blackburn 1998).

Farmer participation, however, is not neutral, but can be utilised for various political purposes and organisational means (Brohman 1996: 251; Blackburn and Holland 1998: 1–2; Robb 1998). Many questions need to be clarified: *who participates* (an elite group or ordinary people), *what they participate in* (sharing information and benefit or being involved in decision-making) and *why they participate* (as a means towards poverty alleviation or as an end in itself)? As a continuum, farmer participation can be divided into several typologies as described in Box 2.1.

Box 2.1 **Typology of farmer participation**

- *Passive participation*: listening to outsiders without response.
- *Participation in information giving*: for example, filling in a questionnaire.
- *Participation by consultation*: being consulted and having their views listened to.
- *Participation for material incentives*: providing resources (e.g. labour, fields) to outsiders in return for food, cash or other material incentives.
- *Functional participation*: being organised as groups for predetermined objectives.
- *Interactive participation*: joint analysis and decision-making for action plans and institution building under control by outsiders.
- *Self-mobilisation*: taking initiatives independent of external institutions to change the system.

Source: Pretty (1995: 173).

Having such a wide range of meanings, unsurprisingly, the term participation is increasingly popular and widely accepted. One of the popular uses, for example, refers to encouraging local people to contribute their labour to various development projects in return for food, cash or materials; the rural poor will not refuse to do so because they lose nothing. Without the improvement of their skills, organisation and, management capacity, however, 'these material incentives distort perceptions, create dependencies, and give the misleading impression that local people are supportive of externally-driven initiatives' (Pretty and Hine 1999).

In contrast to participation for material incentives, an alternative approach views participation as a means to improve the design and result of a project (Brohman 1996: 251–252). One good example is 'self-reliant participatory development'. According to Burkey (1993: 209), the poor are 'seldom able to initiate a self-reliant development process without outside stimulation'. As a result, such development is largely dependent upon the promotion of the poor's self-awareness and self-confidence, which need 'an education and empowering process'.

Both types of participation mentioned above, however, are initiated and manipulated by outsiders, and only rely, in turn, on the emergence of 'new professionals' (Chambers 1983, 1997). Reflecting the progress and achievements in this respect, NGOs, the 'third sector' for rural development, have become major actors, equally important, if not more, to government agencies (Edwards and Hulme 1992; Bebbinton and Farrington 1993). Compared with government organisations, NGOs have many characteristics and advantages, including small size, flexibility, 'shallow hierarchies', quick responses and rapid decision-making, which would be beneficial to poverty alleviation, participatory development and rural technological innovation (Bebbington and Farrington 1992; Brohman 1996: 254–257).

However, NGOs themselves also face many constraints, such as limited size and sources of funding, lack of a long-term approach and difficulty in reaching the poorest (Bebbinton and Farrington 1992; Edwards and Hulme 1992; Robinson 1992). These issues, according to Brohman (1996: 221), are related to 'a top-down, paternalistic manner that afforded little opportunity for local organisations to participate meaningfully in decision-making'.

Due to the above limitations, outside NGOs have to rely upon local community organisations that provide a channel or 'vehicle' for farmer participation and empowerment. The so-called 'community development' is, however, actually based upon the assumption that 'individuals, groups and classes in village communities have common interests which are strong enough to bind them together' (Burkey 1993: 43). Unfortunately, 'local organisations are often open to influence and control by local elite, who will then continue to make decisions in their own interests under the cover of a participatory organisation structure' (Lane 1995). One lesson that can be learnt from such 'community development' is that the SRL may not be achieved without improving or promoting social capital.

Whilst overwhelming attention has been paid to external initiative or sponsored organisational development, equally important questions remain untouched: do the rural poor have the capacity to initiate and manage an organisational process by themselves without external assistance, incentives or inducement? By what kinds of conditions and mechanisms can such a process occur, be sustained and scaled-up? What contribution can farmer self-mobilisation make to the SRL? The above issues are discussed in subsequent sections.

2.1.4 Concluding remarks

Reviewing the debates of rural development and sustainability in the developing world, this section attempts to identify a suitable theoretical base for this book in general, and to establish an analytical framework for farmer innovation studies in particular. In the light of the former, the SRL approach offers insights into unsustainable development practice in the past, which can be attributed to the depletion or imbalance of five assets: natural, social, human, physical and financial capitals. Concerning the latter, it is argued that the objectives of the SRL for poor regions and groups might not be achievable without technical and organisational changes, which involves interfaces between endogenous and exogenous dynamics.

Under the umbrella of the SRL, however, there is still a wide range of roles for the rural poor to play. Taking farmer participation and empowerment as an example, significant progress has made in acknowledging the contribution of the poor, although overwhelming attention has been paid to the exogenous dynamics and organisation.

Two factors may account for the neglect of intrinsic dynamics and the farmer self-organising process. First, it is very common to assume that the marginal areas are poor, not only in natural, physical and financial assets, but also in human and social capital. Second, the focus of research methodology in this stage is on the dialogue between urban professionals and the rural poor, rather than internal communication and co-operation among farmers. The former may be called as 'organisation bias' because it assumes that all poor are the same or similar in terms of organisational needs, capacity and potential. The latter may be named 'participatory bias', which assumes that what outsiders see is equal to the real world in which the poor live.

If we take account of the complexity of the marginal areas in the developing world, the above-mentioned assumptions are questionable. First, the rural poor are not homogenous in terms of human or social capital. Neglecting the heterogeneity among the poor may lead to an underestimation of the complexity of local environment and an overstatement of the role of outside initiatives. Second, externally led participation and empowerment are means but not the end of rural development. The aim is to enhance the poor's capacity of technology learning and organisation, and external initiatives are merely one of many possible formats. Over-emphasis on farmer participation may lead to neglect of farmers' own innovative potential and organisation capacity. Finally, although there may be no formal organisation to facilitate rural technological change, the poor have their own networks to support their survival and development (Narayan *et al.* 2000).

To reveal the limitations of exogenous development, the next section will examine the exogenous organisation process of technological innovation.

2.2 Exogenous technological innovation in marginal areas

Sustainable rural livelihoods cannot be achieved without technological and organisational innovation. Regarding the marginal areas of the developing world, both involve two types of dynamic sources: endogenous and exogenous. Whilst the previous section considered exogenous organisational change (e.g. reconstruction of government intervention or scaling-up of NGOs) for farmer participation, this section turns to exogenous technological innovation, defined as a technical change that is initiated, collaborated or controlled by outsiders (either government or urban professionals). The central focus is on the role of the rural poor in the innovation process and their relationship with the professionals. To avoid theoretical ambiguity, the term *innovation* will be defined in the beginning, and this will be followed by an 'environmental analysis' on the marginal areas. The main innovation approaches, including technology transfer, participatory research and induced innovation, are examined and compared. The section ends with a summary and comment on innovation studies.

2.2.1 Whose innovation? Farmer as primary innovator

The term innovation,[1] which originated from Schumpeter (1934), refers to the introduction, adoption or creation of new things, which can cover a wide range from new goods, production method or materials, to new markets and organisational structures. Despite great variation, it commonly contains either or both elements of 'new knowledge' (ideas, skills or experience) and 'new organisation' (principles, forms or mechanisms). Regarding the former, three approaches can be identified: the application of scientific principles; the accumulation of experience or techniques; and the integration of the two. With respect to the latter, various approaches to organisation of innovation can be distinguished: the linear model of research and extension, the individual inventor-entrepreneur and the network organisation comprised of all actors (Rycroft and Kash 1999: 59–61).

Combining knowledge system and organisational process, the term innovation as used in this book refers to a new social practice with the aim of improving and securing rural livelihoods. The broad definition above highlights three aspects of innovation. First, the innovation process cannot be separated from innovators. Whereas Schumpter and his followers emphasise entrepreneurship as the core of innovation (Sundbo 1998: 4), so that the rural poor can hardly be included in the lists of innovators, the social practice approach emphasises that farmers are real or potential innovators in nature, depending upon the specific environment or condition. Furthermore, the primary innovators in the marginal area are neither outside professionals, nor government agencies, but ordinary farmers. In contrast with a narrow focus on knowledge, professional, local elite or entrepreneur, this definition gives opportunities for researchers to observe and reflect innovative activities among ordinary people.

Second, two broad categories of innovation can be distinguished: technological and organisational. The former is related to development and application of 'new knowledge' (experience, skills, know-how, processes, methods or products) to on-farm or non-farm production. The latter is concerned with a new form of communication and interaction among rural households, and between farmers and professionals through either formal or informal institutional arrangement.[2] Initiated and completed by the same actor, farmers, the social practice approach emphasises on the interdependence between technological and organisational innovation.

Finally, neither technological nor organisational innovation in marginal areas can be fully understood unless the particular environment and demands of the rural poor are fully taken into account. In this sense, innovation can be viewed as a process of interaction between farmers and their environment (in both natural and social aspects). It is, thus, crucial for development professionals to understand the complexity of the rural innovation environment, which involves both natural and social factors.

Applying the 'social practice' approach to innovation studies, the next section highlights 'environmental features' in marginal areas.

2.2.2 Marginal environment and innovation

Innovation as a social practice is inseparable from and shaped by an *environment* composed of all relevant natural and social factors. Due to differences in academic traditions and disciplinary division, not surprisingly, images of the environment may vary greatly. Whatever definition is adopted, 'environmental analysis' of its scope, composition and potential impacts should be undertaken before any technology choice is made or innovation is planned. This raises the questions: what factors should be taken into account regarding rural innovation (project or policy)? What differences can be distinguished regarding the innovation environment between marginal and core areas? What environmental factors are particularly important for marginal areas, which may lead to a different innovation model from other regions, or to different results from adopting the same model that has succeeded in other regions?

Regarding the environmental factors of rural innovation, uneven resource distribution has been widely recognised, and may be expressed in various terms such as 'poor region', 'resource-poor areas' or 'low-potential areas' (World Bank 1990; Ellis 1998). More than the natural or resource dimension, according to the International Geographic Union (2001), the term *marginal* indicates 'inequality, disadvantages, neglect . . . [which] is linked to the prevailing socio-economic and political system . . . [and which is] not bound to any particular region or society of the world nor to any specific scale'. In this sense, no single criterion or dimension is capable of reflecting the constraints from marginal areas, because all constraint factors (or dimensions) are interconnected or interwoven into a whole, namely the 'marginal environment' (Jussila *et al.* 1998, 2000).

The term marginal environment requires a complete view of constraints against technological innovation in marginal areas. In other words, both technological and organisational innovation in marginal areas can be seen as the process and result of the rural poor's struggle against marginal environments. In this sense, a systematic

***Box 2.2* Environmental features of the marginal areas**

- Geographical remoteness.
- High ecological fragility or natural hazards.
- Dispersed, heterogeneous populations living at subsistence levels.
- Poor physical and social infrastructure, and lacking access to outside.
- Economic backwardness or depression.
- 'Low productivity' and potential but high risk for investment.
- Little or no political influence on the decisions affecting their lives.

Source: Ruddle and Rondinelli (1983).

and comprehensive picture of 'marginal environment' will aid understanding of the constraints, choices and demands of the farmer innovation in these areas. Focusing on the local level, Box 2.2 highlights some features that particularly constrain convenient technological innovation in marginal areas.

'Marginal environment' does not merely refer to constraints from natural and physical conditions, but also involves various development biases such as 'roadside', 'seasonal', 'project' and 'professional' (Chambers 1983). One of the negative effects of the marginal environment is that the voice of the rural poor are hardly heard by outsiders (Holland and Blackburn 1998; Mullen 2000; Narayan *et al.* 2000).

Regarding the impacts of marginal environment on agricultural innovation, it is increasingly recognised that a conventional technological system such as 'green revolution' (GR) agriculture is not suited to these resource-poor regions (Conway and Barbier 1990; Redclift 1990). Instead, a new category, called complexity, diversity and risk-prone (CDR) agriculture, has emerged to reflect environmental complexity, small farmers and heterogeneous demands in these areas (WCED 1987; Chambers *et al.* 1989; Pretty 1995).

In summary, the marginal environment can be seen as a sum of various natural and social factors that impede the application and diffusion of modern technology. To understand rural technological and organisational innovation in marginal areas, the following environmental features are very important:

- *Wholeness* of various natural and social factors. It is, thus, difficult to sort out one issue without improving other relevant variables, factors or conditions.
- *Complexity* not only in local geographic and resource environment, but also in farmers' demands and the social environment.
- *Communication barrier* between the poor and professionals related to both remote location and various social biases.
- *High cost and risk* due to a dispersed residence pattern, small production scale and complex climatic conditions, resulting in both ecological and market risks.

- *Relative division* between core and marginal areas, related to research issues, hierarchy and time factors. A detailed discussion of these will be found in Chapter 3.
- *Marginalisation* process referring to increasing economic difference and social inequality between marginal and core areas.

The above list does not cover all the unfavourable factors and features facing marginal areas, but is intended to show how important the environmental differences and constraints that influence technology choice and adoption are. Different understandings of the rural environment are, thus, an important factor responsible for different approaches to rural innovation.

2.2.3 Classic technology transfer

To cope with the challenges from ecological degradation and rural poverty, three innovation schools can be distinguished from each other: the classical, neo-liberal and neo-popular approaches.

Following the conventional development paradigm, the classical approach assumes that the solutions to ecological challenges and rural poverty are well known, and the problem is how such knowledge can be adopted and implemented by local people. Taking ecological degradation as an example, it diagnoses that technical solutions are available, but cannot be implemented properly due to one or many factors, such as mismanagement, over-population or subsistence fundamentalism (Blaikie 1985: 53).

The innovation strategy in this school is, thus, based upon 'transfer of technology' (TT) and state intervention. The former supposes that modern technology is universal in application for all circumstances and conditions, and its diffusion is a linear top-down process from research centres via extension stations to farmers.[3] The latter involves the institutional (organisational) base of TT, by which government uses various means of institution (e.g. establishment of research and extension institutions) and policies (e.g. fiscal budgets and subsidies) to support technological diffusion and adoption. A good example of the TT model is the diffusion of GR agriculture, which was invented in international research centres, and has been widely adopted due to government intervention and subsidies (Conway and Barbier 1990).

Despite great success in resource-rich areas, the extension of GR technology into the marginal areas is questionable, due to many issues such as: *technological immaturity* from the perspectives of ecology and environment; *discontinuity* between new technology and traditional farming systems; and *systems dependency* on a wide range of supporting services and infrastructure (Bhalla and James 1988). These issues, according to Conway and Barbier (1990: 11), 'are not simply second or third generation problems capable of being solved by further technological adjustment. They require an approach that is equally revolutionary, yet very different in its conceptual and operational style'.

The issues of the GR agricultural extension are not unique, but expose the limitations of the classical innovation school itself. Not only does it ignore the complexity of the CDR environment in the marginal areas, but equally important, it suffers a 'lack of any account of the position of the participants and the reliance on experts' (Biot *et al.* 1995: 4). If any failure occurs, 'escape hatches' are employed, whereby the blames is associated to 'unfavourable weather, lack of co-operation by different government departments, lack of political will, or lazy and unco-operative farmers' (Biot *et al.* 1995).

It would be unfair to say that nothing has been achieved within the classic approach. Realising the complexity of rural environments, an important improvement has been made by Farming Systems Research, which requires a multiple-level, interdisciplinary approach in order to understand farming practice within the context of wider ecological, technical, economic and social constraints (Long and Villareal 1993). Limited feedback occurs from farmers to extension agents, then to research centres. Instead of a single TT, the technology package, which includes a whole set of technological elements and encouragement policies (e.g. credit, financial and other benefits), has become a standard procedure of agricultural extension (Ellis 1992: 227).

Despite these improvements, as Anholt and Zijp (1995) suggest, there are still many shortcomings existing in public agricultural extension, including unresponsiveness to the variation in farmer needs; lack of ownership by the intended beneficiaries; failure to reach poor and women farmers; limitation in the quality of field and technical staff; and high and unsustainable public costs. It seems that mini-repair or adjustment in innovation policy and institution are not enough to cope with the challenges mentioned above.

To conclude, the classical approach, holding a top-down perspective, excludes the farmers from the list of innovators, resulting in a neglect of their knowledge and creativity. Not only does it fail to take account of the complexity of the marginal environment, it also assumes the homogeneity of farmers, neglecting the diversity of their demands and capacity. Depending on state intervention, it pays little attention to indigenous communication networks, leading to omission of farmers' own learning process and organisation practice.

2.2.4 Neo-populist participatory research

In contrast to large-scale, standardised, modern TT and state intervention, the neo-populist approach prefers small-scale, diverse, traditional technology and farmer participation. Believing 'small is beautiful', Schumacher (1974) called for a novel innovation path to help the rural poor who own an abundance of labour but have limited employment opportunities and scarce capital. Despite great variety in terminology,[4] a common element shared by scholars in this school of thought is that farmers are not outside the innovation process, but positive contributors and important collaborators with urban professionals. In contrast to professional and government-dominated TT, the alternative approach can be called participatory research (PR), which emphasises equality in collaboration between farmers and professionals (Hagmann *et al.* 1998; Holland and Blackburn 1998).

Compared with the TT model, many differences can be identified in the neo-popular approach. Instead of the 'package of practices' found in the former, the latter prefers a 'basket of choices' so as to meet the diverse demands of small farmers (Chambers 1988). In contrast to the agricultural intensification path of the former, a 'low external input and sustainable agriculture' is recommended by the latter, as this is said to be more adaptive to local ecosystems, resource endowment and, more importantly, indigenous knowledge and farmer capacity (ILEIA 1989). Unlike the top-down procedure in the former, the PR approach offers a circular process, in which the starting point of innovation is 'not new technology but the analysis of existing farming systems, *in situ*, to determine needs, problems and constraints to which subsequent technological innovation is directed' (Conway and Barbier 1990: 114–115).

The key to the neo-populist approach is a rethinking of the value of indigenous knowledge systems (IKS) in the face of a marginal environment. Some scholars (Richards 1985) emphasise that the diversity, heterogeneity and complexity of farming systems require a locally specific strategy of technology. Compared with urban professionals, it is said that peasant farmers have many characteristics such as 'wealth of knowledge of their own environment', 'specific skills to use in this environment' and being 'very active and creative' in reaching their objectives (ILEIA 1989: 4). Unlike the TT model, the farmer in the PR model is seen as 'an active strategist who problematises situations, processes information and brings together the elements necessary for operating his farm' (Long and Villarreal 1993).

It would be misleading, however, to exaggerate the value of the IKS. Rejecting the somewhat romanticised or idealistic view, Thrupp (1989) argues that not all resource-poor farmers have valuable indigenous knowledge and many of their practices are ineffective for the people's own interests. Roling and Engel (1989) emphasise: 'Opportunities for [rural] technology development grow out of synergy between IKS and science-based knowledge and technology'. It is fair to say that indigenous and modern scientific knowledge are complementary in their strengths and weaknesses. As Chambers (1983: 75) points out, 'combined they may achieve what neither would alone'.

It is crucial for the PR approach to reveal the real linkages and interface between these two kinds of knowledge systems (Pottier 1993; Scoones and Thompson 1994; Walker *et al.* 1995). In contrast to formal research and development (R&D), Biggs utilises the term 'informal R&D' to identify the farmers' own innovation activities. The difference between them is that the former is 'centralised, powerful and visible' while the latter is 'dispersed, weak and hard for professionals to see' (Chambers *et al.* 1989: 166). Related to the various roles of farmers in formal and informal R&D, Biggs distinguishes four types of relationships between scientists and farmers (as shown in Box 2.3).

According to Biggs's taxonomy, there is a wide spectrum of roles farmers can play from passive receivers (the TT model in the first two categories) to dominant innovators (the PR model in last two categories). As a result, the difference between them lies not in different mechanisms but in the extent of farmer participation.

Box 2.3 Biggs' taxonomy of farmer's roles in agricultural innovation

- *Contract*: scientists use farmers' resources, mainly land, for their trials.
- *Consultative*: like a doctor, scientists diagnose, design and control process.
- *Collaborative*: sustained interaction between farmers and scientist equally.
- *Collegiate*: to strengthen informal R&D at the farmer and community level.

Source: Chambers *et al.* (1989: 167).

The TT model, however, is not constant but subject to continuous evolution and adjustment. It emphasised technological delivery directly from the formal R&D system to the farming system at first, and later a feedback channel through the farming system research approach was added. Since it devalues indigenous knowledge, not surprisingly, there is no room for informal R&D in the TT model. In the PR model, by contrast, informal R&D is located as the centre of rural innovation in resource-poor farming systems, which leads to a redefinition of innovation channels and mechanisms. According to the schema, it is most likely that communication between professionals and farmers first occurs between formal and informal R&D systems and then between informal R&D and the wider farming system.

Compared with the 'black box' approach in the TT model, the PR might be viewed as a 'grey box' due to the acknowledgement of farmer innovative capacity and collaborative relationships with professionals. There is, however, still a lack of consideration of the differences in farmer innovative capacity and learning mechanisms; farmers are still seen as homogeneous in this approach, which leads to a somewhat overstated or idealised view of farmer innovation. As Long and Villarreal (1993) emphasise, 'farming populations are essentially heterogeneous . . . [which leads] to differences in farmer management styles, cropping patterns and levels of production'. In reality, it is not easy to achieve the combination of different knowledge systems because professionals and farmers 'differ so greatly that they do not allow for communication between the parties' (Load and Villarreal 1993). Since it is dependent on outside initiative and facilities, it is questionable whether this approach can 'be applied on a widely expanded, let alone, universal basis [because] successful examples are often subsidised and unsustainable, and unreplicable on a large scale' (Boit *et al.* 1995: 6).

One of the conclusions that can be drawn out from the above comparison of models is that a narrow focus on knowledge systems seems inadequate to understand farmers' innovation potential and their real interface with the outside. Instead, there is a need for an organisational (institutional) dimension for knowledge diffusion and integration, which is the theme of the section on 'Methodology for farmer innovation and self-organisation'.

2.2.5 Neo-liberalist-induced innovation

Differently from the naive neo-populist idea, the neo-liberal approach tries to reveal the realistic constraints from sustainable resource utilisation and technological innovation. Applying an 'economic approach' to environmental and developmental issues, it pays special attention to the 'structure of incentives' for both farmers' adoption of appropriate technologies and professionals' delivery of new technologies (Biot *et al.* 1995: 6). According to Hayami and Ruttan (1985), technical change is induced by changes in the availability and cost of major production factors. In this sense, rural innovation in marginal areas is largely dependent on what kind of a new regulation system can be established, and how, in order to promote the demand and supply of new technologies.

Compared with the classical school, the neo-liberal approach acknowledges the complexity and particularity of the marginal areas, due to their limited potential for growth, poor skills of farmers, low access to infrastructure and supplies, and serious environmental degradation (World Bank 1990: 71–72). It rejects the conventional assumption of farmers' ignorance and conservativeness, and diagnoses that rapid population growth, ineffective regulation of common-property resource, commercialisation of agriculture, and so on, have forced these poor to intensify 'traditional farming methods such as slash and burn agriculture [which] has damaged the productivity of these marginal areas' (World Bank 1990: 71–72).

In contrast to the classical bias against traditional farmers, a cornerstone of the neo-liberal approach is the assumption of 'rational farmers'. Schultz (1964) viewed small farmers not only as sensitive to prices and other market factors, but also as capable of allocating resources effectively, given the information, institutions and technology that were available to them. Unlike neo-populists, neo-liberalists avoid focusing on the nature and source of technological innovation, but assume that new, appropriate technologies will be available if proper incentives are provided (Hoff *et al.* 1993). In this sense, rural poverty and livelihood insecurity in the marginal areas are seen not as a matter of technology, but as an institutional issue, that is, lack of appropriate or sufficient incentives (support) for the poor to adopt new technologies. In addition, instead of viewing farmers as homogenous, the neo-liberal emphasises on the role of entrepreneurs, though it views entrepreneurship not as a precondition of rural technological change, but as the result of political and economic institutional changes.

Compared with the classical and neo-populist schools, many advantages can be seen in the neo-liberal approach. First, the assumption of rational farmers gives more scope for the rural poor to participate, not only in technological development but also in institutional innovation. Second, the approach invites rethinking about state intervention and governmental performance, which often conflict with farmer interest and demands. Finally, an important feature of the neo-liberal approach is that it acknowledges the heterogeneity of farmers in terms of innovation demand and capacity, and emphasises a policy environment inducing innovation rather than simply administrative intervention.

Despite its many advantages, the neo-liberal approach has its own limitations. Bemoaning the 'tragedy of the commons' (Hardin 1968), it focuses predominantly on individual rationality, while social rationality, related to collective benefits or social profit within a community or region over the long term, is largely neglected (Hoff *et al.* 1993: 13). In addition, the neo-liberal approach seems to pay little attention to the impacts of imperfect information and deficient infrastructure on the marginal areas, which constrain the communication and interaction both vertically (between the farmers and outsiders) and horizontally (among farmers themselves). With its narrow focus on the economic rationale, the neo-liberal approach faces the dilemma: how can market mechanisms enhance the adaptive capacity of the rural poor rather than enlarge the rural technical gap and income inequality? Finally, the neo-liberal school seems to share with the classical approach a tendency to hand over research affairs to urban professionals, at the expense of farmers' experience and participation in agricultural research.

2.2.6 Concluding remarks

From the SRL perspective, the classical approach of TT is inappropriate to the marginal areas for two reasons. One is the complexity and particularity of the marginal environments (comprising both unfavourable national and social factors), which conflict with the assumptions of universality (of modern scientific knowledge system) and linear process (of knowledge production and application). Another is the role assigned to traditional farmers, who are assumed to be passive users (receivers) and are ignorant, backward and conservative in facing technological change.

Revising the conventional innovation paradigm, the neo-populists emphasise the validity of the IKS in the marginal environment, which leads to emergence of a PR approach with the aim of promoting equal communication and collaboration between the farmers and professionals. Similarly, the neo-liberal approach challenges the validity of top-down state intervention, which neglects the fundamental function of market mechanisms on the one hand, and the rational selection and decision-making of farmers on the other.

Rather than conflicting with each other, the neo-populist and neo-liberal schools are complementary in some respects, such as technical and institutional, micro and macro, outside engagement or farmer self-selection. Focusing on exogenous organisation or institutional change, they share a common deficiency in the simplistic view of the marginal environment in which the majority of the poor have little chance to communicate with professionals and whose decision-making is seriously constrained by limited information and infrastructure. These limitations lead to a call for methodological innovation to observe and reveal farmers' own innovative potential and organisational practices. This is the theme of the next section.

2.3 Methodology for farmer innovation and self-organisation

Technical innovation, according to the previous section, cannot be separated from but is constrained by the institutional environment that determines the professionals' room for manoeuvre and relationship with farmers. With their focus on the exogenous organisation format and intervention mechanism, the three innovation approaches in the previous sections share a common deficiency in that they neglect the intrinsic dynamics and self-organising process of farmers for their innovative purposes. It is reasonable to ask: whether and how is it possible for traditional farmers to accumulate and strengthen their innovative capacity by themselves? By what kinds of network and mechanisms can they learn, diffuse and share new technologies, knowledge and methods? What interfaces exist between farmers' self-organisation and outside intervention (participation, assistance)? To address the above-mentioned questions, the organisational dimension of farmer innovation needs to be introduced and developed. Accordingly, in the beginning of this section, we clarify the position of farmer innovation through an overall review of innovation organisation studies. This is followed by a focus on social networks and function. To interpret the phenomenon of farmer innovation and self-organisation, the third section considers the role of social capital and its implications for institutional change.

2.3.1 Farmer innovation and self-organisation: definition and typology

The term farmer innovation here is used to emphasise the nature of the farmer as the first actor of rural technological and social change. Bearing in mind the interrelationship between technical and institutional changes, in this book, farmer innovation is defined narrowly as a technological change selected and determined by farmers themselves. The theme of this book can be expressed as a study of the organisational environments, conditions and mechanisms of farmer innovation in the marginal areas of China.

The notion *organisation* may mean different things to different people. Whilst the main attention of previous sections is paid to the formal, institutional and urban-led innovation organisations, it is equally important to understand these informal social networks, processes and mechanisms, which are more closely related to the genuine life of the poor. The term *organisation* in this book is used to include all formal and informal social linkages, functional relations and interactive mechanisms, which are used by farmers to carry out their production processes directly or indirectly, and to achieve their objectives of livelihood, growth or security.

Farmer innovation as an organisational process or collective action can be carried out by many channels, forms, means and mechanisms. The term *self-organisation* is a useful concept that encompasses not only organisational forms dominated by farmers themselves, but also an organisational (or evolutionary) process from simple to complex, from informal to formal. Originating from Nobel Laureate Ilya Prigogine's work on thermodynamic system and complexity (Nicolis and Prigogine 1977; Prigogine and Stengers 1985), self-organisation has been increasingly fashionable in systems research (Schieve and Allen 1982; Silverberg *et al.* 1988; Krugman 1996). Defined as 'the capability of some systems to reorder themselves into ever more complex structure' (Rycroft and Kash 1999: 61), self-organisation has been widely applied to interpret the complexity related to information technology and the economy.

Turning to marginal areas, farmer self-organisation here is broadly used to reflect a process of technological, social or institutional change, which is totally initiated, controlled and managed by farmers themselves. Furthermore, this process can be viewed as a focus of social communication, which is comprised of interaction between information (new ideas, knowledge or know-how) and communication channels. Accordingly, farmer self-organisation can be defined as a process of interaction between information (knowledge) systems and communication (social) networks, with the aim of securing rural livelihoods.

Combining knowledge (information) systems and communication networks together, a significant contribution to farmer innovation studies has been made in a research on 'indigenous communication' (Mundy and Compton 1995). Parallel with the distinction between the IKS and exogenous (scientific) knowledge, a communication channel can also be divided into indigenous and exogenous categories. The indigenous communication can be viewed as the system 'which existed before the arrival of mass media and formally organised bureaucratic systems, and is still in existence today despite changes' (Mundy and Compton 1995). Unlike exogenous channels, most indigenous communication channels are interpersonal, traditional, localised, informal and without bureaucratic organisation.

Rather than being separate from each other, the knowledge system and communication channel (organisation networks) are actually interconnected, and interactive, leading to the existence of different organisation patterns. Based on the nature and functions of communication networks, Mundy and Compton (1995) distinguish four types of innovation organisations (networks) (Box 2.4).

Box 2.4 Mundy and Compton's classification of rural innovation organisation

- *Exogenous communication of exogenous information.* Good examples are public education systems, mass media and agricultural extension networks, which are mainly employed by the government for modern technology transfer.
- *Exogenous communication of indigenous information.* The efforts of IKS documentation and farmer participatory research fall into this category. The wide application of traditional Chinese medicine in contemporary China is an example.
- *Indigenous communication of exogenous information.* Beside exogenous channels, some kinds of exogenous information and technologies can be also delivered through indigenous channels. A successful new crop variety, for instance, can be spread quickly through direct observation and unorganised channels between farmers.
- *Indigenous communication of indigenous information?*

Source: Mundy and Compton (1995).

Mundy and Compton's classification provides a valuable insight into the diversity of rural innovation organisation. Of many organisational types for technological innovation, according to Box 2.4, TT and farmer PR belong to the first two categories, in which there is involvement, and most likely, domination by external professionals. In contrast to exogenous intervention or engagement, the neo-liberal approach assumes that scientific research (exogenous information) would be able to meet the technological demands of rural producers, leaving the choice of organisational forms or mechanisms (either exogenous or endogenous) to market forces and farmers' own choice.

Compared with the first two types of innovation organisation predominated by outsiders, the second two categories in Box 2.4 are dominated by farmers. This is particularly true for the marginal areas where the rural poor find it difficult to access exogenous resources on the one hand, and a GR agricultural package is not necessarily suited to the marginal environment on the other. The focus in this book is, thus, on indigenous communication networks and mechanisms that have functions to diffuse either modern agricultural knowledge (exogenous information) or farmers' own experience or techniques (indigenous information).

Regarding the organisational format and mechanisms of farmer innovation, 'diffusion school' and social network studies are particularly relevant, which are briefly introduced in the next section.

2.3.2 Farmers' innovative capacity and social networks: diffusion school

Learning lessons from mainstream innovation schools, two conclusions can be drawn. First, related to the complexity of marginal environment, the rural poor are not homogeneous in terms of innovation demands and capacity. Second, heterogeneous farmers are not totally independent, in line with the assumption of the 'rational economic man', but are more likely interwoven in response to both challenges and opportunities. Taking account of the above factors, the diffusion school has made significant progress in understanding farmers' innovative capacity and mechanisms.

Needless to say, not all farmers in a society are the same in terms of adopting new knowledge, skill or methods. This provides a base to observe and measure technology diffusion amongst farmers. Rogers (1983) employed the notion of innovativeness to reflect the differences in innovation adoption within a social system. By a linear time series, all members of the system are classified into five categories of adopters (Rogers 1983: 241–251), namely: (i) *innovators* – venturesome; (ii) *early adopters* – respectable; (iii) *early majority* – deliberate; (iv) *late majority* – sceptical; (v) *laggards* – traditional.

To interpret the variety of innovativeness, he identifies three factors, including: *socio-economic status,* related to education, social status, upward social mobility, access to scarce resources, etc.; *personality variables* such as empathy and rationality, attitude, ability to cope with uncertainty and risk, and achievement motivation; and *communication behaviour*, which refers to social participation, contact frequency or interpersonal communication channels. For Rogers, innovativeness is universal and predetermined by socio-economic status and personality variables. Being based upon a linear assumption of technology substitution, Rogers' classification system actually excludes traditional technology and skills, and views most of the poor, if not all, as laggards in terms of both attitude to innovation and capacity to adopt modern technology.

Avoiding a strict hierarchy or rank index such as that of Rogers, Mundy and Compton (1995) point out the complexity and diversity of innovative capacity. For instance, 'a person may be a highly skilled smith but know little of farming, another may be held in high esteem for her midwifery or gardening skills'. For them, five different types of innovative sources in the indigenous knowledge system can be recognised (Box 2.5). In contrast to Rogers' emphasis on time order, Mundy and Compton's classification pays more attention to the width and depth of knowledge or technique. Compared with the former, the latter scheme seems less 'professionally biases'.

Farmer innovation involves a communication channel or network to carry or facilitate information communication and knowledge diffusion. As regards the flow of information, Rogers (1983) views interpersonal links as an important factor influencing the adoption of an innovation. Specifically, Mundy and Compton (1995) divide indigenous communication channels into several types, such as: *indigenous organisations:* for example, religious groups, village meetings, irrigation associations; *deliberate instruction:* a form of education and innovation diffusion ranging widely from child-rearing practices to any individual learning and habituating something throughout the entire life cycle; *unorganised channels:* spontaneous and informal meetings and talk in wider settings such as at home, in the fields, on the road, at the market; *direct observation:* referring to the kind of innovation where the source does not have to be another person.

***Box 2.5* Types of innovation sources in indigenous knowledge systems**

- *Indigenous experts* in broad areas such as crop or livestock raising who are frequently sought out for advice.
- *Indigenous professionals*: for example, blacksmiths, veterinarians, healers, midwives, etc., whose skills are mainly gained through long apprenticeship or on-the-job training.
- *Innovators* are a major source of indigenous innovation through deliberate experimentation by themselves or introduction of new ideas from outside.
- *Intermediaries* do not originate but report information to association members.
- *Recipient-disseminators* are informal intermediaries in the information chain. As links outside the local society, 'they are important conduits for the lateral exchange of both indigenous and exogenous innovations'.

Source: Mundy and Compton (1995).

Despite the many forms or channels of technological communication, in reality, not all people have equal access to desired information. Concerning the relationship between communication and innovation, Rogers (1983) distinguishes pairs of interactive individuals as heterophiles (different) and homophiles (similar) in certain attributes such as beliefs, education and social status. In his view, 'more effective communication occurs when two individuals are homophilous' while the communication of innovation often takes place where 'the participants are usually quite heterophilous'. As a result, the homophile is viewed as 'a barrier to diffusion' while the heterophile faces dilemmas 'in securing effective communication' (Rogers 1983: 19).

The heterophile–homophile distinction indicates the possibility of knowledge transfer from one group to another. Equally important, how is new knowledge diffused and shared among group members, which may vary from one group to another? To address this issue, the term proximity is employed to measure the degree to which personal communication networks overlap (Rogers 1983: 295).

Generally, communication occurs within the border of cliques through strong ties (i.e. high proximity). Due to the nature of the homophile, however, close friends in each clique 'seldom know much that the individual does not also know'. In contrast, the low-proximity link is an important channel for the flow of information between cliques. As a result, the weak tie is 'strong' in 'its potential for carrying information between the two unlike cliques and thus playing a crucial role in the diffusion of innovativeness' (Rogers 1983: 298).

By combining homophily (or heterophily) with proximity dimensions, personal networks can be classified into different patterns, which may be representative of various types of society with different innovation function and potential. At one end of the continuum, a traditional society characterised by closeness in personal contact, similarity in personal qualities (high homophily) and collectivism in value system (high proximity) is more likely to be poor in innovativeness. At the other end, modern society is more diverse (high heterophily) in labour diversity and individualist in value system (low proximity), which would lower the social barriers to innovation. As a result, traditional personal relationships cannot contribute to, but block, innovation.

In summary, Rogers' approach provides a worthy but sad picture in which various kinds of societies should be transformed to individualist societies, if innovative capacity (innovativeness) is the objective of development. It seems difficult to deny that there is a positive relationship between heterogeneity and innovation capacity. It is questionable, however, whether traditional social relationships and a collectivist value system are necessarily barriers to technology innovation. As a counter to the above biases, the social capital debate offers an opposite picture to traditional organisations.

2.3.3 Social capital and organisational innovation

While the diffusion school considers the process of innovation, the interpersonal network is seen as largely unchangeable. As a part of social change, however, not only are knowledge systems and communication networks subject to continuous adjustment and change, but also the two processes are interconnected and interactive with each other. In this sense, it is reasonable to assume that farmers are the first actors of both technological change, and organisational innovation, leading to new or formal organisations. Many questions arise: How is it possible for the poor to initiate, run and manage organisational innovation by themselves? What is the relationship between the technical and organisational innovation? What are the implications of farmer innovation and self-organisation for institutional change against rural poverty and marginalisation? These questions may be difficult to address without a social capital dimension. The following paragraphs, therefore, introduce the concept of social capital, and the implications for farmer innovation organisation studies.

Although there is great variety in its definition and utilisation, the term *social capital* can be identified as having four core aspects: (i) relations of trust; (ii) reciprocity and exchanges; (iii) common rules, norms and sanctions; and (iv) connectedness, networks and groups (Coleman 1990; Putnam *et al.* 1993; Carney 1998; Grootaert 1998; Ostrom 1998; Pretty and Ward 2001). In contrast with vertical approaches to the interaction between outside professionals and rural poor, the concept of social capital considers the horizontal dimension, which pays particular attention to the role of farmer cohesion and co-operation in strengthening their innovative capacity. In this sense, social capital is a capacity of the poor working together to cope with common challenges from unfavourable environments, and to use and share knowledge and skills for resource and production management..

Focusing on reciprocal and co-operative linkages amongst farmers, 'social capital' can be increased through accumulation (e.g. growing frequency of communication and mutual aids between households) or creation (e.g. establishment of new co-operative partnership and groups). Social capital may also be diminished through the expansion of individualism and conflict. It cannot be assumed that social capital is always a good thing without any side impacts. An important, though often neglected, aspect of social capital is the way it relates to innovation. In the face of growing uncertainty, about economies, climates and political processes, the capacity of people both to innovate and to adapt known technologies and practices to suit new conditions becomes vital for rural development and innovation in marginal zones. An important question is whether forms of social capital can be accumulated to enhance such innovation (Boyte 1995; Hamilton 1995; Pretty 1995; Röling and Wagemakers 1997).

Accumulation and creation of social capital have functions to not only enhance the adaptive and innovative capacity of the rural poor, but also a potential or real function to back up, lead to or accelerate social change. In this sense, farmer innovation and self-organisation can be approached as a process of social organisational and institutional change. As an institutional process, farmers' self-organisation is indirectly supported by Pretty (1995: 132–134), who suggests that local organisations (called 'indigenous collective management systems') have played the dominant role in agricultural development until the establishment of modern agriculture extension institutions in the twentieth century. One of the lessons learned from agricultural modernisation, in his view (Pretty 1995: 162), is that the suffocation of local institutions led to 'increased degradation and the decreased capacity in local people to cope with environmental and economic change'. It is not surprising, therefore, that organised farmers can manage to continue their collective activities after project completion, while the lack of institutional variables is often linked to the failure or unsustainability of a large number of projects.

Since it involves various demands and interest contradictions between various participants, farmers' self-organisation cannot be idealised. Related to the heterogeneity of rural people and varied access to scarce resources, Pretty discovers that the organisation or institutional process often involves traditional institutions and existing groups that are full of local biases and may not be representative of the poor (Pretty 1995: 142–143). Calling for an 'actor-oriented approach', Long and Villarreal (1993) emphasise the interplay and mutual determination of 'internal' and 'external' factors and relationships. Rejecting a simplified explanation of 'state–peasant relations', he emphasises an 'interface analysis' of the discontinuities in social life and organisational culture. Instead of being completely independent without any interaction, or absolute co-operation without any conflict interest, the rural poor are better seen as a sum of heterogeneous individuals who have both common demands and conflicts of interest. The key to innovation studies is to understand first the interfaces of various farmers (including economic interest, social identification and value orientation) and then the connection mechanisms that involve the various indigenous organisations or networks. Rather than vertical relationships between the top and the bottom, it is more important to reveal horizontal interest interfaces between various groups in rural society, and between rural and urban people as well.

In summary, farmer innovation and self-organisation can be viewed as a process of accumulation and creation of 'social capital', with the function of enhancing the capacity to adapt to and cope with various challenges and uncertainty. Social capital is particularly important for marginal areas where the marginal environment impedes the communication between the rural poor and urban professionals. To cope with the shortage and constraints of other assets, there is no choice but to use and enhance the social capital for the purposes of technology learning and innovation cooperation. The role of social capital, therefore, cannot be overstated, because internal networks are not isolated but are shaped by external organisation or institutions. This claim, however, needs to be verified by empirical evidence, which will be the theme of following chapters.

2.4 Conclusions: environment, sustainability and farmer innovation

By way of introduction to an empirical study on sustainability and innovation in rural China, this chapter has taken a 'tour' around the debate about the Third World's rural development and innovation. With the aim of identifying a suitable conceptual framework and research methodology, it has drawn special attention to three questions: what is the meaning of SD for the rural poor? What role can they play in technological innovation in order to improve and secure their livelihoods? And by what organisational patterns can their innovative capacity be enhanced to cope with various challenges and uncertainties? The main findings have been summarised next.

First, SD as distinct from convenient development means not only a change of the priority to the demands of the rural poor, but also a rethinking of development procedure to allow them to participate in development decision-making and to contribute their experience and knowledge. Focusing on their adaptation and coping capacity against various challenges and uncertainties, the SRL approach provides a basis for a focus on balance and harmony among five assets: natural, human, social, physical and financial capitals. Under the umbrella of the SRL, however, the role of the rural poor varies significantly from one school to another. These schools can be further distinguished according to various emphases and composition of four elements or dimensions: exogenous vs. endogenous, technological vs. organisational (institutional). Whilst the interaction and interfaces between external and intrinsic dynamics cannot be overstated, a major issue facing developmental professionals is that we have actually known little about intrinsic dynamics and developmental potential among the rural poor. Many questions arise: how can we identify the intrinsic dynamics and development potential among the rural poor? Why is endogenous development so important for the marginal areas and rural poor to cope with various challenges against livelihood improvement and security? By what kinds of organisational patterns or institutional arrangements can the intrinsic dynamics and development potential of the poor be fully used and released? And where is the interface between endogenous and exogenous dynamics, between farmers and professionals?

Second, the SRL cannot be achieved without technological innovation in which the rural poor can play different roles, depending upon different understandings of both the environment and innovation. In the classical approach, the assumed similarity of the environment of technology application and homogeneity of the producers allow a linear process of TT from research centres to rural users, and is dominated by government and urban professionals. By contrast, the neo-populists shed light on the complexity of the marginal areas and the validity of the IKS, leading to a call for novel collaborative relationship between the rural poor and 'new professionals'. In contrast to the narrow focus on either material factors or knowledge system, the neo-liberal approach emphasises an appropriate institutional environment and policy levers, which would induce desired knowledge supply and technological demands. Whilst overwhelming attention has been paid to the relationship between the farmer and outsiders, we have known little about whether the rural poor have the capacity to learn, improve and even create new technologies by themselves. If so how heterogeneous is the innovative capacity among them, and what factors influence the distribution of the capacity? By what means and policy intervention can their capacity be enhanced, and what lessons can be learnt from unsuccessful intervention in the past?

Finally, the importance of farmer innovative capacity for the SRL leads to a call for a methodological innovation to observe the social networks and self-organisational mechanisms employed by farmers for their own innovation practices. Constrained by unfavourable natural and social factors, the rural poor cannot rely solely upon external assistance but must use and enhance social capital, a capacity of the poor working together to cope with common challenges. Many questions arise regarding the relationship between sustainable livelihoods, social capital and farmer innovation. Why and in what way is social capital important for the rural poor to secure their livelihoods in general, and to enhance their innovative capacity in particular? Is there any correlation between marginal environment, social capital and farmer innovative capacity? If so, how can it be measured and verified? By what patterns and mechanisms do farmers use, maintain and develop their social capital for the purpose of enhancing their innovative capacity? What are the implications of social capital and farmer innovation for SD and innovation in marginal areas of China?

The following chapters attempt to address these questions.

3 Marginal areas and marginalisation in rural China

Farmer innovation and self-organisation, as shown in Chapter 2, is particularly important to the marginal areas, not only because the marginal environment constrains communication between farmers and professionals, but also because the CDR of the environment are constraints on the application of convenient technological systems and innovation models. The necessity of farmer innovation and self-organisation is particularly important in the era of economic liberty and globalisation, wherein more capital flows from marginal to core areas, resulting in increasing regional gap and income inequalities. In this respect, perhaps, China's experience is particularly salient due to both its impressive achievement in economic transition from a planned to a market system, and its concentrated efforts against rural poverty and regional inequality. Many questions arise: Where are its marginal areas and how seriously has China suffered from the marginalisation process? What are the impacts of marginalisation on rural poverty reduction and environmental sustainability? How effectively has the Chinese government coped with challenges of marginalisation in general and rural poverty and ecological degradation in particular? These issues are addressed in subsequent chapters. This chapter attempts to conceptualise the core–marginal division, the marginalisation process and the impacts on the government's PRP in China's market economic era, whilst Chapter 4 takes Shaanxi province as an example to reveal the environmental effects of marginalisation, and of the government innovation strategy. The next section briefly introduces the geography of rural China, leading to a core–marginal division. This is followed by a description of the regional development and marginalisation process. Section 3.3 draws attention to the impacts of marginalisation on the government's PRP. Linked with the theme of SRL, the final section summarises the findings from secondary data analysis and raises a list of further questions, which the fieldwork in rural Shaanxi sought to answer.

3.1 Geography for China's rural change? A core–marginal division

Due to its huge land area and complex geographical environment, rural China can hardly be viewed as a homogenous whole. It is particularly true that market-oriented reform since the late 1970s has reshaped its landscape, requiring an updated geography of rural China (Leeming 1993). Of the work to be done, regional division should be put at the forefront. Accordingly, this section begins to examine the complexity of China's physical environment, then compares the major regional division systems. Based on a combination of geographic features and economic change, Section 3.3 proposes a new division system for rural study in the era of market economy.

3.1.1 Complexity of China's physical environment

With regard to the regional division of rural China, a notable feature is the complexity of the geographic environment and resource distribution, which results in various images, according to the perspective taken.

From the topographical perspective, China is a mountainous country: two-thirds of its land is covered by numerous mountains and hills with a wide range of altitudes, from earth summit over 8,000 m above sea level to −50 m in some areas. Despite its mountains and hills being wide, spread broadly speaking, a three-step 'staircase' can be distinguished from the Qinghai-Tibet Plateau in the west, via the Inner Mongolia, Loess and Yunnan-Guizhou plateaus, to the eastcoast (Cannon and Jenkins 1990).

Due to its large span of both longitude and latitude, China's climate pattern is also very complex. One of the outstanding features is its uneven distribution of precipitation resources, which range from over 2,000 mm/year in the southeast to less than 200 mm in the northwest. As a result, the surplus rainfall supply in the south is in sharp contrast to severe shortage of water resources in the north. With respect to aridity, China can be divided into many zones: humid, semi-humid, semi-arid and arid. These zones are arranged from the southeast to the northwest, leading to a geographic division, namely the 'Aihui–Tengchong division', which divides China into two parts. Northwest China is constrained by arid or semi-arid climatic conditions which are unfavourable for agricultural production; thus, animal husbandry predominates. By contrast, southeast China is characterised by humid or semi-humid climate conditions where agriculture is predominant (Goodman 1989).

Related to geographic and climatic conditions, the distribution of China's population is uneven. More than 90 per cent of the population live in only a little more than 30 per cent of the country's land area where the population density is over 350 persons/km^2. By contrast, 10 per cent of the population are spread in 70 per cent of the land, with an average population density of less than 20 persons/km^2 (Heilig 1999). One conclusion can be drawn out. Rural China cannot be viewed as a homogeneous whole, nor can the regions be distinguished by a sole factor (e.g. topography, climate or soil conditions) because they do not necessarily match each other. It is incorrect, therefore, to assume that there is a universal model or solution for all of rural China.

Bearing in mind the extreme complexity, rural China can be divided into four rims whose main features and estimated resource distribution can be summarised as shown in Table 3.1. Regardless of economic and political factors, the four rims

Table 3.1 Estimation of population and resource distribution by rural division

Indicators	*Rim I*	*Rim II*	*Rim III*	*Rim IV*
Total land (%)	25–35	10–15	25–30	25–30
Total population (%)	70–75	15–20	10–15	<2
Population density (people/km^2)	>270	100–200	50–100	<10
Altitude (m)	<500	500–1,000	1,000–3,000	>3,000
Yield potential (tonne/ha)	6–13	4–6	<4	0

Source: Based upon information from Heilig (1999).

in Table 3.1 represent four different environment types, levels of carrying capacity and production potential within Chinese territory. At one end, about 30 per cent of China's land is resource-rich, high-potential areas that are occupied by over 70 per cent of the national population. At the other end, the remaining 30 per cent of its territory is almost uninhabited due to its extreme climatic conditions and lack of natural resources. Between the two ends of the spectrum, one-third of national land and population is shared by Rims II and III.

The purpose of Table 3.1 is not to seek for an absolute benchmark for regional division, but to provide a rough idea of how unevenly China' population and resources are distributed, and what regional pattern most closely reflects the real distribution.

In contrast to absolute static division systems, Table 3.1 offers an insight into the dynamic process of China's environmental change. Assuming Rims I and IV to have stable status in terms of production potential and carrying capacity, Rims II and III are more likely to be unstable on the one hand, and have different or even opposite trends of environmental change on the other. Under a similar amount of environmental investment, it would be easier for Rim II to improve its environmental quality and carrying capacity than for Rim III. Under similar population or economic pressure, it is likely that the latter would go downward to Rim IV.

The above division seems to be in line with China's present ecological environment. For instance, whilst one-third of the land is threatened by desertification, it is necessary to distinguish the desert and gebei (Rim IV) from the degraded land (Rim III), which is still used by farmers for their livelihoods, despite rapid decline in carrying capacity. Similarly, soil erosion as a big issue challenging China's environment can be further recognised to fall into two categories: light erosion with great production potential (Rim II) and severe erosion (Rim III) tending towards waste land (Rim IV).

Regarding China's environment change and sustainability, three conclusions can be drawn. First, the above classification system is not limited within conventional regional division systems and, in principle, can be applied to all regions, no matter how big or small. Second, within this huge territory and variety of ecological zones, special attention should be paid to the transition areas (Rims II and III) along the 'Aihui–Tengchong division', not only because of their geographic position between the crowded southeast and harsh northwest, but also because of their ecological fragility and instability that influence the environmental systems of the downstream Yangtze and Yellow Rivers. Finally, although they share many common features, there would be significant differences between Rims II and III in terms of both resource endowment and environmental trends. The top priority in China should be given to Rim III, to reverse the trend of rural poverty and environmental degradation.

3.1.2 Comparison of regional division systems

Reflecting differences in geographical environment and resource endowment, there are many regional division systems used in China. Two main division systems are used according to purpose: administrative division and agricultural planning.

Of the many regional division systems, the most popular is the administrative division, which classifies rural China according to the borders and hierarchy of administrative units: provincial, county and township. At the national level, rural China is divided into three strips: east, middle and west, of which the basic unit of statistics and measures is the province (Autonomous Regions or Municipalities).

Within the present political system, the administrative division has the advantage of facilitating collection and comparison of regional development information. As a regional study and planning tool, however, it has many deficiencies. First, the administrative division does not necessarily reflect the borders of natural and ecological systems, resulting in a decline in the accuracy of regional comparison. Second, since the emphasis is on inter-regional difference, it is easy to neglect the differences and complexity in intra-regional development. Finally, considering the range of variation, the big differences in population density within the western region raises question of comparability among western provinces (e.g. Sichuan vs. Tibet, Shaanxi vs. Xingjing). Similar criticisms can be applied at the province and county levels.

An alternative system focusing on agricultural resource distribution and regional features is the agricultural resource and regional planning system, which was established in the 1980s (Sun *et al.* 1994). Following a standard process and methodology, thousands of professionals and experts from a wide range of academic backgrounds were gathered to conduct a resource inquiry. This resulted in a comprehensive regionalisation system from county to national levels. At the national level, for instance, there are nine agricultural zones instead of the 'three strips' in the administrative division, and each of these is further divided into several parts, resulting in a total of thirty-eight secondary zones.

By contrast with administrative division, much progress has been achieved by the agricultural regionalisation system. First, agricultural resources and ecological factors have been fully considered in the new system, which has provided more accurate information about local ecological systems and resource distribution. Second, breaking through the administrative border, the new system can take a balanced account of administrative and ecological factors, which aids understanding of the complexity and diversity of rural environment and development.

However, the new system has some disadvantages that have limited its application and development. First, since it originated with the planned economic system, it is increasingly difficult to account for the change and uncertainty of the market-demand environment. Second, its main concern is with natural factors and professionals' voices at the expense of social factors and farmers' voice. Finally, since it does not match the administrative structure, it is difficult to maintain and update system information.

It seems that the two regional division systems each have advantages and disadvantages. Whilst the administrative division is more easily used to collect and compare official statistical information, agricultural division is more accurate in reflecting the differences in agricultural resources and ecological environment. Both, however, share a top-down approach to various degrees and over-simplify the rural environment.

3.1.3 Definition of China's marginal areas

Reflecting the economic transition from a planned to a market system, it seems necessary to introduce a new regional division system in order to overcome the limitations existing in the present regional division systems. For this purpose, three criteria can be set up in advance. First, the new system should be able to reveal the change and trend of local ecological environment. Second, it should be in keeping with the transition towards a market economic system. Finally, it should be compatible with other regional division systems to facilitate use and comparison of available data/information.

To satisfy the above criteria, China's territory can be divided into three parts: *core, marginal* and *sterile areas*. Core areas are those regions, zones or locations where natural and/or man-made environments are so favourable or attractive that the majority of population, economic activities and social wealth are concentrated there. By contrast, sterile areas are those locations, areas or regions where natural, ecological or human environments are not suitable for human beings to settle unless man-made environments or facilities are available. Intermediate between the core and sterile categories, marginal areas are featured by resource shortages and unstable ecological environments.

From the perspective of physical geography, the term marginal areas would be helpful to clarify the nature, scope and trends of China's environmental change. By contrast with core areas, which are resource rich and characterised by high carrying capacity, marginal areas suffer constraints not only from deficient resources and low carrying capacity, but also from ecological fragility and high risks. In contrast to sterility, which is another 'stable status', the marginal areas are actually in a state of environmental instability, which has potential of either improving towards the condition of the core areas or continuing to degrade towards environment collapse or sterility (Zhu and Wang 1993). In this sense, the marginal areas are crucial for both China's environmental sustainability and its food security in the twenty-first century (Brown 1995).

Under the market economic environment era, marginal areas have both advantages and disadvantages. Regarding the former, marginal areas have more land

and minor resources, but less population and capital stock. As population, capital and wealth accumulation in the core areas increase, the marginal areas will become increasingly attractive to outsiders (from the core areas) due to their cheaper labour, land and potential market. As a result, the marginal areas would sooner or later be integrated into the outside market. Regarding the latter, marginal areas have three barriers: poor infrastructure and high costs of production and transportation; poor stock of human capital; and high ecological risks.

The above assertions, however, seem too simple to reflect the complexity of rural environment and development in the marginal areas. As Section 3.1.1 has shown, rural China can hardly be viewed as a homogenous whole, and the successful experience in Rim I might not be valid for replication in other regions, because of the large inter-regional differences. Taking into account the heterogeneity of rural resources and economic development, the marginal areas can be further divided into two parts: semi-peripheral and peripheral zones, which may be matched with Rims II and III displayed in Table 3.1. The difference between the two zones is not confined to quantitative elements such as the distance to economic centres or the stock of natural and physical capital, but is also qualitative, related to the environments' carrying capacity and the trend of environmental change. Although both zones are short of physical and human resources, the peripheral zone, in particular, suffers from increasing ecological degradation and outflow of other capital, in contrast to the relative stability and even improvement of these assets in the semi-peripheral zones. In this sense, the semi-peripheral zone can be viewed as an intermediate area between core and peripheral zones, which share the characteristics of both and can absorb resources from both sides. The existence of an intermediate zone offers opportunities to observe and interpret the imbalance of capital and information exchange between the central and peripheral zones.

Like the administrative division system, the core–marginal division can be applied to various levels from nation to township, depending on the research questions and objectives. Although it does not necessarily conflict with the administrative division

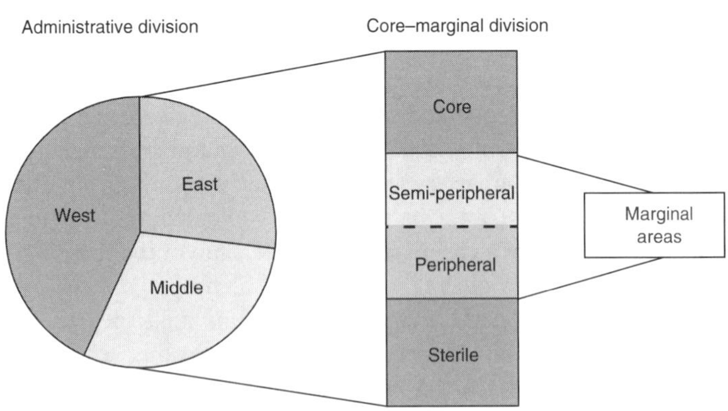

Figure 3.1 Comparison of regional division: administrative vs. core–marginal.

system, the core–marginal division emphasises on the heterogeneity and complexity of rural development. Besides geographic environmental constraints, in particular, it draws attention to various social and political biases, which are favourable to the core zone against the peripheral zone. Figure 3.1 illustrates a comparison between the administrative and core–marginal divisions.

The core–marginal division provides a useful tool for this book to identify the regional change response to the generation of the market economic system, and to understand 'policy biases' against peripheral zones and the rural poor in particular. Applying the new regional division system, the next section describes the process of regionalisation and Section 3.3 focuses on policy biases related to poverty reduction.

3.2 Rural change and marginalisation in market economy era

The necessity of the core–marginal division will be clear if China's rural change and marketisation are taken into account. Due to the great variation in resource endowments and economic conditions, a similar development strategy or policy intervention might have different impacts on different regions, resulting in an increasing (or decreasing) regional gap. To understand various impacts of rural reform on regional development, this section begins by outlining rural institutional change. This is followed by discussion of the adjustment of rural economic structure in part two and the effects on its core areas in part three. Reflecting China's uneven development, marginalisation is also discussed, paving the way to a discussion of impacts on rural livelihoods in Section 3.3.

3.2.1 Overview of China's rural change and economic development

The complexity of rural China is not only due to its land area and landscape type, but also due to its unique social change in the last half a century. To understand the process and impacts of the rural change, the following paragraphs outline the broad background of China's rural institutional change with reference to the relationship adjustment or reconstruction amongst farmers, land, market and government.

Before the 1950s, rural China was dominated by a feudal land system and self-sufficient household farms that had weak linkages with the outside world. The key barrier to rural development was the centralisation of land resources with a small proportion of landlords, leaving the mass landless peasants without a secure livelihood. For instance, according to a national survey conducted in 1952, the rich accounted for less than 10 per cent of the rural population but over half of the nation's farmland area whilst the poor accounted for over half of the population but held less than 15 per cent of the land (MOA 1999). Equal distribution of land and social wealth was the dream of Chinese peasants for thousands of years.

Learning lessons from the country's history, the Communist Party adopted 'land reform' as an important strategy in its struggle for national power and to initiate rural development. The radical 'land reform' in the early 1950s led to equal distribution of land resources among rural residents, without changing the nature of private ownership. Afterwards, a farmers' production organisation, called 'mutual-aid group', was encouraged by the government. The gradual process, unfortunately, was interrupted by a radical collectivisation in the late 1950s, which led to a fundamental change of land ownership from private farmers to collective organisations on the one hand, and the reshaping of rural production and social systems from individual households to a large-scale CCS on the other. The new system was further integrated into and controlled by a top-down state planning system. Besides the contribution to national industrialisation, the main functions of the CCS institutions were to ensure self-sufficiency of grain and to provide a comprehensive social welfare security to all community members (Glaeser 1987; Lin and Zhang 1997).

Despite impressive achievements in social equality and agricultural infrastructure improvement, the CCS could not survive, due to the failure to satisfy the basic demands of rural residents. Since Deng Xiaoping's reforms started in the late 1970s, a series of changes have occurred in rural China:

- A household responsibility system (HRS) has been introduced to replace the CCS. Unlike private farms, all land resources in the HRS still belonged to the collective (community).
- Market mechanisms have become a dominant factor driving the rural economy. Under the umbrella of a 'socialist market economy', the impacts of government intervention in the rural economy and social affairs cannot be underestimated although it may very greatly from one region to another.
- Related to collective ownership of rural land resources, the ideal institution is neither the private farm nor the traditional commune system but a two-tier economic system consisting of household farmers and their community economic organisations. Together with the HRS, it is expected that the collective (community) economic system will be able to develop so as to provide various production or technological services to small farmers.

In response to rural reform and the HRS, farmers' enthusiasm and productive potential have been released, providing a powerful dynamic for rural economic growth. Compared with 1978, according to official statistics, by 1998 the net income of rural residents of increased 4.6 times nationwide, an average growth rate of 7.9 per cent annually (MOA 1999).

Regarding rural economic change, Table 3.2 shows the evolution of the rural economic structure since 1978. By contrast to the predominance of agriculture in 1978, the non-agriculture sector has become the dominant force of economic growth, accounting for more than three-fourths of gross rural outputs twenty years later. Turning to agricultural products, Table 3.2 indicates the declining trend of crops from 80 per cent in 1978 to just over a half in 1998, in contrast to the doubling of livestock in the same period. Focusing on crops themselves, the increase in sowing area for cash crops reflects the growing trend towards cash agriculture in the rural economy, although the area given to cash cropping may not fully reflect the size of its contribution to rural livelihoods.

Table 3.2 Change of China's rural economic structure

Category	*Sector*	*1978*	*1990*	*1998*
Gross value (products)	Agriculture	68.6	57.1	22.3
	Non-agriculture	31.4	42.9	77.7
Agriculture (products)	Crops	80.0	64.7	56.2
	Livestock	15.0	25.7	30.8
	Others	5.0	9.7	13.0
Crops (sowing area)	Grain	80.4	76.5	73.0
	Cash and others	19.6	23.5	27.0

Source: Edited according to MOA (1999).

Compared with over three-fourths of gross output values, however, non-agriculture had only 30 per cent of the rural labour forces in 1998 (MOA 1999). This suggests that neither does all rural non-agricultural growth in China contribute to rural labour transition to non-agricultural employment, nor have all rural residents received benefits from non-agriculture activities. Examination of the structure of the agricultural economic system reveals that the role of grain production has significantly declined whilst animal breeding and cash cropping, which are largely dependent upon urban markets, have become increasingly important.

Three conclusions can be drawn from the rural economic transformation. First, taking account of relatively equal access to farmland resources and participation in grain production, rural economic growth in the reformed China has been achieved through a transformation of the rural output structure, resulting in non-agricultural dominance. Second, farmers do not share equally the benefits from rural economic growth, because of unequal opportunity of non-agricultural employment and access to urban markets. Finally, rural economic transformation is largely a process of rural reorganisation, because individual households cannot enter a distant market without information channels and a suitable organisational format (either formal or informal).

3.2.2 Regionalisation: rural industrialisation and commercialised agriculture

As a consequence of both its history and present institutions, rural China is still in the process of economic transformation from a homogenous and agriculture (especially grain) dominated economy to a heterogeneous and predominantly non-agricultural one. Parallel with the economic transformation, and equally important, rural China is on the way to a reorganisation whereby individual and small households will be able to enter a wider market. This raises questions: How is rural reorganisation matched with economic transformation? What are the impacts of environmental factors? Both issues are closely related to the geographic environment, which generates two different paths or patterns: rural industrialisation and commercialised agriculture.

It seems difficult to imagine how an economic miracle can occur in rural China without a process of rural industrialisation, referring to continuous increase and dominance of rural non-agricultural products in overall rural outputs. The role of non-agriculture in rural economic development can be verified from the following facts. By year 1998, rural industry nationwide provided: 78 per cent of rural gross outputs and 60 per cent of rural economic growth at current year; 125 million employment opportunities, a share of 27 per cent of total rural labour or 50 per cent of rural surplus labour; 32 per cent of rural net income; 28 per cent of national gross domestic product (GDP), 35 per cent of national export value and 20 per cent of the tax revenues (MOA 1999).

Rural industrialisation cannot be separated from the process of rural organisational innovation, resulting in the spread of TVEs. By 1998, the number of TVEs nationwide had reached about 20 million, 97 per cent of which were registered as individual or private companies (MOA 1999). Besides rural employment and income growth, and not less important, the TVEs have contributed to urbanisation and infrastructure improvement. This is particularly true for the collective TVEs that have played a positive role in agricultural technological advance through investing in or subsidising agricultural infrastructure.

Despite impressive achievements in rural non-agriculture, the majority of rural livelihoods are still dependent upon agriculture. Whilst the equal distribution of farmland resources provides a sound base for household food supply, differences in rural income are largely related to the scale and extent of household specialisation in the areas of cash crops, economic forestation or animal breeding, or others products produced for market demands. The term *commercialised agriculture* is used to reflect such a process and trend whereby, besides conventional grain crops, household income is increasingly dependent upon one or two products in which there exists comparative advantages in either production skill or scale. The trend to commercialised agriculture can be illustrated through the following statistical data (MOA 1999):

- from 1978 to 1998, the crops per capita increased for grain, 1.24 times; cotton, 1.50 times; vegetables, 3.56 times; fruits, 6.38 times; meat, 6.61 times;
- from 1985 to 1997, the total trade value of agricultural products increased 27.6 times;
- about 19 million households nationwide specialise in commercialised agricultural production.

Similar to the roles of the TVEs in rural industrialisation, FTAs or similar organisations are well developed, and play a crucial role in terms of interconnection and interfaces between farmers and the market (Yao *et al.* 1996). Despite great variety in format and extent, the FTAs provide an organisational base or 'platform' for hundreds of thousands of farmers to access and share market information, and to learn new techniques or skills by themselves. It is estimated that a total of 11,800 FTAs nationwide offer various production, technology or information services to their members (MOA 1999).

Since many factors and conditions are involved, the development of TVEs and FTAs has been uneven. It seems clear that the TVEs have been highly successful in the advanced regions of the eastcoast or suburbs of cities. Parallel to rural industrialisation, alternatively, commercialised agriculture is rapidly expanding in the inland regions that may not have resources or opportunities for the TVEs but have advantages of agricultural resources such as fertile land and irrigation facilities with good transport linkages. The term regionalisation is used to reflect such a process and trend of rural economic development. It is defined as the 'advantage area of products (or services)' according to market environment and local (regional) resource endowment and, equally important, guides the flow of local (regional) resources (capital, labour, technology, etc.) to release their potential.

Regionalisation in rural China, according to the definition above, involves many elements (e.g. market demands, resource endowments), sectors (e.g. agriculture, transport, credit) and complex interactions amongst elements, sectors or actors. Accordingly, three issues are crucial for successful regional development. First, what is the meaning of 'advantage area' for a region, which may exist in the form of potential in most circumstances, and which may vary region by region and from one period to another? Second, how can the potential of advantage areas be fully released or utilised, and the risk of failure avoided or minimised? Finally, by what organisational strategy can local resources and conditions be utilised and combined to achieve large-scale benefits?

Bearing in mind the uneven geographic and resource distribution, many lessons can be learnt from the rural economic development practices in the past. First, there is no universal model or path that is suitable for the whole countryside. It is not surprising that a high frequency of failure has occurred when poor regions tried to copy the experience of the TVEs from more advanced regions.

Second, as a result of many factors and conditions, each region may have a few 'advantage areas' in which regional resources are expected to be used and released to the maximum. With its dense population, advanced transportation, craft tradition and limited land resources, the central zone is more suitable for rural industrialisation, whist the semi-peripheral zone, which is rich in land resources but far way from industrial centres, may be more fitted to commercialised agriculture than rural industry. Without a distinction between semi-peripheral and peripheral zones in the marginal areas of China, it is often assumed that the experience of the former would be suitable for all marginal areas, leading to a failure in application in the peripheral zones.

Finally, geographic division cannot determine, but provides the possibility of applying a specific 'technical strategy' (or pattern) for regional development. Equally important is rural organisation strategy, which involves many actors and complex interactions at various levels. Linked with the dissolution of the CCS and the popularity of the TVEs and FTAs in core areas, it can be suggested that rural disorganisation is both a cause and effect of economic backwardness in marginal areas.

3.2.3 Marginalisation: definition and features

Whilst rural reform has successfully promoted economic development and income improvement, the distribution of benefits is uneven, depending on geographic location and selection of development pattern. Generally, rural industrialisation seems to be more popular in the central zones, where farmers enjoy high-profit non-agricultural income. By specialising their production and sales, farmers in semi-peripheral zones can also gain benefits from commercial agriculture and economies of scale.

Reflecting uneven development, rural income difference and inequality have received increasing attention. Regardless of geographic factors, the Gini coefficient for per capita income rose from less than 0.20 in the late 1970s to more than 0.40 by the late 1990s (Benjamin *et al.* 2000). By aggregating provincial data, many researchers have confirmed the increasing income gap between east, middle and western China (Johnston 1999; Kanbur and Zhang 1999). A similar picture can be applied at the intra-provincial level (Lyons 1998).

Many conclusions can be drawn from China's uneven development. First, even though the vast majority of rural residents, if not all, have received benefits from rural reform and development, the distribution of income and welfare growth is very uneven. Second, the unevenness is closely related to geographical factors, which can be distinguished by the core–marginal division at various levels, from national to local. Finally, the differences and inequalities in regional development seems not to have been reduced but have even widened. The term marginalisation is used to refer to this process and trend of development leading to an increasing gap and inequality between core and marginal areas at various levels.[1]

The definition above emphasises that marginalisation is not a development status or stage, but a process leading to continuous enlargement of regional difference and inequality. It seems to suggest that marginalisation is neither caused by a particular policy deficiency nor solvable by one or two policy improvements; rather, it needs a fundamental change in development policy system. Furthermore, marginalisation is not limited to a particular region or specific level, but rather, exists at all levels from national to local, and involves all sectors and actors, inside and outside. In this sense, it is impossible to alleviate or reverse the marginalisation process at a particular region or level, unless the whole dynamic system and environment can be changed or improved.

The division between core and marginal areas, however, is not absolute but relative. In this respect, the semi-peripheral zone is the key to understanding the marginalisation process and ineffectiveness of government intervention. First, the semi-peripheral zone, sharing some of features with the peripheral zone, is likely to be viewed as representative of all marginal areas, leading to an oversimplification of the environment there. As a result, the particularity of the peripheral zones and the demands of the rural poorest are largely neglected. Second, without a distinction between semi-peripheral and peripheral zones, the former is assumed to be representative of all marginal areas by outside professionals, to demonstrate either the validity of 'technical patterns' ('development experience') from the core areas or the feasibility of 'new designing' ('new solutions'). This results in weak impacts on these remote locations. Finally, for most of the visitors from outside, the semi-peripheral zone is perhaps the most distant place they can see or approach. Even if some of them have a chance to reach the 'peripheral land', they may not have enough time or opportunities to observe or compare the difference within marginal areas.

Although generated from the statistical information, the definition and assertions mentioned above need to be verified and consolidated by empirical evidences. Accordingly, the next section examines the government's 'anti-marginalisation' approach by reviewing the national PRP, whilst Chapter 4 illustrates the marginalisation process and the impacts on ecological environment and technological innovation, with reference to the case of rural development in Shaanxi province.

3.3 Impacts of marginalisation on government intervention

Whilst marginalisation is often blamed on the 'blank' market, it raises the question whether government intervention can alleviate, stop or even reverse the process. In this respect, China's national PRP provides good opportunities to test the government's wiliness, capacity and effectiveness to deal with rural poverty. Starting from the mid-1980s when it became aware of the slowdown of rural poverty reduction and the increasing regional development gap, the central government has been committed to eradicating rural poverty, first by the 1980s and then by the end of the twentieth century (Zhu and Jiang 1996). Since then, substantial poverty funding associated with large-scale political mobilisations and administrative intervention seem to have produced positive results in a rapid decline of the number of poor from 125 million in 1985 to less than 40 million by 1998, according to official data. Despite these impressive achievements, however, many studies have shown that there is a long way to go to eliminate rural poverty in China, and the government's development interventions suffer many limitations (Yao *et al.* 2000; World Bank 2001b). This section does not attempt to assess the PRP strategy itself, but to examine whether and how marginalisation influences the PRP. Applying the framework of the core–marginal division to the secondary information, it tries to address questions such as: what area and people were targeted by the government aid? How much benefit have the rural poor gained from the PRP and what change has occurred regarding their livelihood security? Regarding the interdependence between rural and urban livelihoods, what lessons can be learnt from the government's development intervention? To address the above issues, this section begins to view the targets of government's PRP through examining the concept of 'poor areas'. This is followed by an analysis of the trend of poverty reduction. In the light of the uneven distribution of poverty reduction, the next section turns to government performance, to reveal the deficiency of the institutional environment and the impacts on rural development.

3.3.1 Target of government intervention: questioned 'poor areas'

The concepts of 'marginal areas' and marginalisation explained in the previous sections provide useful insights into the government's development approach and poverty-reduction policy. Rather than detailed examination of government policy design and implementation, the following paragraphs focus on the 'poor areas', a term used by the government when allocating government poverty-reduction funding. Starting from 1986, around one-fourth (331 later 592) of counties nationwide were selected as 'nationally designated poor counties' by the central government. Selection, however, was based solely on rural income, but was also affected by political consideration (Zhu and Jiang 1996).

Reflecting regional difference and inequality, for example, 36.8 million of a total of 80.7 million poor people nationwide were concentrated in the west region, nearly doubling its share of national rural population by 1993. Of these rural poor, 58.6 million or 72.7 per cent were located in the 592 'nationally designated poor counties' targeted by the central government. Among these 'target counties' nationwide, 52 per cent were concentrated in the west region, where the poverty incidence was twice the national average.

Although it is in line with the present political system, the concept of 'poor areas' can be questioned in many respects. First, over one-fourth (27.3 per cent) of the poor population were actually outside the government target.[2] This is particularly true for the east and middle regions, where over 40 and 30 per cent of poor households were missed from the national PRP, respectively. Second, as the basic unit of the 'poor areas', these targeted counties themselves can hardly be viewed as a homogenous whole, as less than 30 per cent of the rural population were below the national absolute poverty line. Without a further distinction, government funding could be put into the central zone or intermediate (semi-peripheral) zones, leaving the peripheral zone untouched.

Regardless of political factors, the issues mentioned above seem to expose the methodological deficiency existing in the concept of the 'poor areas'. First, in reality, it is hard to identify a clear division between 'poor' and 'non-poor' areas; there is a wide spectrum between prosperous and poor countryside. Unable to reflect the above-mentioned circumstances, the 'poor areas' include 'non-poor' locations on the one hand and exclude real poor locations on the other. Second, there is no logical linkage between 'poor county' and 'poor households', because the former refers to an administrative unit that consists of many actors (farmers are only one of them), whilst the latter is an economic and social concept, referring to people who do not live in 'a poor county' but in particular villages. In other words, between 'poor counties' and 'poor households', it seems that there are some missing linkages in the PRP, which has led to ambiguity or confusion about the real target: 'poor county' or 'poor house'? Finally, rural poverty is not static, but is a dynamic process, and involves natural environmental change as well. With its narrow focus on farmer income by county average, the term 'poor areas' cannot reflect the evolutionary process within the 'poor areas' on the one hand and neglect environmental change and trends on the other.

3.3.2 Distribution and trends of poverty population

Bearing in mind the deficiency of the government's targeting systems, it would be not surprising that a considerable number of rural poor and the poorest in particular are easily missed in the PRP. To support for the above assumption, the following paragraphs will examine poverty-reduction trends and distribution through two indicators: poverty incidence and poverty gap. The former indicates the percentage of the rural poor among the total rural population within selected regions, whilst the latter takes accounts of the severity of poverty suffered by poor households. From the view of rural geography, the former considers the spatial dimension and inter-regional inequality, whilst the latter reflects temporal dimensions and intra-regional inequality. Using official data, Table 3.3 provides a regional comparison of poverty reduction in selected years.

Regarding poverty incidence in years 1988 and 1996, Table 3.3 shows an impressive progress in poverty reduction nationwide. Compared with other regions, however, western China including its southwest and northwest regions suffered more severe rural poverty, and less progress was made in poverty reduction. This is particularly true for the northwest, where poverty reduction went on slower, so that its poverty incidence was triple the national average.

By contrast with the rural population in first two columns, Table 3.3 shows uneven distribution of rural poverty among regions and the changing trends during the period of government intervention. Despite the general decline of poverty

Table 3.3 Regional comparison of rural poverty by selected years

	Rural population (1996)		*Poverty incidence (%)*		*Share of national poor total (%)*		*Squared poverty gap*	
	Million	(%)	*1988*	*1996*	*1988*	*1991*	*1991*	*1996*
North	83.6	9.1	15.2	4.6	9.8	7.6	1.32	0.27
Northeast	55.0	6.0	10.2	4.7	4.6	5.1	1.36	0.52
East	272.0	29.6	7.0	1.2	14.9	6.4	0.76	0.03
Central	233.3	25.4	13.6	2.6	23.1	11.3	1.05	0.17
Southwest	198.3	21.6	20.5	10.5	31.9	41.2	0.77	0.49
Northwest	77.2	8.4	26.3	18.6	15.7	28.4	1.75	1.45
National	919.4	100	13.9	6.3	100	100	1.19	0.59

Source: World Bank (2001b: 4–5).

Notes
North: Beijin, Tianjin, Hebei, Shanxi.
Northeast: Liaoning, Jilin, Heilongjang.
East: Shanghai, Jiangsu, Zhejiang, Anhui, Fujian, Jiangxi, Shandong.
Central: Henan, Hubei, Hunan, Guangdong, Hainan.
Southwest: Chongqing, Sichuan, Guizhou, Yunan, Tibet, Guangxi.
Northwest: Inner Mongolia, Shaanxi, Gansu, Qinghai, Ningxia, Xinjiang.
Poverty incidence = number of poor/rural population.
Squared poverty gap is an index to measure the income that would be necessary to bring a poor person up to the poverty line. The greater index value indicates greater severity of poverty.

incidence, Table 3.3 shows clearly a trend of poverty centralisation in western China (southwest and northwest) where the share of national total poverty population significantly increased from less than a half in 1988 to 70 per cent by 1996. In this respect, again, the northwest shows its 'leading position', with its share in national poverty over three times its share in population size.

Narrow calculation of the percentage of poverty incidence, however, cannot indicate how seriously the poor suffer from shortage of livelihood. Taking squared poverty gap as a means to measure the severity of poverty, Table 3.3 shows that the suffering of the poor in the northwest was much higher than the national average. The message behind the figure is that these remaining poor in the northwest received little or no benefit from external assistance, over a period of eight years.

Bearing in mind the government's involvement during the period, the trend of poverty centralisation and severity seems to suggest that whilst the majority of the rural poor received benefits from government assistance, the distribution greatly varied from one region to another. The uneven distributions mentioned above are difficult to interpret by either the *ecological model* (which emphasises geographical factor) or the *socio-economic model* (poverty as an individualised issue) (Riskin 1994). According to the World Bank (2001b), about half of the rural poor are actually outside 'nationally designated poor counties', and have unfortunately received little assistance from the government. Even within these poor counties, according to the report, there is 'a very substantial leakage of assistance to the non-poor', which may account for 90 per cent of local population.

Many conclusions can be drawn from the phenomenon of poverty centralisation. First, despite remarkable achievements, the government's PRP is not free from marginalisation, which can be seen in its geographic bias, favouring the central or 'semi-peripheral' zones, and giving the peripheral zone and the rural poorest less help. Second, the decline of poverty reduction is not necessarily a result of government intervention. Otherwise, it is difficult to explain the decline of those poor who were outside of the 'poor areas' or 'nationally designated poor counties'. Besides government intervention, there may be other mechanisms with a function of poverty alleviation, which may be outside scientific observation. Finally, within government-targeted areas, the effects of the governmental intervention may vary from one location to another, resulting in great variation in terms of both the decline of poverty incidence and the alleviation of poverty severity. This seems to suggest that a homogenous approach on the poor areas is too simplistic to reflect the complexity of the geographical and social environments in the marginal areas.

3.3.3 Marginalised institutional environment

The trend of poverty centralisation to the peripheral zones can be attributed to neither the 'ignorance' of the professionals nor to the government's poverty-targeting system itself. In fact, it is widely realised that the majority of China's absolute poor are concentrated in remote and mountain townships and villages. The division between poorer mountain settlements and better-off townships, according to the World Bank (2001b), can be easily distinguished by topographic features: the former are 'in higher elevation outlying areas (*shanqu*)' whilst the latter are 'around the county seat and in wide valley floors (*baqu*)'. This raises the question: which should be given priority in the PRP, semi-peripheral or peripheral zones? Poor or poorest?

Under the strategy of economic-growth-oriented poverty reduction, the answers will most likely be in favour of the former, resulting in an increasing inequality within the marginal areas. In an analysis on the impacts of 'food-for-work' projects in the early 1990s, Zhu and Jiang (1996) found that villages with more favourable economic conditions and higher populations were more likely to host the projects, whilst the poorest villages were less likely to gain such opportunities. Location biases may be explained by an economic rationale, because the poorest villages are often dispersed in areas of low economic return and high project risk.

Marginalisation is unlikely to be attributable to geographic environment itself or to the local government's performance, but is more likely related to the institutional or policy environment that can be reflected in many factors, such as biases against agriculture, an imperfect fiscal system and out-of-date bureaucratic system.

Dominated by agricultural production, the marginal areas and the poor households are particularly vulnerable in the face of a policy environment that favours urban development and the industrial sector. It has resulted in an outflow of financial capital from marginal to central areas, from agriculture to industrial sectors. According to Zhang and Chui (2002), the share of the agricultural sector in central government fiscal expenditure declined from 10.3 per cent in 1991 to 8.3 per cent in 1997, which is in sharp contrast to the three-fold growth of government fiscal revenue from the agriculture sector during the period. It is even true for government poverty reduction funding, of which 31 per cent was used for industrial development in 1991–5, 2 per cent higher than in the agricultural sector (World Bank 2001b: 43).

As a result of decentralisation and reconstruction of the fiscal system, governments at various levels are asked to achieve fiscal 'self-sufficiency'. As a result, local government revenue and savings per capita become the 'key factors determining the level of development in various localities, confirming the key role of "local state corporatism" in regional development in China' (Gu *et al.* 2001). Under the present fiscal system, unsurprisingly, the local governments face 'strong incentives to use poverty funds in ways that quickly generate local fiscal revenues' (World Bank 2001b: xvii). Even focusing on rural infrastructure and agricultural production areas, poverty funding is more likely to be put into better-off areas and high-value products such as fruit, tobacco, speciality crops and livestock, which could be helpful to generate fiscal revenues for government, even if alternative locations or projects may be more economically efficient and of more benefit to the poor.

The selection of 'revenue-starved governments' seems to be understandable if the pressure of expenditure demands is taken into account. According to official statistics, for instance, nationally designated poor countries had a fiscal surplus in the first half of the 1990s, but suffered from fiscal deficiency in the second half, reaching 2.3 times on the ratio between revenues and expenditure in 1999 (NBS 2000). Due to serious fiscal deficiency and debts, unsurprisingly, the large percentage of poverty-reduction funding was actually transferred from rural to urban uses including simply paying back wages to employees on the government payroll (Han 2000; World Bank 2001b). This resulted in 'greater inequality in the provision of public goods and services, and created incentives for local governments to stress revenue mobilization at the expense of other distributional and growth objectives' (Park *et al.* 1996). As a result, 'self-reliance and hard budget constraints deprive poorer localities and provinces of the most basic revenues needed for survival purposes, not to speak of productive investment' (Selden 1997).

Marginalisation in the marginal areas is not confined to the fiscal system, but is also related to the traditional bureaucratic system. First, it is still dominated by a top-down approach in which the voice from the remote locations and rural poorest can hardly be heard, and the government's objective from the top overwhelms the genuine demands from the bottom. Second, the short-term approach taken by government agencies at various levels encourages 'rational activities' towards high-return, low-cost and mini-risk projects, to which peripheral locations and poorer communities are not suited. Finally, rapid expansion of the government body in addition to sector-separate working styles have imposed multiple administrative burdens on county and township governments. To cope with the situation, local governments had to enlarge the number of government employees to match the line managerial system, resulting in an increase in farmers' tax and fee burden, a decline in efficiency of the government public service function and increasing intension between farmers and government (Zhang and Chui 2002).

3.4 Marginalisation and farmer reorganisation: concluding remarks

Before initiating an empirical study on farmer innovation and self-organisation in rural China, many questions need to be addressed, such as: where are the marginal areas and how do they differ from its core areas? What has happened in the marginal areas since rural reform and government development intervention? As a part of the 'environmental analysis' of farmer innovation and self-organisation, this chapter particularly aims to clarify: what is the meaning of 'marginal environment' in the context of China's market economic era? How seriously do marginal areas suffer from the marginalisation process? Is the top-down approach able to attack the challenges of marginalisation and rural poverty, and why? Accordingly, many conclusions can be drawn as follows.

First, rural China is extremely complex, and administrative division or focus on a single dimension is too simplistic to address its environmental constraints and farmers' demands. It is particularly true that rural reform has led to a dramatic change of 'landscape', which requires a revision of rural geography to take increasingly complexity, diversity and heterogeneity into account. A combination of natural environment features and socio-economic change has led to the emergence of a core–marginal division, which distinguishes rural China at various levels into three areas: core, marginal and sterile areas. Instead of a static division, marginal areas are viewed as unstable in terms of both ecological environment and rural development. In this respect, the distinction between semi-peripheral and peripheral areas is helpful to understand the two different and sometimes opposite change processes and development trends.

Second, applying the core–marginal division system to observe China's rural reform and development, different 'models or paths' of regional economic development can be interpreted in relation to the geographic environment. Whilst rural industrialisation has successfully brought prosperity into core areas, marginal areas suffered numerous failures in copying the model until an alternative model of 'commercial agriculture' emerged, which emphasises local resource potential and the interface with the urban demand for agricultural products. Without a distinction between semi-peripheral and peripheral zones, however, it is misleading to assume that the alternative model would be suitable for all marginal areas; such a view is likely to be responsible for many failures in agricultural extension. This seems to suggest that, besides rural industrialisation and commercialisation of agriculture, China needs to explore a novel development path for the marginal areas and rural poor, to use local resources and secure their livelihoods. The above assertions, however, need to be tested by empirical evidence.

Third, related to differences in resource endowment and development conditions, rural China has tended towards marginalisation, a development process and trend leading to increasing regional gaps and income inequalities between core and marginal areas. Related to economic globalisation world-wide and the institutional transition from a planned to a market economic system in China, marginalisation seems not to be limited within a particular region or sector, but has spread and influenced the whole of rural China. Therefore, two questions need to be asked and examined in the light of empirical evidence: what are the impacts of marginalisation on rural sustainability? And where is the dynamic against marginalisation?

Fourth, the Chinese government has exerted great efforts against rural poverty and marginalisation, with mixed results. Generally, impressive progress has been made in the decline of the absolute poverty population, and in promoting the economic growth of semi-peripheral zones. Constrained by its regional perspective together with deficiencies in urban and political systems, however, the government approach has been unable to avoid the impacts of marginalisation, resulting in a trend of centralisation of rural poverty and increasing severity of the remaining poor. This seems to suggest that the capacity of government intervention against marginalisation cannot be overstated, whilst its side-impacts cannot be underestimated. Based upon secondary information, however, the above assumptions need to be verified.

Finally, thinking about China's experience in rural industrialisation and commercial agriculture, rural organisational innovation, leading to a generation of TVEs or FTAs, seems to have played a vital role. It seems to suggest that dis-organisation is an important barrier against poverty reduction and rural sustainability. Again, the above statement needs to be verified by empirical evidence.

4 Environment and innovation in rural Shaanxi

Marginalisation as a form of uneven development has not only impeded rural poverty reduction, but also exacerbated ecological degradation. If a sustainable rural livelihood is to be achieved in China's marginal areas, it is commonly recognised that technological innovation will play a vital role. In view of the impacts from the marginal natural and social environment, it may be difficult to find a universal solution for technological policy and innovation organisation. The complex relations between the marginalisation process, ecological degradation and innovation organisation can be illustrated by the experience of Shaanxi province where an empirical survey was conducted in 1996–7. Accordingly, this chapter attempts to address the representatives of rural Shaanxi; to clarify the process and effects of marginalisation and to examine the government innovation strategy and policy. The above targets are addressed by a combination of statistical analysis, field observation and key informant interviews. The chapter consists of four sections. The first presents a picture of rural Shaanxi through both inter- and intra-regional comparisons. This is followed by a focus on the environmental challenges in north Shaanxi. Responses to rural poverty and environmental challenges in the form of government policy on agricultural research and extension are examined in the Section 4.3. Summarising field observations and analysis of secondary data, the final section provides concluding remarks.

4.1 Marginalisation in rural Shaanxi: an introduction

Shaanxi province is a good example of the marginalisation in rural China, due to its great variation in geographic environment and resource endowment. Through a statistical analysis of uneven economic development in rural Shaanxi, this section will clarify the concepts of marginal areas and the marginalisation process, and show how the province is representative of rural China. Accordingly, it begins by overviewing Shaanxi's resources and development; Section 4.1.2 describe income difference and inequality. Section 4.1.3 examines the distribution of rural poverty and government intervention whilst Section 4.1.4 indicates the impacts from local economic development.

4.1.1 Complexity of rural Shaanxi

As a medium-small sized province, Shaanxi contains 2.1 per cent of the country's land and 2.9 per cent of its population. Located at a crossing region between the east and the west, the north and the south of China, Shaanxi is unique in many aspects, of which the complexity of its topographical and climatic patterns is outstanding. It is similar to Britain in shape and area; its 205,600 km^2 land takes a strip-like form, in which its middle plain lies between the two highland areas in the north and the south (see Map 1).

As one of the cradles of the Chinese nation, Shaanxi was the political, economic and cultural centre of China before the tenth century. Interestingly, Shaanxi province was also the cradle of the Chinese revolution in modern history, and was adopted as a capital of the Communist Party and its 'Red Army' (1936–47). Since the new China foundation (1949), Shaanxi has been suffering from a 'double economic structure', which has separated rural and urban systems and is still impeding communication and interaction. As a result, intensive high-technology industries such as space and aircraft manufacture in the middle of Shaanxi contrast sharply with the low-technology (or primitive) agriculture that predominates in its north and south.

To understand the complexity of its resources and environment, rural Shaanxi can be divided into six zones from north to south. Desert, hill and gully areas in the north belong to the semi-arid rim, where elevation is more than 1,000 m above sea level, and precipitation ranges from 300 to 600 mm yearly. In the middle are the Weibei plateau and Guangzhou Plain, which span the semi-arid to semi-humid rims. In these less-elevated areas (300–800 m) there is more rainfall (550–700 mm). Different again is south Shaanxi, with its mountainous topography and humid climate rim, where the higher temperature and precipitation are more suitable for agricultural production. These regional differences are reflected in Table 4.1, which presents a summarised resource comparison among the six zones.

Table 4.1 shows the great variety of geographic environment and resource endowment within rural Shaanxi. It is noticeable that the crowded Guanzhong

Table 4.1 Division of agricultural zones in Shaanxi province (1985)

Division	*Desert*	*Hill and gully*	*Plateau*	*Plain*	*L mountain*	*H mountain*
Land share (%)	8.8	23.4	19.7	11.3	14.1	22.8
Popn share (%)	2.3	9.8	19.9	40.0	18.3	9.8
Density (p/km^2)	38	61	147	518	189	63
Cropland (mu/p)	6.6	9.8	3.9	2.0	1.8	2.5
Irrigated (mu/p)	1.3	0.3	0.6	1.4	0.5	0.2
Precipitation (mm)	316–434	330–610	550–730	529–586	700–1,200	683–1,340

Source: Shaanxi Agricultural Regionalisation Office (1989: 85–86).

Notes
Land and population share refer to the provincial total. All area of land usage including cropland, irrigated land, forest and pasture land are based upon average of rural population. 1 ha = 15 mu.

Plain is no different from the eastcoast China in terms of population density, which is almost ten times higher than the marginal hill and gully and high mountain zones. The least densely population area is the desert zone, where the irrigation system can support only a limited population.

From the perspective of climate variation, Table 4.1 shows a range of precipitation from one zone to another. Generally, three statuses can be recognised: *relatively stable* in both plain and desert zones; *moderate variable* in plateau and low mountain zones; *highly variable* in the hill and gully and high mountain zones. In terms of rural livelihood security, this would suggest that the hill and gully zone in the north and high mountains in the south are high-risk zone, in contrast to the ecological stability of the plain and desert zones.

Many conclusions can be drawn regarding the uneven resource distribution. First, the core–marginal division can be applied to rural Shaanxi, in which its middle falls into the category of core areas, whilst both north and south Shaanxi can be viewed as the marginal areas. Second, each of the divisions above can be further divided into core–marginal zones. Finally, the core–marginal division can be used to reflect environmental status and ecological risk. To avoid sterilisation and natural disasters, special attention should be paid to the hill and gully zone in the north, and to the high mountain zone in the south.

4.1.2 Marginalisation in Shaanxi: inter- and intra-regional comparison

From the perspective of economic performance, rural Shaanxi falls into the bottom group of China (twenty-eighth of thirty-one provinces). Related to its uneven distribution of resource endowments, unsurprisingly, Shaanxi is a victim of marginalisation, as can be seen in the increasing economic gap at both inter- and intra-provincial levels. Regarding the former, Figure 4.1 illustrates the process and trend of rural net income between Shaanxi and the national average.

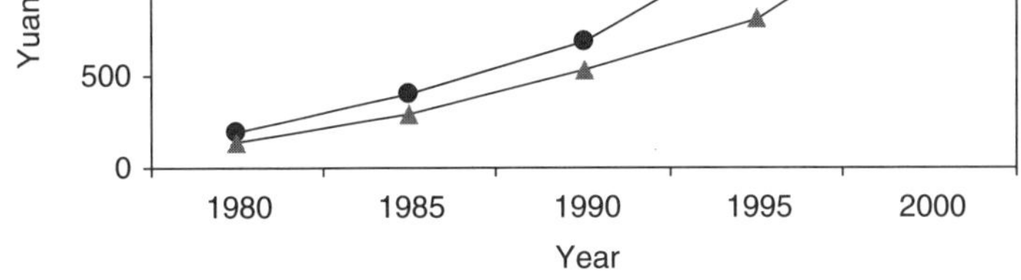

Figure 4.1 Rural income gap between Shaanxi and national average.

Sources: NBS 2000, 2001.

Table 4.2 Regional comparison of rural income distribution in Shaanxi (1985, 1995)

Division	*No. of counties*	*1985*		*1995*	
		Yuan/person	*% of total*	*Yuan/person*	*% of total*
Desert	5	157	70.1	665	78.2
Hill and gully	15	160	71.2	749	88.1
Plateau	24	223	99.5	837	98.4
Plain	28	305	135.9	1,114	131.0
L mountain	19	191	85.0	711	83.6
H mountain	11	198	88.3	673	79.1
Total	102	224	100.0	850	100.0

Sources: SARO (1989) and SAD (1996).

Note
There are totally six counties in the desert division, of which one, Fugu, is not included.

Despite impressive increase in Shaanxi's rural income from 1980 to 2000 (142–1,406 yuan), the difference from the national average has also enlarged; whereas in 1980 Shaanxi's income was about three-fourths of the national average, the percentage has declined to around 60 per cent in 2000.

Turning to the internal development gap within Shaanxi province, Table 4.2 compares rural income distribution by region and selected year. Roughly, four levels can be distinguished by comparing the regional income to the provincial mean. The highest income is in the Guzhong Plain, followed by Weibei Plateau as the mean, leaving hill and gully and low mountain in third place and the desert and high mountain with the lowest income.

Table 4.2 shows no evidence to suggest an increasing income difference between the core (e.g. middle Shaanxi) and marginal (e.g. north and south Shaanxi) areas. What has happened during the period, however, was a reshaping of regional economic position within the marginal areas, resulting in an exchange of position between the north and the south. In the light of the national PRP, it is reasonable to ask: has government intervention led to a mitigation or even reversal of marginalisation in rural Shaanxi? Why did the north but not the south have a chance to speed-up its economic growth? To answer these questions, rural poverty distribution needs to be examined in detail.

4.1.3 Rural poverty distribution

Aggregated rural income cannot reflect how seriously Shaanxi suffers from rural poverty and marginalisation. The unevenness of rural development in Shaanxi can be revealed by looking at the distribution of poverty reduction and the impacts of government intervention.

Table 4.3 shows the achievements and problems in Shaanxi by comparison with the national average. Despite a decline in poverty incidence from one-fourth to just one-sixth from 1988 to 1996, it shows that the progress in Shaanxi has

Table 4.3 Comparison of rural poverty between Shaanxi and national average (1996)

Indicator	*Population*	*Poverty incidence (%)*		*Squared poverty gap*	
	Million, 1996	*1988*	*1996*	*1991*	*1996*
Shaanxi	27.5	24.9	17.5	1.79	2.88
National	919.4	13.9	6.3	1.19	0.59
% of national	3.0	5.3	9.6	—	—

Source: World Bank (2001b: 4, 82, 85).

been much slower than the national average. As a result, Shaanxi's share of the national poverty population has increased from 5.3 to 9.6 per cent during the period. Regarding the severity of poverty in the population, Shaanxi's situation is even worse, as the squared poverty gap has increased from 1.79 in 1991 to 2.88 in 1996, which is in sharp contrast to the declining trend nation-wide. Many questions arise immediately: why is Shaanxi so poor in poverty-reduction performance? What is wrong with government intervention?

To address the above questions, the government's poverty-reduction projects need to be examined in detail. As targets of the central government's PRP, 50 of Shaanxi's 102 rural counties (districts or 'county-level' cities) were listed as 'nationally assigned poor counties'. These targeted counties, according to the Provincial Poverty Reduction Office, however, accommodated only 2.5 million poor by 1996, which amounting to just over half (52 per cent) of the provincial poverty population. To help those 'poor counties' excluded from the national lists, the provincial government assigned another nineteen counties as 'provincial poor counties' in which 0.5 million rural poor were identified. Taking both lists together, this means about 3 million poor were recognised by the government. Considering that about 4.8 million rural poor lived in rural Shaanxi by 1996, this means that the remaining 1.8 million or 38 per cent of the rural poor were actually outside the government's assistance programme.

The limitations of the government's targeting mechanism is revealed by Table 4.4, which contrasts the distribution of poor population with nationally targeted counties. It shows clearly the 'regional biases' in the government's PRP. For instance, the north had 16 per cent of the province's population and 24 per cent of its poor but accounted for 40 per cent of the nationally targeted counties. By contrast, the south with nearly 30 per cent of the province's population, and over half of its poor, contained just 36 per cent of the target counties. As a result, the south suffered more serious rural poverty than the north but was allowed less poverty-reduction funding.

The regional biases of government aid is further confirmed by the distribution of the government's poverty-aid target. By 1996, for instance, mean poverty incidence in the fifty 'nationally assigned poor counties' was 21 per cent, just slightly higher than the provincial average (17.5 per cent). One conclusion can be drawn from the distribution of poverty in rural Shaanxi: being based upon the administrative regional division system, the government's PRP was unable to

Table 4.4 Comparison of Shaanxi's rural poverty by region (1997)

Region	*Population*		*Rural poor*		*Target county*	
	Million	(%)	*Million*	(%)	*No.*	(%)
North	4.32	15.8	0.71	24.5	20	40
South	7.77	28.4	1.57	54.1	18	36
Middle	15.30	55.9	0.62	21.4	12	24
Total	27.39	100	2.90	100	50	100

Source: Calculations based upon information from SPRO (1997).

reflect the complexity of rural environment and poverty distribution. As a result, poverty-reduction funds were diverted to some non-poor population on the one hand, and a considerable number of the rural poor were not entitled to gain assistance from the government on the other.

4.1.4 Local economic environment

Marginalisation in rural Shaanxi cannot be separated from the local economic environment, which is composed of many factors such as local economic performance, industrial structure and the capacity of fiscal revenue. Similar to agricultural resource endowment, the local economic environment is also important in stimulating or constraining rural income growth. To reflect the marginalisation process and impacts on rural development, GDP and local fiscal revenue (balance) are used to reveal the difference in local economic systems.

The position of Shaanxi's economic development can be indicated by comparing its GDP with the national average. By 1999, Shaanxi's GDP per capita was 4,101 yuan, less than two-thirds of the national average of 6,392 yuan (NBS 2000). Focusing on poor counties' economy, the mean GDP per capital in Shaanxi's 'nationally assigned poor counties' was 2,313 yuan/person, slightly lower than the average of either rural Shaanxi (2,786 yuan/person) or the 592 'nationally assigned poor counties' (2,573 yuan/person). It seems to suggest: (i) there is a large division between rural and urban Shaanxi in terms of local economic structure and development; (ii) rural Shaanxi can be viewed as a representative of the marginal areas of China; (iii) the distinction between 'nationally assigned poor' and non-poor counties is not obvious in terms of local economic development.

Turning to the variation in local economic development within rural Shaanxi, all ninety-two counties[1] are divided into six groups according to their GDP per capita from less than 1,000 yuan/person to more than 5,000 yuan/person. Figure 4.2 indicates the distribution of these counties by both GDP and their status in the national poverty-reduction system. It is clear that the majority of 'nationally assigned poor counties' (thirty-seven of fifty) are located in the lower groups. Whilst an overlap exists between poor and non-poor counties in the median GDP

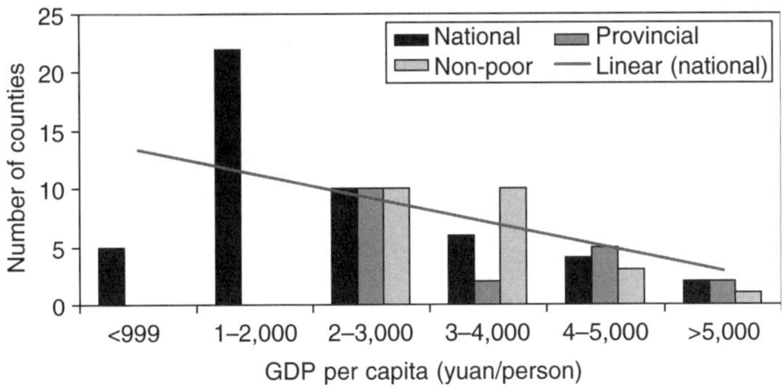

Figure 4.2 Distribution of Shaanxi's counties by GDP grade and aid nature.

Sources: Author's computation based on the category of poor county from SPRO, 1997, and county economic statistical summary in NBS 2000.

group (2–3,000 yuan/person), the graph shows that a number of 'nationally assigned poor counties' achieved quite good economic performance (located in groups over 4,000 yuan/capita).

Regarding the factors shaping the distribution of GDP per capita, the local economic structure plays a crucial role: the higher the secondary industrial share, the higher the GDP per capita. As a result, acceleration of local industrial development becomes a central focus of the local government. Bearing in mind the underdeveloped rural industry in the marginal regions of China, including Shaanxi province, the main source of secondary production is mineral exploration. This is particularly true for north Shaanxi, where the national energy demand and special treatment for local enterprises participating in mineral resource development provided a strong impetus to local economic development. This is an important reason why north Shaanxi seems to have experienced a more rapid economic growth compared with its southern and even central counterparts in the last decade.

The importance of local GDP is largely related to local fiscal revenues, the source of urban livelihood security and social welfare growth. According to official data (NBS 2000), fewer than one-fifth of Shaanxi's counties have fiscal revenue above 200 yuan/person, whilst nearly one-third of the counties' fiscal revenues are below 100 yuan/person by 1999. The limited capacity of fiscal revenue generation is far from meeting the increasing demand of local fiscal expenditure, resulting in a serious fiscal deficiency. Of a total ninety-two counties of rural Shaanxi, for instance, ninety-one counties suffer fiscal deficiency to various extents, and the mean percentage of local fiscal sufficiency rate is only 58 per cent by year 1999. Regarding the trend of local fiscal balance, unfortunately, the deficiency has been enlarged from 33 per cent of the revenue in 1989 and 20 per cent in 1993 to 73 per cent in 1999. Whilst fiscal deficiency is a common challenge facing local government, it is particularly serious for those fiscal-poor counties where the mean fiscal expenditure is 3.7 times more than the revenue.

Local fiscal crises in marginal areas have not only impeded the urban livelihood supply and social welfare improvement, but also had serious impacts on rural development. First, they constrain ability of urban professionals to produce and deliver public products and services to rural residents. Second, they are barriers to rural welfare (e.g. education and medicine) improvement and exacerbate farmer burden. Finally, to cope with fiscal deficit, priority in allocation of scarce funds is given to urban industry, TVEs or any other projects, whose products may increase local fiscal revenue, at the price of delay in agricultural development and poverty alleviation.

Regarding the local economic trend, all counties in Shaanxi province are grouped into three levels according to their position of 1999's GDP per capita from low (<2,000 yuan/person), middle (2–4,000 yuan/person) and high (>4,000 yuan/person) groups. Similarly, they are classified into another three groups, low (<300 yuan/person), middle (3–400 yuan/person) and high (>400 yuan/person), according to their GDP positions in 1989. Integrating the two results together, data analysis shows that a small number of 'poor counties' have had the chance to join the 'middle class', leaving the majority of poor counties unchanged.

In summary, the secondary evidence mentioned above shows clearly that rural poverty in marginal areas of Shaanxi cannot be separated from 'urban hunger' in terms of both their livelihood security and welfare growth, which involve complex issues related to China's urban development and political system reform. Without a good improvement in the local economic and political environment, rural poverty and marginalisation in these marginal counties can hardly be remedied. As a result, a substantial amount of the government's poverty-reduction funds has been paid to urban projects or central areas in these 'poor areas', leaving the poor locations and the poorer households increasingly marginalised.

4.2 Environmental challenges and impacts on rural livelihoods

Marginalisation has not only impeded poverty reduction, but also exacerbated ecological degradation. Taking the Loess Plateau of Shaanxi as an example, this section attempts to reveal the scale and extent of environmental challenges, and to identify the impacts on rural livelihoods. It consists of four sections. The first introduces environmental issues in the Loess Plateau, followed in Section 4.2.2 by a case study on reservoir reduction. Regarding rural livelihood sustainability, Section 4.2.3 examines the grain growth and fluctuation. Section 4.2.4 summarises the research findings, highlighting the environmental effects of marginalisation.

4.2.1 Environmental issues in the Loess Plateau and Shaanxi

The Loess Plateau is located in a transitional area between the arid northwest and eastern monsoon regions, and between semi-temperate and semi-humid zones as well. Accounting for about 4.3 and 7.0 per cent of national land and population, respectively,[2] the Loess Plateau contains six provinces (or regions). North and central Shaanxi share 27 and 29 per cent of its land and population, respectively.

One of the important advantages in the Loess Plateau is its farmland resources. Whilst it has around 5 per cent of the national land area, the Loess Plateau accounts for about 10 per cent of the cultivated land (ARPI 1992: 55). In particular, the area of cultivated land in north Shaanxi is as great as 8.2 mu/capita, 2.9 and 4.6 times more than the provincial and national averages respectively (SARO 1989). With regard to farmland quality, however, only 16 per cent of farmland in the Loess Plateau falls into the category of highly productive land (usually plain and irrigated), 5 per cent lower than the national average, whilst 57 per cent is low productive land, 16 per cent more than the national average (ARPI 1989: 12–13). Amongst the nine agricultural zones nation-wide, the Loess Plateau ranks the last in terms of farmland quality.

The potential of land resources in the Loess Plateau is seriously constrained by its scarce water resources. The average quota of water sharing in this region is 840 m^3/capita or 238 m^3 per farmland (mu), only 30 and 13 per cent of the national average respectively (Shan and Chen 1993: 215). As a result, 70 per cent of farmland in the former falls into the category of water-constrained land, accounting for more than one-fourth of the national total (ARPI 1992: 27). Uneven distribution of water resources is much more severe in north Shaanxi, where the water share by farmland is only half that in the central area.

Related to the shortage of water resources, frequent drought is the main natural disaster that is alarming for the agricultural producers of the region. According to historical statistics, the frequency of drought in the Loess Plateau during the last five centuries was as high as 36 per cent, while the figures in north Shaanxi were around 6 per cent higher, making it the most seriously affected area (Shan and Chen 1993: 28–30).

It is said that more than a half of the Loess Plateau was covered by forest 2,000 years ago (Fang and Xie 1994; Ye *et al.* 1995). Due to population growth and numerous wars, unfortunately, forest resources were nearly exhausted by 1949, and the wood coverage of the Loess Plateau was only 7.2 per cent by the end of the 1980s, just over half of the national average (CAS 1991: 7).

Due to loose earth and devegetation, the Loess Plateau and north Shaanxi, in particular, are suffering from serious soil erosion (ACCA 1998). For example, of a total of 1.8 million km^2 eroded land nation-wide, the Loess Plateau accounts for nearly one-fourth (23.9 per cent) and Shaanxi 7.7 per cent. Of a total 5 billion tonnes of soil loss each year in China, one-fourth (32 per cent) is contributed by the Loess Plateau, of which half come from Shaanxi. Soil loss in Shaanxi is particularly concentrated in the north where the sediment delivery mould (SDM) is about 100–220 tonne/ha yearly, in contrast to 10–50 tonne/ha in the centre (SARO 1989).

The fragility and harshness of the ecological environment in north Shaanxi are, thus, an important factor that constraints agricultural and rural development. An unfavourable natural environment, however, can be improved or exacerbated, depending upon the social and political conditions. In this sense, it is reasonable to assume that the marginalisation would lead to worsening ecological degradation, as will be shown by empirical data.

4.2.2 Trends of environmental change: case of reservoirs reduction

Related to rural institutional change from the collective to household responsibility systems, the ecological environment in the Loess Plateau has been subject to many challenges and shocks. Without attempting to cover all aspects, the following paragraphs offer an insight into the environmental issues in the market economy era, based on information about water resource management.

Of many constraints to agricultural development in the Loess Plateau, the most outstanding is perhaps the high frequency of drought. According to the Shaanxi Water Resource Department (SWRD 1997a), since 1950 drought has become increasingly serious in terms of both frequency and severity. Of a total 47 years from 1950 to 1995, for instance, 24 years are recognised as drought years. Breaking down these droughts to the seasonal level (e.g. a year can be distinguished as 3 droughts from spring to autumn), an increasing trend can be founded: 7 drought seasons in the 1950s, 11 in the 1960s and 14 in the 1980s. In total, 22 out of 47 years have received funds for severe drought, defined as the loss of over 30 per cent of normal grain production. Of these, 9 years affected north Shaanxi itself and another 9 years affected both north and middle Shaanxi together. The scale of yearly grain loss has increased from less than one million tonnes in the 1970s, to 1.5 and 3 million tonnes in the 1980s and 1990s, respectively.

Reservoirs and irrigation systems are the main measures to secure grain production and livelihoods against frequent drought. Related to rural change since 1949, Shaanxi's water resource management systems have experienced many changes (see Box 4.1). Since rural reform, the system has suffered increasing challenges that can be identified from the decline of reservoirs in terms of both number and the volume of water stored.

According to the same source from the Shaanxi Water Resource Department, the total number of the reservoirs over 1 million m^3 province-wide was 341 in 1980, 296 in 1990 and down to 252 by 1999, meaning over one-fourth of reservoirs have disappeared in the last two decades. Regarding the dynamics of reservoir disappearance, Table 4.5 offers an insight into their geographic distribution and the dominant factor in the loss of those resources.

Comparing 1990 with 1980, a significant trend of irrigation decline can be found, due not only to the decline in the number of reservoirs, but also to an increase in sedimentation, leading to a decline in the effective water storage capacity. This is particularly true for north Shaanxi, whose reservoirs decreased from nearly 60 per cent of the provincial total in 1980 to less than 40 per cent in 1990. As regards the cause of the system decline, there is no doubt that soil erosion is a predominant factor responsible for the rapid increase of sedimentation resulting in both decline of reservoir number and increase of sedimentation in the remaining reservoirs.

Regarding the rapid decline of reservoirs in north Shaanxi, serious soil erosion is one of the important factors. Furthermore, soil erosion in China and the Loess Plateau as a whole is largely related to over-cultivation referring to unreasonable

Box 4.1 **Impacts of soil erosion on Shaanxi's agriculture (an expert on soil control)**

Soil erosion is a serious issue against Shaanxi's agriculture, which can be partly reflected by the decline of provincial reservoirs from 341 in 1980 to 296 in 1990. In official statistics, annual sedimentation has also declined from 100 million tonnes in the late 1970s to 60 million in the late 1980s. It can be explained by two factors. One is the achievement of soil erosion control in the upstream of rivers where so many small dams and ponds built in the period of 'Cultural Revolution' have played an active role in blocking the flow down to the soil. Another is related to the disappearance of these reservoirs from the lists of over 1 million m^3 category whose sedimentation is actually excluded from the calculation. Taking account into above factors, soil erosion is still a serious environmental issue facing Shaanxi.

Regarding the agricultural sustainability of Shaanxi province, the impacts of soil erosion is actually more serious than normal because all 341 reservoirs above were built in the period between 1949 and 1980. Since then, no new reservoir (1 million m^3) has been built, simply because neither can farmers be organised to do so, as in Mao's era, nor can government provide sufficient funds. The impacts of soil erosion are particularly serious in north Shaanxi where the decline of reservoirs has further weakened the capacity of the local agricultural system against increasing drought and water shortages.

Soil erosion cannot be controlled unless the traditional farming system is totally prohibited. According to the national law of water and soil conservation, cultivation on slopes over 25° is not allowed and should be stopped. Until now, unfortunately, governments have not yet taken their responsibilities to stop the over-cultivation, to provide necessary subsidies to farmers and to enhance reservoir management.

Table 4.5 Sedimentation in Shaanxi's reservoirs by selected years (1980, 1990)

Category	*North*		*Provincial total*	
	1980	*1990*	*1980*	*1990*
No. of reservoirs	160	111	341	296
Total capacity (million m^3)	1,800	1,686	3,997	4,078
Sedimentation (million m^3)	564	663	803	1174
Sedimentation ratio (%)	31.3	40.3	20.1	28.8

Source: Shaanxi Water Resource Department (1997b).

Note
The size of reservoirs recorded here is above 1 million m^3.

cultivation or the use of steep slopes (>25°) for grain production. According to a national land survey in the late 1980s (ARPI 1992), the total area of China's cropland was nearly 40 per cent higher than the official statistics. Unauthorised cultivation is widespread in the mountains and hilly counties nation-wide. It is particularly serious in north Shaanxi, where the real area of cropland was 50 per cent higher than the official statistical data (SARO 1989: 207).

Over-cultivation will not secure grain production but will only exacerbate soil erosion. According to a field measure (Ye *et al.* 1995: 87), steep cropland (>25°) in the centre of the Loess Plateau could produce 35,000 tonnes of sand per km^2 yearly compared with 25,000 and 10,000 tonnes on the slopes (15–25°) and gentle slopes (<15°), respectively. To understand the nature and cause of over-cultivation, Table 4.6 compares the cropland composition in north Shaanxi with provincial, regional and national averages. From the view of cropland per capita, north Shaanxi is about three times higher than the provincial and regional averages, and four times higher than the national average. This large area of cropland is actually based upon the high rate of cultivation, about double the average of the Loess Plateau. In terms of topography, more than 90 per cent of its cropland is located on the slopes, in contrast to only 55 per cent of the regional average, whilst one-fourth is over-cultivated, 77 per cent higher than the regional average.

Over-cultivation has been prohibited officially since the early 1960s, accompanied by modern agricultural extension and large-scale cropland construction. After three decades of efforts, however, over-cultivation is far from being remedied and even seems to be worse. According to an empirical inquiry in parts of north Shaanxi, from 1949 to 1985 the population in this region roughly doubled (2.22 times) whilst the cultivation grew even faster, an increase of 3.67 times (Ye *et al.* 1995: 84–89). Compared with a less than 10 per cent cultivation rate (i.e. proportion of cultivation area in total land) in 1964, the figure had jumped to 30 per cent by 1985. Of the added cultivated land, particularly, about 40 per cent was over-cultivated

Table 4.6 Comparison of cropland between regional and national averages (%)

	Hill and gully	*Shaanxi total*	*Loess Plateau*	*National*
Cropland (mu/person)	8.0	2.6	2.9	1.8
Cultivation rate (%)	37.1	27.0	19.3	13.8
Share of slopes (%)	92.5	51.4	55.0	35.1
Over-cultivation ratio (%)	24.9	20.7	14.1	5.5

Sources: SARO (1989) and ARPI (1992).

Notes

The term Loess Plateau includes Shaanxi, Shanxi and Guanshu Provinces; whilst hill and gully zone is limited to the territory within Shaanxi province. Cropland refers to the area from agricultural surveyed land in the 1980s. Cropland per capita accounts for total population. Cultivation rate = (surveyed area of cropland)/(total land area). Share of slopes is defined by (cropland in slopes)/(total cropland area). The term slope is slightly different: <6° for cases of hill and gully zone and Shaanxi but <8° for the Loess Plateau and the national average. Over-cultivation ratio = [cropland in steep (>25°)]/[total cropland area].

(Ye *et al.* 1995: 86–88). Unbelievably, such serious over-cultivation does not appear in official statistics, so that the total cropland of Yanan (one of two Prefectures in north Shaanxi) by 1985, for instance, was only 5 million mu in official statistical data, but 14 million mu in the land surveys (Sun *et al.* 1994: 326).

Although there are many unsolved issues, the case of reservoir reduction and over-cultivation seem to confirm the escalating trend of environmental degradation in north Shaanxi. Related with rural change in the market economic era, this seems to suggest that not only is the environmental degradation related to marginalisation, but also both are linked with technological change, which is examined in a later section.

4.2.3 *Impacts of environmental degradation: case of grain issues*

As a result of the environmental degradation, agricultural development in Shaanxi is facing increasing challenges. Taking grain production per capita as an example, Figure 4.3 shows that Shaanxi experienced two decades' grain growth during the period of the 1970s and 1980s. From the 1990s, however, grain growth has entered a stage of stagnation, resulting in a decline of grain product per capita on the one hand and wide fluctuation on the other.

Bearing in mind the great variety of Shaanxi's resources and ecological environment, Figure 4.3 may not be able to reflect the impacts of grain fluctuation on rural livelihoods. Whilst the mean provincial grain production was 362 kg/capita in 1999, a good harvest year in Shaanxi (about 90 per cent of the national average), grain production in the hill and gully zone was 200 kg/person, 55 per cent of the provincial average.

To reflect the extent of grain shortage and impacts on rural livelihoods, the county's grain product in 1999 can be divided into four bands: <200 kg/person; <2–300 kg/person; 3–400 kg/person; >400 kg/person. Of the total ninety-two

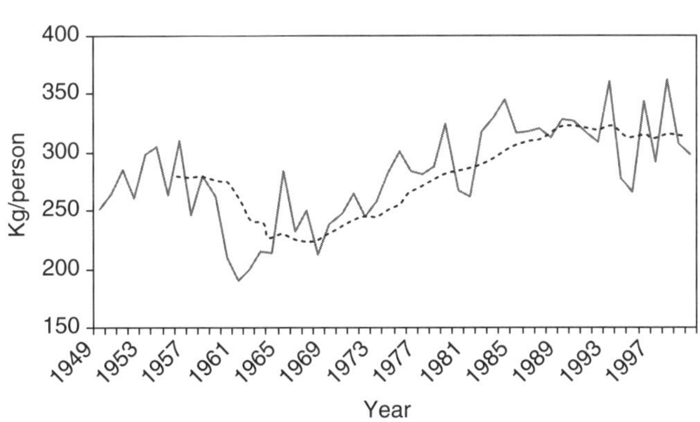

Figure 4.3 Grain growth and fluctuation in Shaanxi province.

Sources: SBS 1990; broken line as five-year average.

counties recorded, eleven are in the bottom group and sixteen in the middle-low level, meaning that in total, twenty-seven or about 30 per cent of the counties actually suffered food shortage to various extents. Turning to the distribution of available grain by population, nearly half of the population actually shared less than 300 kg/capita, putting them in the food insecurity category. This was particularly true for north Shaanxi, where over two-thirds of counties fell into this category.

The distribution above, however, reflects merely the 'harvest year' of 1999. Considering the fluctuation of both agricultural production and the county's economy, it seems that grain production and security are still challenging issues facing the rural poor in the north Shaanxi.

4.2.4 Concluding remarks

Concerning rural livelihoods in the marginal areas of Shaanxi, this section has tried to reveal the interconnection between environmental degradation, traditional technology and grain security. Bearing in mind the marginalisation process mentioned in Section 4.1, the following main conclusions can be drawn:

- Shaanxi is still suffering the challenge of unsecured grain production, which can be shown by the low level of grain per capita province-wide, stagnation of grain growth and increasing fluctuation in the late 1990s.
- Stagnation and insecurity of grain production seem to be closely related to ecological degradation, which has become increasingly serious in marginal areas (e.g. north Shaanxi).
- Ecological degradation and unsecured grain production cannot be separate from but are closely related to the traditional farming system, which is more likely to be concentrated in the 'poor counties' where little progress has been made in agricultural production and ecological environment compared with others.
- All the above issues cannot be isolated from, and are related to the transition of rural institution from the collective to household responsibility systems, which has produced many negative impacts on rural infrastructure, environmental protection and agricultural technology improvement.

Integrating the above facts, it seems clear that marginal locations (regions), ecological fragility and traditional technology are interconnected and interwoven in the complex challenge efforts of poverty reduction and technological innovation. It is not clear, however, what are the impacts of rural institutional change on farming technological systems, and what role has the government played in technological and organisation innovation?

4.3 Rural innovation and re-organisation in marginal areas

In the battle against rural poverty and marginalisation, technological innovation has been thought of as a crucial element. This is particularly true for rural Shaanxi where the strength of agricultural research is in sharp contrast to the poor agricultural productivity. To understand the main barriers against the diffusion of agricultural technology, this section draws attention to rural innovation system and policy, based on field observation and key informant interview. It consists of four sections. The first provides an overall picture of Shaanxi' agricultural research and extension system. This is followed by an explanation of the regional technical pattern. Section 4.3.3 outlines government innovation strategy for coping with environmental and technological challenges, whilst Section 4.3.4 highlights some policy and organisational issues.

4.3.1 Agricultural research and extension systems in Shaanxi: an overview

By contrast to its poor economic performance, Shaanxi is a leading province in scientific research, high technology and higher education; it ranks third in China in its capacity for scientific and technological development. In particular, central Shaanxi accommodates a national agricultural scientific base that consists of eleven research and education institutes and more than 4,000 scientists and technicians covering most of the disciplines in agriculture, animal husbandry, forestry and irrigation. In 1997, the first national agricultural high-tech development zone was established here.

The strength of agricultural research, however, has not yet led to technological solution to the low agricultural productivity. Similar to its rural income per capita described as Figure 4.1, the gross output value (GOV) of agriculture (including farming, forestry, animal husbandry and fishery) in Shaanxi was just 60 per cent of the national average in 1999. So was the yield of cereals per area of cultivated land, in which Shaanxi falls into the bottom group of the total of thirty-one provinces, municipalities and regions nation-wide (NBS 2001).

Among the many factors impeding Shaanxi's rural economic development, the deficiency of agricultural technology is an important one, of which many instances can be cited. The total power of farming machinery by farmland, for instance, is about 2 kW/ha, just over half of the national average, whilst the consumption of electricity is 58 per cent of the average. Although its grain production per cropland is only 60 per cent of the national average, Shaanxi's consumption of chemical fertilisers is over 80 per cent of the national average (NBS 2001).

In contrast to its advantage in agricultural research and education, unfortunately, Shaanxi seems to have a shortage of extension staff. According to the first national agricultural survey (NBS 2001), the mean agricultural extension personnel in all production fields (e.g. farming, machinery, animal husbandry, forestry) at township level in Shaanxi is 7.4 personnel, just over half of the national average (14 persons/township). As a result, there is only one technician for every two administrative villages of Shaanxi, or 2.4 extension personnel per thousand households. Regarding the skill of these extension personnel in Shaanxi, about three-fourths of extension staff are identified at the preliminary level (usually no systematic training) and only 2.5 per cent are of the senior level, similar to the national average. This suggests that the advantages of Shaanxi's agricultural research and education have not yet brought direct impacts on agricultural extension at the grassroots level.

Concerning the technical division of agricultural extension, the farming system (grain cropping) accounts for about one-fourth of total agricultural extension staff nation-wide. Regardless of the skills of these staff and availability of time (a considerable number of them are actually involved in agricultural extension only on a part-time basis), on average, each township in Shaanxi has fewer than two extension staff (1.8/township) or about six professionals per 10,000 rural households, whilst each member of staff is responsible for nine administrative villages. In particular, over one-fifth (21 per cent) of Shaanxi's townships do not have an extension station, compared with only 6 per cent in the nation as whole (NBS 2001).

By contrast to its poor capacity in convenient agricultural production technology, Shaanxi has taken a leading role in orchard technique innovation in which 6 per cent of its rural households have participated in various training programmes, compared with a national average of 1.6 per cent. To explain the above phenomena, the impacts of geographic environment and government innovation strategy need to be taken into account.

4.3.2 Difference of rural technological environment

The gap between Shaanxi's agricultural research and extension is related to many factors, including both rural infrastructure and farming systems. The former impedes the diffusion of knowledge from research centres to users in remote villages, whilst the latter is related to the conflicts between the modern agricultural system and the local technological tradition.

Regarding the former, the difference of rural Shaanxi can be identified through many indicators such as road, communication, school and market facilities. By the end of 1996, according to the first national agricultural survey (NBS 2001), nearly one-fifth (17.2 per cent) of administrative villages in Shaanxi were difficult to access by outsiders due to lack of road connection, about 5 per cent higher than the national average. Furthermore, there were only two market facilities available for agricultural trading for every three townships, compared with about four markets per township nationally. With the rapid expansion of information and communication technology, the difference between rural Shaanxi and the national average is even wider: only 2.5 per cent of rural households in Shaanxi have access to telephone networks, compared with 7.5 per cent in the nation as a whole.

Regarding the composition of provincial agricultural extension system, according to the Provincial Station of Agricultural Extension in Shaanxi Agricultural Development, there were a total of 10,000 employees at various levels in 1996, of which about three-fourths (72.6 per cent) were professional extension staff. Among these professionals, over a half worked at the county level or above, leaving the remaining 48 per cent at the township level. Besides these formal employees, there were a total of 24,000 farmers who were designated by the government as 'peasant technicians' (usually part-time and unpaid). These indigenous experts, however, are available in 52 per cent of the administrative villages, leaving nearly half of all villages without such expertise (SAD 1997).

Related to the uneven distribution of agricultural resources, the farming system in rural Shaanxi varies greatly, as can be seen from Table 4.7. To avoid the impacts of agricultural fluctuation, an average of grain product across years 1992, 1995 and 1999 is used and compared by both geographic location and poverty target, for all ninety-one counties. It shows that there is no big difference in labour productivity of grain production among these regions. By contrast, land productivity is significantly different, varying widely from just over 500 kg/ha to over 3,600 kg. Focusing on the variation of land productivity, it seems that there is some correlation between grain production per area of cultivation land and the inputs of production elements such as farming machinery power and chemical fertilisers.

By contrast with poverty target and location, Table 4.7 seems to suggest two alternative technical routes with similar results in grain production: capital-intensive and labour-intensive agriculture. Regardless of climate factors, the former can be explained by the higher element inputs in the centre, whilst the latter can only be explained by more intensive labour inputs. Besides the two patterns above, clearly, north Shaanxi seems to fall into another technical path: farmland-extensive agriculture (FEA), referring to high inputs in farmland area for grain cropping, but low inputs in both labour and productive elements. The existence of the FEA can be shown by the fact that against a 15 per cent share in provincial labour, the north owns 42 per cent of the farmland, consumes 11 per cent of the fertilisers and produces 13 per cent of the grain. As a result, grain production per area of farmland in the north is only 30 per cent of the provincial average, whilst the use of chemical fertilisers per farmland is one-fourth of the latter. Furthermore, the FEA is hardly explained by rural poverty, otherwise it conflicts with case of the south.

Table 4.7 Regional division of agricultural technology within Shaanxi

Criterion	*Division*	*County* (no.)	*Grain* (kg/p)	*Grain* (kg/ha)	*Machinery* (kW/ha)	*Fertilisers* (kg/ha)
Poverty target	National	49	686	1,096	0.99	122
	Provincial	20	912	2,265	1.61	247
	None	22	894	3,657	3.60	532
Geographic location	North	25	695	551	0.70	60
	Middle	38	852	2,730	2.74	413
	South	28	769	2,740	1.48	225
Total		91	804	1,818	1.64	228

Sources: Author's computation based upon SARO (1989) and NBS (2000).

Notes

Grain production is averaged over three years (1992, 1995 and 1999), and is divided into two columns, by rural labour (1994), and by cultivation land based upon the area of the agricultural regionalisation survey (1985). So are machinery power and chemical fertilisers, both of which are divided according to the same source of cultivation land.

4.3.3 Rural innovation and organisation strategy

Realising both the technological difference and development potential in rural Shaanxi, the government has highlighted agricultural innovation as the core of its poverty-alleviation programme. Accordingly, the government innovation strategy contains many objectives related to grain and income growth and improvement of the ecological environment. In contrast to the traditional FEA in the north, the rural innovation strategy comprises the following elements: infrastructure development, high-yield agriculture and pillar industry.

It is widely recognised that the poor infrastructure is a bottle-neck against technological diffusion and applications. A good example is the construction of terraces, which has been listed as a main target of the poverty-alleviation programme. Associated with improvement of cropland quality, the transformation of the traditional farming system is equally important because the outputs and effect of high-quality land are largely dependent on the inputs of production elements. Instead of low labour and external element inputs in the traditional FEA, highly efficient agriculture (HEA) emphasises intensive element inputs and cropping management through a package of wide-furrows, high-yield seeds, fertilisers, plastic sheet and subsided credit.

Parallel to grain growth and security, income growth is equally important for both farmers and local government. In the light of lessons learned from unsuccessful TVEs in the past, generally, the focus of the government's innovation strategy in the 1990s was on full use of local resources and interfaces with outside markets. This resulted in the popularity of commercial agriculture, called the 'local pillar industry' (LPI) with the aims of both rural and urban income growth. Related to the objective of local fiscal revenue, the LPI is not totally open to households, own their selection and decision-making, but is influenced by local government to ensure the adoption of technology and the effects of scale. Without a 'blueprint' for technological choice or a strict procedure to guide local government decision-making, however, it is better called a process of 'trial and error' in which local authorities and farmers gradually identify their resource advantages and the market potential of various available technologies and products.

A wonderful example in this aspect is fruit production and apply plantation in particular, in which Shaanxi has taken a leading position nation-wide. Compared with its twelfth place among fruit producers nation-wide in 1985, Shaanxi has jumped to fourth position, whilst fruit product per capita is in first place nation-wide since 1998. The success of apple plantation seems to indicate an alternative path of local economic 'take-off' and farmer income growth in the marginal areas. Compared with non-agricultural development, marginal areas seem to have an advantage in commercialised agriculture, although the realisation of this potential is largely dependent on the co-operation between local government and farmers.

One important experience learnt from Shaanxi's fruit development is that local government has played a positive role in initiating, encouraging or facilitating various farmer innovation organisations. According to official statistics (SAD 1997), by 1996 there was a total of 1,670 FTAs with 176,000 members province-wide. Furthermore, there were 426,000 'specialised households', or 6.5 per cent of rural households, who are actively learning and applying new techniques.

4.3.4 Unsolved issues

As a novel innovative path, no doubt, Shaanxi's experience in 'orchard technological development' has the potential to be applied and diffused to other areas. Due to the complexity of the rural environment and development, however, the success of fruit plantation has so far been limited to these semi-peripheral zones that have a favourable climate and soil elements for fruit plantation and transport access for information and flow of production. This raises the question whether the pattern of commercial agriculture is also suitable for the peripheral zones. In the face of high risks (both market and ecological environment) and challenges (both rural and urban poverty), how can the government satisfy the demands of rural economic development and enhance the capacity of the poor to cope with risk and uncertainty? During the period of system transition from market to market economy, what role can the local government play? The following paragraphs do not aim to answer these questions, but to highlight the necessity of further research based upon field observation and interviews.

First, it is not seldom that an innovative objective is established through a top-down procedure without taking account of local circumstances and the urgent demands of the rural poor. The case of electricity connection in Box 4.2 illustrates the limitation of top-down decision-making, which, far from helping, might actually bring trouble to the poor. More than access to the power system, the case raises the question: whose development and innovation is at stake in marginal areas? What procedure and regulation should government follow if they want to make decisions on behalf of farmers?

Second, it is not new that most agricultural extension institutions suffer from the shortage of fiscal budget. Because of the local fiscal deficit, it is very difficult for extension staff to find a small amount of funding to support their extension activities. For them, it would be good enough if they could receive their salaries on time. Without fiscal support, unsurprisingly, most extension staff can actually do nothing but stay in the county town. This has resulted in an outflow of professionals from extension stations to administrative departments of the county government on the one hand, and an inflow of more unskilled staff to occupy the 'vacancies' in these stations on the other. Regarding the extension style, the main focus of these active personnel, according to field observation, was on establishing and maintaining various 'model' plots, villages or zones for the purposes of technological 'demonstration', like 'controlled experiments' in a scientific laboratory. Such demonstration bases are actually the results of the intensive inflow of external resources (including capital, fiscal and manpower) while taking no account of cost. Such expensive models, however, are too far remanded from the local simulation to be learnt and stimulated by others.

Box 4.2 **Is accessing electricity urgent to sort out? (an assembly of field observations)**

Access to electricity networks in all villages of the north Shaanxi was listed as an objective of poverty reduction by the provincial government in 1996. To achieve it, the provincial government provided one-fourth of its development funding, which accounted for about one-third of the project costs; the remainder was to be provided by both county government and by potential benefactors, who would also contribute their labour.

Whilst the county government could have used other resources to fulfil their responsibilities, this plan indeed brought trouble for the rural poor. Having dreamed of access to power and light for a long time, they appreciated the government offer. However, suffering from poverty, most of them were not be able to stand such costs. Since it was a political task, neither local government nor the rural poor could be excused from the project. As a result, a large number of households had to take out high-interest loans to fulfil their responsibilities.

Bearing in mind the fact that most of project-targeted areas were actually located in the marginal areas of these poor counties, the sharing of project costs between government and potential users has actually created new inequality because those villages with power access in the core areas had been connected free of charge in the past. Furthermore, by various fiscal channels outside of local government, many villages (mainly those in intermediate zones) were able to have their costs paid, leaving the real poor people to bear such high costs.

Whilst the government claimed that the project has succeeded and all villages in north Shaanxi have access to electricity, the field observation seemed to disprove this claim because the term 'village' used by the government is actually 'administrative village', which is not equal to the natural villages in which households are living. In mountainous areas, it means another 5 or 10 km of power line needs to be installed if they really want to access power. Even if power lines are available in their villages, many households may not be able to afford to consume such a luxury.

Third, a common 'location bias' seems to be shared by the government and professionals, resulting in increasing regional inequality. For the government, the priority in project selection is always given to those villages with the resources, transport access and powerful leadership to ensure the projects' success. Professionals have no way to access their marginal villages, unless the local government requests their involvement. As a result, various project designs and demonstrations are based upon the conditions of central or semi-peripheral zones, which may be significantly different from those of the peripheral zones. Without a clear distinction between core, intermediate and peripheral zones, unfortunately, various extension or innovation projects are based upon the border of administrative unit, with a serious underestimation of the complexity of the local natural and social environments.

4.4 Why a farmer innovation study is needed? Concluding remarks

To initiate an empirical survey on farmer innovation and self-organisation, this chapter has 'toured' around rural Shaanxi with the broad questions: what is the position of Shaanxi province in China's rural development and agricultural innovation? What environmental and development issues impede against poverty reduction and livelihood security? How are these challenges related to technological systems and innovative capacity of the rural poor? What kind of the innovative strategy has the government adopted and does it work well? Despite a wide-ranging introduction to Shaanxi's environment, technology and development, the central objectives set up for this chapter were to see the impacts of marginalisation on ecological environment and sustainable rural livelihoods in rural Shaannxi, and whether top-down development intervention and innovation organisation can tackle these challenges or dilemmas. Based on a combination of secondary information with field observation and interviews, many conclusions can be drawn.

First, the complexity of Shaanxi's environment and development suggests that no universal solution or development model can be found for the marginal areas and the rural poor. This is even true for the 'nationally assigned poor counties', some of which benefit more from government assistance than others. Learning the lessons from the case of Shaanxi, development professionals need to take serious account the particularity of local circumstances and the voices of the rural poor in particular.

Second, marginalisation in Shaanxi is much more serious than normally expected, so that the top priority of the local government is not to help the rural poor but to secure urban livelihoods and welfare growth. Beyond a large-scale and standard technological package, it is very difficult for the local government or development professionals to consider or meet any specific demands from these marginal locations and groups, resulting in a significant difference between government supply and farmer demand.

Third, Shaanxi's ecological environment is subject to accelerated degradation, which can be seen in increasing drought hazards, stagnation and fluctuation of grain production, serious over-cultivation and soil erosion. Related to agricultural resource endowment and ecological fragility, rural poverty and insecure livelihoods are still serious issues challenging Shaanxi's development. It seems increasingly clear that the challenges of rural poverty and ecological degradation in Shaanxi, cannot be separated from but are interwoven with marginalisation. Limited by the theme of this book, however, this chapter has not dealt with the linkage and mechanisms between them.

Fourth, to cope with the various challenges and uncertainties facing the rural poor, rural technological and organisation innovation plays a vital role. Whilst success in fruit technical innovation encourages positive exploration of novel technological and organisation models for marginal areas to enhance their innovative capacity, the complexity of the marginal environment and diversity of the poor's demands suggest that the government and development professionals should be aware of the limitations of their knowledge on the one hand, and develop trust and collaborative relationships with the rural poor in the peripheral zones on the other. All the above-mentioned point depend upon a novel approach to farmer innovative demands, capacity and potential.

Finally, uneven development in rural Shaanxi seems to suggest the necessity of a broad institutional approach to address the urban economic and political institutions. It is important to understand, for instance, why the rural poor in marginal areas need to initiate and manage their own 'innovation projects', and what lessons can be learnt from government intervention and assistance in the past. Where is the potential interface between farmer self-organisation and outsiders' participation or intervention? Parallel to the technological process, farmer innovation and self-organisation is also an institutional process in which farmers are more than demanders of sustainable rural livelihoods, but are also creators or constructors of a novel institution in the new century.

The above conclusions can be seen as both a rationale for empirical survey in north Shaanxi, and working hypotheses to be tested or further clarified in later chapters.

5 Environmental and development challenges in Zhidan

The necessity and reality of farmer innovation and self-organisation in the marginal areas of China can be shown by a tailored survey in Zhidan, one of the 'nationally assigned poor counties' in north Shaanxi. Conducted during the period 1996–7, it was implemented by an integrative methodology consisting of secondary information collection, key informant interviews, participatory environmental observation, household questionnaire surveys and case studies. The results of data analysis are displayed in Chapters 5–7. Before detailed examination of farmer innovative potential and organisational patterns, this chapter attempts to introduce Zhidan's environment, development and innovation in general, and identify its challenges and dilemmas related to rural sustainability in particular. The above objectives are addressed in five sections. To begin, Zhidan's population, resource and ecological environment are outlined. It is followed by its economic environment and development challenges. Section 5.3 concerns the evolution of rural innovation strategy whilst Section 5.4 examines institutional contradictions and their impacts on agricultural innovation. The final section summarises the research findings and raises further questions and foci for village and household surveys.

5.1 Zhidan's resources and ecological environment

Zhidan is located in the heart of the Loess Plateau, a conjunction between Shaanxi, Gansu and Ningxia provinces (36°21′–37°11′N; 108°11′–109°03′E) (see Map 2). It was selected as a sampling county not only because of the representativeness of its resources and ecological environment, but also because of its leading position in soil erosion control recognised by the provincial government. Accordingly, this section briefly introduces Zhidan's population and resource environment, with special attention to ecological change and trends. It begins by describing the background and regional division, followed by an examination of its population growth and the land utilisation pattern. Section 5.1.3 focuses on ecological change and environmental risks. Section 5.1.4 gives an outline of the change and trend of Zhidan's agri-ecological environment.

5.1.1 Topography and regional division in Zhidan

Zhidan has a long history as a border town between the Hans and the minority nationalities. As a county, it was formally established by the frontier force of the Song Dynasty in 977 AD with the name of *Bao An*, meaning peace and safety could be preserved forever. The present name of the county was given in 1936 when Chairman Mao and his 'Red Army' settled down in Zhidan after the 'Long March' (ZCEG 1997).

Zhidan is a mountainous county, its total area of 3,781 km^2 (or 5.67 million mu) being covered by numerous hills and gullies. Elevation ranges widely from 1,741 m above sea level in the northwest to 1,093 m at the exit of the Luohe River in the southeast. Of a total of 256 hills, 90 per cent are above 1,400 m. As a result of this mountainous topography, 82 per cent of Zhidan land is of slopes ($>15°$) of which about half (47 per cent) is steep ($>35°$), while the plains ($<5°$) account for only 3 per cent (ZARO 1985: 3). Historically, Zhidan was a mixed area of agriculture and animal husbandry.

In the absence of an industrial basis and urbanisation, 90 per cent of Zhidan's population live in the rural area (ZPSO 1996). Over 100,000 rural people make up 20,200 households, which are distributed among 1,091 sub-villages (villages hereafter) of 189 administrative villages (ad-villages) in 12 townships. On average, each village consists of nearly 20 households and owns about 3.4 km^2 (or 5,000 mu) land. The county's population density was 30 persons/km^2 (ZPSO 1996).

In terms of its topographical features, Zhidan can be divided into four zones: north, south, east and west. Located in the up-stream areas of the main rivers throughout the county, the north is characterised by high elevation (1,300–1,741 m), extensive gullies and poor vegetation. In contrast, the south, being low in both altitude (1,093–1,680 m) and population density, is covered by dense wood and vegetation, but is poor in transport facilities. Between them, the middle land is relatively gentle in topography, dense population and good agricultural facilities. This zone can be further divided into two parts: the west is located in the watershed of the Luohe River (a branch of the Yellow River), whilst the east consists of the watersheds of the Zhouhe River (a branch of Luohe River) and the Xinhe River (a branch of the Yanhe River). Using official data, Zhidan can be distinguished as four zones, as shown in the survey Map 2.

Data on the distribution of population, land and forest resources are shown in Table 5.1. Compared with the large proportion of steep land (around half of the land), the area of forestland is low (26.2 per cent). In particular, two-thirds of the county's forest resources are concentrated in the south, while the forest coverage rate in other zones is around 10 per cent, which is too little to conserve soil and water (ZARO 1985). One of the important factors responsible for the poor forestation is high cultivation rate (around 40 per cent, except in the south), and over-cultivation in particular. The exception is the southern zone of Zhidan because it is part of the provincial forest zone, which is controlled and managed by the state.

Table 5.1 Regional division by resources and environment in Zhidan

	East	*West*	*North*	*South*	*Total/Ave.*
No. of townships	4	3	3	2	12
No. of ad-villages	61	44	47	37	189
Land area (%)	24.4	23.7	20.7	31.2	100
Population (%)	31.3	26.4	22.6	19.7	100
Steep (>35°, % of land)	50.5	56.6	56.0	31.5	46.5
Forest (% of land)	11.2	16.3	9.5	56.6	26.2
Pasture (% of land)	27.2	27.3	29.7	15.9	27.6
Cultivation rate (%)	37.1	40.4	36.5	16.3	31.6
Over-cultivation (%)	25.3	39.5	30.9	18.0	39.0
Sheep/goats (% of total)	26.7	18.8	18.3	36.2	100

Sources: All data from ZCEG (1997), but population from (ZPSO 1996) and over-cultivation from (ZCAD 1990).

Note
Regional division is based on the administrative border of township; cultivation rate is the figure of 1989.

The poor forestation in most of Zhidan's land is also related to its conflict with animal husbandry. Although it accounts for over one-fourth of the county's land, Zhidan's pasture is poor in carrying capacity in general, suffering over-carrying of animals (mainly sheep and goats) in particular. Overgrazing combined with nomad breeding styles are harming the safety of young trees. Regarding the regional distribution of these sheep and goats, according to Table 5.1, the south shares 36 per cent of the county's total, more than double its share of the county's pasture land, which is in contrast to the figures in the north and west.

To conclude, Zhidan is characterised by its huge area of land, high cultivation rate and uneven distribution of population and resources. Despite the relatively low population density, over-cultivation is an outstanding issue, which has invaded the pasture land and caused conflict between animal breeding and forestry. Irrespective of its forest zone in the south, Zhidan's topography and resource environment can be considered representative of the hill and gully regions of north Shaanxi.

5.1.2 Evolutionary pattern of population and land utilisation

Due to numerous wars, Zhidan's landscape has experienced fundamental change in the last two millennia. Zhidan has, however, been free from war interruption since 1949, and during this period the population has rapidly expanded from 35,000 in 1949 to 114,600 in 1995. Alongside this expansion came significant changes in land utilisation.

According to official data (ZARO 1985; ZCAD 1990), more than half of Zhidan's land (3.2 million mu) was covered by forest in 1949 whilst less than 10 per cent (0.5 million mu) was utilised for agriculture. Ten years later, however, the area of forestland had rapidly declined to 1.8 million mu, that is, 44 per cent of the forest had disappeared, although the area of cultivated land did not greatly

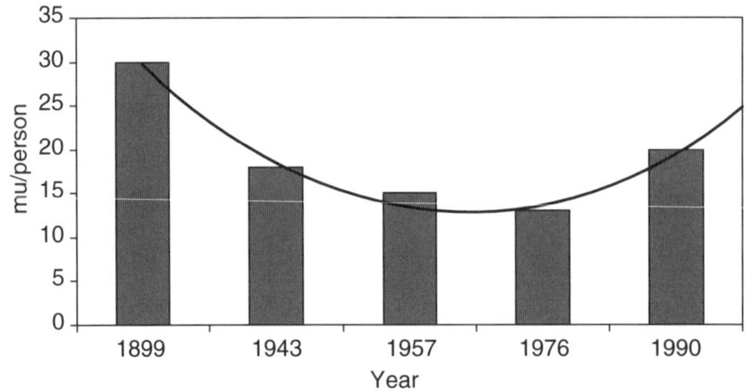

Figure 5.1 Change of Zhidan's farmland per capita.

Sources: Zhidan's population from ZCEG 1997 and land from ZCAD 1990.

change. Cultivation growth reached 1 million mu, the maximum area of reasonable cultivation (i.e. the area of land with slope less than 25°) by the end of 1970, when the area of forest reached its lowest (1.1 million mu). Since 1980, over-cultivation has become a serious issue and the total area of farmland had risen to 1.8 million mu by 1989. Figure 5.1 illustrates the evolution of cultivation per capita over the course of one century.

Although the accuracy of Figure 5.1 may be questioned, the graph offers an overall picture of the evolution of Zhidan's land use. It indicates that the traditional farming system, that is, FEA, is not a new issue but had its roots in the last century, when each person owned as much as 30 mu (2 ha) farmland. During the period of 1950s and 1970s, a technology change occurred, enabling farmland to be used more intensively, which led to a continuous decline of farmland per capita. Since the early 1980s, in contrast, the tendency of technology change seems to have reverted back to traditional FEA (an increase in cultivated area per capita), which led to a big jump of Zhidan's cultivation area. The total addition of farmland in the 1980s was equal to the sum for the first eight decades taken together. Such unusual cultivation will be discussed in Section 5.3.

The over-cultivation in the 1980s can be further confirmed by contrasting two land surveys that indicated an increase in farmland from 1.65 million mu in 1984 to 1.80 million mu in 1989, an increase of 9 per cent. With respect to the farmland quality, four grades are used to assess the farmland according to the degree of slope, from flat (0–5°), through gentle slope (6–15°) and slope (16–25°), to steep (>25°). Figure 5.2 shows the change in the pattern of farmland distribution between the early and late 1980s.

Figure 5.2 shows many issues related to land utilisation. First, although Zhidan is rich in land resources, farmland of high and medium productivity, that is, plains (0–5°) and gentle slope (5–15°) accounted for less than 30 per cent in 1989 while more than 70 per cent of farmland was very low in productivity.

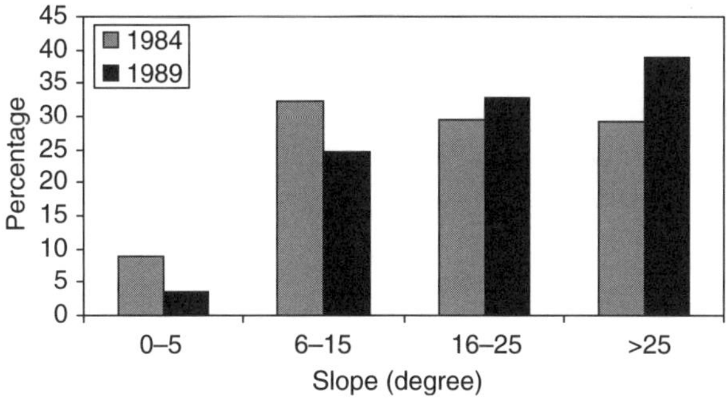

Figure 5.2 Contrast of Zhidan's farmland distribution by slope and year.

Second, of the total farmland in 1989, nearly 40 per cent was located on steep (>25°) areas, which were over-cultivated. A further 30 per cent was low-slope farmland (15–25°). Thus, a total of 70 per cent of Zhidan's cropland was in areas that are unsuitable for agricultural production, exacerbating ecological degradation.

Finally, the growth of farmland in Zhidan in the 1980s was based upon over-cultivation on steep areas, a 10 per cent increase in a short period from 1984 to 1989. Among many factors contributing to over-cultivation, according to Figure 5.2, an important one was related to the decline of high-quality land for non-agricultural purposes.

To conclude, the evolutionary pattern of Zhidan's land utilisation in the second half of the twentieth century does not support the assumption that the utilisation of land resources in the Loess Plateau has improved since rural reform compared with the previous era (World Bank 2001a). Rather, evidence from Zhidan's case shows that a return to the farming system occurred in the 1980s, resulting in a rapid expansion of cultivated land area and over-cultivation. Whilst the change of land utilisation pattern remains to be confirmed, it raises the question whether and how it is related to rural technological and institutional change, which will be discussed in Sections 5.3 and 5.4.

5.1.3 Environmental change and impacts

Generally, Zhidan's ecological environment is fragile and its agricultural production strongly influenced by climatic conditions. The continuous degradation of Zhidan's ecological environment can be explained by many indicators. Yearly rainfall, according to Zhidan Meteorological Observatory Station, has experienced a declining trend from an average of 524.5 mm during the period of 1957–83 to 475.6 mm during 1985–95. The trend of higher-temperature winter growth has become another serious ecological issue in recent years, resulting in increasing incidence of pests and diseases.

Related to large-scale deforestation, the area of soil erosion in Zhidan expanded from 44 to 72 per cent of the county's land during the period of 1949–80

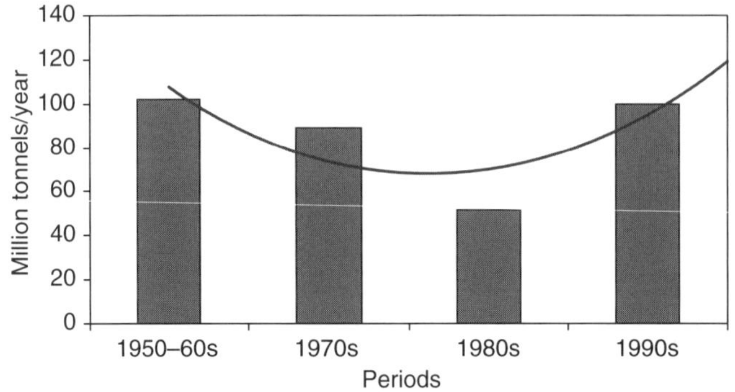

Figure 5.3 Change and trend of sediment delivery through Luohe River.

Source: Calculation based on data collected from Shaanxi Hydrological Observation Station.

(ZCEG 1997: 210). On average, about 37 million tonnes of soil and sand are sent to the Yellow River each year, and the sediment delivery mould (SDM) thus accounts to about 100 tonnes/ha yearly. Large-scale and intensive over-cultivation in the 1980s has unavoidably exacerbated soil erosion. This is partly reflected in hydrological measures of sediment delivery in the Luohe River. Figure 5.3 illustrates the change of soil loss in Zhidan and its neighbouring county during the last few decades.

Similar to the pattern in Figure 5.1, Figure 5.3 confirms that the process of soil loss declined during the 1970s–80s and then increased. The change of sand delivery in the Luohe River system is influenced by many factors and seems to match with the rural technological and institutional changes in the last decades, because large-scale farmland and irrigation projects were introduced into Zhidan after collectivisation in the late 1950s and reached a peak in the 1970s, contributing to the decline of sand delivery from over 100 million tonnes/year during the 1950–60s to half that in the 1980s. Rural reform in the early 1980s, in contrast, greatly weakened the ability of labour mobilisation and erosion control on the one hand, and stimulated large-scale farmland expansion on the other. Its negative impacts on the environment, however, did not emerge directly from the sand delivery of Luohe River in the 1980s, because most of the sand was absorbed by the many reservoirs, dams and pools built in the 1970s. As these irrigation facilities were filled in and became disused, according to a hydrological expert in Shaanxi, the increase of sand delivery in the riverbed in the 1990s was unavoidable. The complex relationship between technology, institution and environment change will be explored in Section 5.3.

5.1.4 Concluding remarks: trends of environmental change

From this review of the evolution of Zhidan's land resource and ecological environment, many conclusions can be drawn. First, compared with half a century ago, Zhidan's landscape has undergone a fundamental change in general, and shown an accelerated trend of ecological degradation in particular. There are many indicators of environmental degradation, including deforestation, soil erosion, climate warming and increasing Spring drought.

Second, whilst the environmental degradation in the Loess Plateau is related to many complex factors including population growth and global warming, Zhidan's experience seems to show the impacts from rural technological and institutional change in the last decades. In particular, the Zhidan experience seems to refute the claim that rural reform and the HRS have contributed to an improvement of land resource utilisation and ecological environment. Rather, the limited evidence displayed in this section shows the reverse: that rural technological progress and ecological improvement in the CCS was interrupted by rural reform, resulting in a return to the traditional farming system, the FEA.

Finally, rather than a homogeneous whole, Zhidan's land can be distinguished into various zones according to resource endowment and livelihood pattern. Whilst the forestry zone in south Zhidan shows the benefits of forestry for carrying capacity, the conflict between the animal breeding and tree plantation is a dilemma challenging local development and environment.

5.2 Zhidan's rural economic development and challenges

The rural economy of Zhidan, as a 'nationally assigned poor county', has faced many challenges and opportunities. Related to its ecological issues described in the previous section, this section attempts to identify the challenges and the impacts of the marginalisation process. Accordingly, Section 5.2.1 outlines its economic development and rural poverty, while Section 5.2.2 focuses on grain production and fluctuation. Section 5.2.3 examines the regional difference and causes. Section 5.2.4 summarises the achievements and problems of Zhidan's rural development.

5.2.1 Background of the county's economic development

Until the 1990s, Zhidan was an 'agricultural county' with little urban industry. Thanks to the discovery and exploitation of oil resources, the county's economy has experienced a 'taking-off' since then and its share of industrial product in the county's gross industrial and agricultural outputs has increased from only 7.6 per cent in 1990 to 29.1 per cent in 1995 (ZPSO 1996: 30). Related to the development of the oil industry, Zhidan's rural income per capita had reached to an average of the provincial total by the mid-1990s.

The urban economic growth in the 1990s has undoubtedly created opportunities for rural non-agricultural development. According to the Zhidan Rural Survey Team (ZRST), non-income in Zhidan fluctuated around 100 yuan/capita for many years in the late 1980s but jumped to over 200 yuan/capita in the mid-1990s. This has become an important factor contributing to rural income growth.

Table 5.2 Structural change of Zhidan's gross agricultural product (1949–95, %)

	1949–65	*1966–78*	*1979–85*	*1986–95*
Crops	61.2	60.6	62.9	53.7
Animal	28.5	23.5	16.2	23.8
Forest	6.0	6.9	15.6	17.0
Others	4.3	9.0	5.3	5.5

Source: Original data from ZCEG (1997: 389–390).

Despite rapid growth in the non-farm sector, according to the ZRST, more than 80 per cent of Zhidan's household income in the period 1990–6 was actually from agricultural production, including grain crops, animals and forest. Focusing on the agricultural economic system, Table 5.2 outlines the structural evolution of the GAP amongst crops, animals and forest since 1949.

Two conclusions emerge from Table 5.2. First, after half a century of evolution, the agricultural economic system in Zhidan was still dominated by grain crops, while the advantages of animal husbandry and forestry had not yet been realised. Second, compared with crops and animal products, the main change has occurred in forest production since the late 1970s. Forests, which accounts for 17 per cent of the county's GAP, is actually comprised mainly of fruit plantations (e.g. apples, apricots and pears). In contrast to ecological forestation in the past, these economic trees have become the mainspring of forestation in the market economy.

Compared with the slow transformation of economic structure, the more challenging issue facing Zhidan county was rural poverty. According to official statistics (ZPSO 1996), for example, half of the rural population in 1995 had an annual net income less than 500 yuan, the national line of absolute poverty, when the average of the county was 816 yuan. In particular, about one-third of the rural population earned below 300 yuan, the line of severe poverty.

Among the many factors responsible for rural poverty in Zhidan, poor education was thought to be the main one. A review of the results of three censuses between 1964 and 1990 shows that the proportion of educated population at various levels (including primary, junior and senior middle school) reached only 37 per cent of the total population in 1990, while the adult illiteracy figure in Zhidan was still very high, at 34 per cent of the total population, or just 10 per cent less than in 1964 (ZPSO 1996: 123). There is a long way to go to eradicate rural illiteracy, an important objective of rural development.

Due to the mountainous topography, poor road accessibility was a serious issue constraining Zhidan's rural development and poverty-alleviation efforts. Although 85 per cent of administrative villages have a vehicle road connected with their townships, most of the rural roads are very poor in quality, and cannot be utilised by large vehicles, or in rainy and icy seasons (accounting for nearly half the year). Moreover, according to field observations, a number of roads exist in name only, due to lack of necessary maintenance. In addition, the notion of 'road accessibility' in mountain areas means that there is at least one village in an administrative village (usually located in low altitude areas) that has access to the road network. As a result, a large number of villages in the remote and high mountains actually have no vehicle road access, and are easily neglected by outside agencies.

The situation of electricity connection is ever worse. By 1995, there were only forty-eight administrative villages and 4,000 households with access to electric power, accounting for merely 25 and 20 per cent of the county's total, respectively (ZPSO 1996: 123). These villages and households, with no exception, are located in the valleys and some low mountain areas.

In a high, frequently dry environment, drinking water is perhaps the most urgent issue for the rural poor. By 1995, 60 per cent of rural people suffered to varying degrees from water shortages. It is very common for people to walk 3–5 km to collect drinking water from streams at the bottom of hills, and the supply is not even secure in rainy, dry and icy seasons.

5.2.2 *Growth and fluctuation of grain production*

Despite a decline in the proportion, according to the ZRST, grain production still accounted for about 40 per cent of household income. From 1949 to the harvest in 1999, according to official data (ZCEG 1997), the production of grain in Zhidan greatly increased from a total of 9,900–57,204 tonnes, increasing 5.8 times (NBS 2000). As regards grain consumption, the product rose from 261 to 504 kg/capita during the same period, increasing 1.9 times. In practice, however, agricultural production in Zhidan has exhibited a complex and fluctuating pattern, as indicated in Figure 5.4.

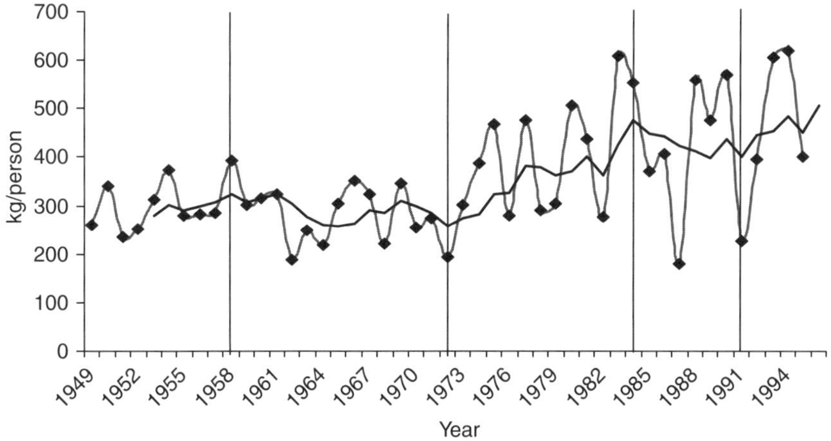

Figure 5.4 Fluctuation of grain production in Zhidan (kg/person).

Source: ZCEG (1997).

Figure 5.4 shows the growth and fluctuation of Zhidan's grain production since 1949. Roughly, five stages can be distinguished, each lasting an average of eight years indicated by the middle line. Before the 1970s, agricultural productivity in Zhidan was low, around 300 kg/person. After the early 1970s, Zhidan had experienced continuous growth resulting in a jump of 100 kg/capita compared with the previous stage. From the mid-1980s, the county's grain production began to decline and was subject to increasing fluctuation. In 1987, for instance, the grain share reached a new low of 179 kg/person, even lower than 188 kg/person in the famine of 1962. The decline in grain production did not stop until the early 1990s, after which a new growth trend has been observed.

When considering dynamic factors behind the growth and fluctuation of Zhidan's grain production, both land and technological inputs should be taken into account (the labour factor here can be ignored due to grain per capita). Referring to Figures 5.1 and 5.2, the expansion of cultivation area could be an important factor contributing to increased grain production in the 1980s, whilst over-cultivation caused increasing fluctuation. Increase of farmland area itself, however, is not enough to explain the continuous growth of grain production without concerning technological change. Otherwise, it is difficult to explain why grain production increased in the 1970s and 1990s, in particular, when the growth of cultivation stopped as over-cultivation reached its peak.

Besides the impacts of land and technological factors, Figure 5.4 shows that growth and fluctuation of Zhidan's grain production are also related to rural institutional change. The land reforms of the early 1950s, for instance, seems to have had positive impacts on agricultural development. The stagnation and decline of agricultural production in the second stage between 1958 and 1972 was related to the rural collectivisation and the CCS system. Under the impacts of rural reform and the HRS, Zhidan's grain production has reached a new level (above 400 kg/person) despite increasing fluctuation.

Two conclusions can be drawn from Figure 5.4. The continuous growth of Zhidan's grain production from the early 1970s to the mid-1980s seems to suggest that agricultural development in the early 1980s cannot be attributed to the rural reform itself but was rooted in the late stage of the collective economic system. Taking into account the expansion of cultivated areas in the 1980s, it seems that the achievements of rural reform have been overestimated, and the contribution of the CCS to the later agricultural development has been underestimated.

Second, under the same institution, agricultural development can be divided into various stages, related to various policies or organisational strategies. In contrast with the decline in the late 1980s, for instance, the growth trends of grain production since the early 1990s cannot be separated from government intervention for poverty alleviation, in which improvement of agricultural infrastructure and extension of modern technology were listed as important targets.

5.2.3 Regional difference and inequality

The impressive achievement in Zhidan's rural and agricultural economy cannot be over-estimated due to the process and impacts of marginalisation. According to

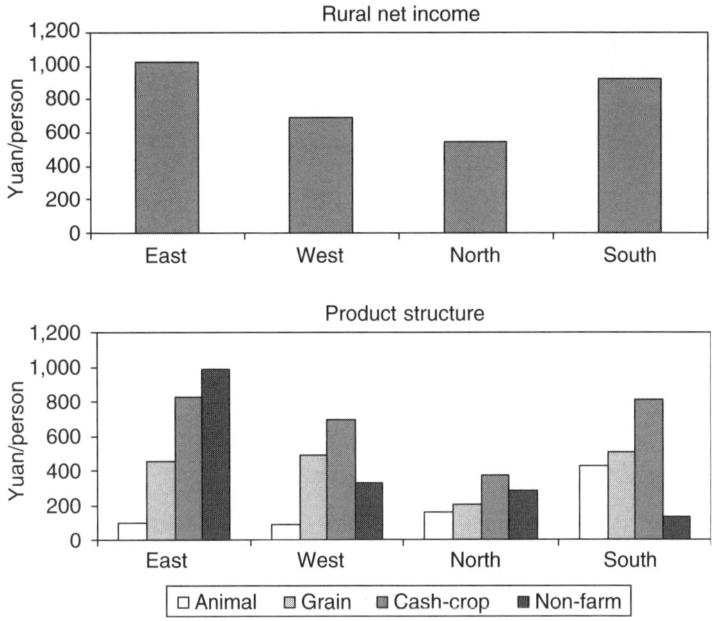

Figure 5.5 Zhidan's rural income and economic structure by region (1995).

Source: Author's calculation based upon ZPSO 1996.

official data (ZPSO 1996), for instance, farmer net income per capita was 804 yuan in 1995, reflecting a wide range from less than 500 yuan/person to over 1,300 yuan/person. Based on regional averages, Figure 5.5 shows the extent of differences in rural income and factors related to product structure.

Some conclusions can be drawn from the schema:

1 Similar to the regional development difference in national or provincial level, Figure 5.5 shows income difference and inequality existing in rural Zhidan, with farmers' net income in the poor north just over the 'national poverty line' (500 yuan), two-thirds of the county's average.
2 Related to uneven distribution of resource endowment and environmental conditions, Zhidan can hardly be viewed as homogenous whole. Behind the uneven distribution of resources and income, there are distinctive patterns of economic structure from one zone to another. Due to its unique conditions of geographic location, transport and oil exploitation, the east has advantages in non-farm production and employment for the urban market. Owing to both its advantage in vegetation and disadvantage in transportation, in contrast, the south relies more on a combination of animal breeding, grain production and cash crops, but has experienced little non-farm employment.
3 With the adaptation to a market economy, cash crops (including fruit trees) have come to dominate industry and household income generation.

Compared with grain production, cash cropping is more dependent on new knowledge and external inputs, which distinguish it from the traditional farming system.

4 Compared with other zones, the north is particularly poor in grain production and cash cropping. It is suggested that improving agricultural technology and conditions is particularly important for marginal locations and the rural poor.

Concerning the distribution of poverty, according to the Zhidan Poverty Reducing Office, the majority of the rural poor in Zhidan are mainly concentrated in remote and high mountain areas, especially in the north and part of the west where the average income of farmers is much lower than in other regions. For example, five poverty townships identified by the provincial government are located in the north and west zones. Of a total of fifty-eight poverty villages, three-fourths are in these two zones.

5.2.4 Conclusions: development challenges in Zhidan

Based on a review of Zhidan's economic environment and rural economic development in the last decades, an attempt in this section has been made to clarify the impacts of the marginalisation process on rural livelihood security. Related to many factors, especially the local oil industry and national poverty-alleviation programme, Zhidan has witnessed an impressive economic growth and agricultural improvement since the 1990s. Due to the relatively high level of grain consumption per capita (>400 kg/person), as well as non-farm and cash crop opportunities, rural Zhidan seems to have entered a stage of economic 'taking-off', in which more and more farmers have changed their roles from traditional farmers to specialised and commercialised farmers, whilst few, if any of the rural population suffer from hunger or food shortage.

Despite these impressive achievements, however, rural Zhidan was not free from the marginalisation process, but faced many challenges including: uneven distribution of rural infrastructure (e.g. road, electricity, educational facilities, drinking water, etc.); increasing economic difference and income inequality; lacking opportunities of non-farming or cash cropping and increasing agricultural fluctuation and decline of infrastructure facilities related to both draught and soil erosion. To cope with the above challenges, technological innovation has played an important role, which is, in turn, related to both geographic environment and rural institution, the themes of the next two sections.

5.3 Evolution of Zhidan's innovation strategy

In coping with Zhidan's environment and development challenges, technological innovation plays a vital role. This section intends to identify the major characteristics and stages of technological change in the last half-century linked with rural institutional change, leaving institutional dilemmas and government coping strategy to the next section. Accordingly, Section 5.3.1 introduces the traditional farming system, to which various innovative approaches are distinguished. Section 5.3.2 concerns innovation strategy in the CCS while Section 5.3.3 examines the adjustment of innovation strategy since rural reform. Summarising field findings, the final section presents conclusions on innovation strategy in response to institutional changes.

5.3.1 Traditional farming system and innovation: an analytical framework

Zhidan's agricultural innovation system to combat soil erosion and the problems of the traditional farming system can be traced back the late 1950s when a county agricultural extension station was set up. Related to the change of economic and political environment, however, the content and priorities of innovation strategy varied from one period to another. To understand the evolutionary process, first, the local traditional farming system needs to be introduced.

In the past, the Loess Plateau and Zhidan were dominated by FEA, a farming system in which agricultural production is heavily dependent on natural processes rather than human control and external inputs (CAS 1991). The main features of the FEA can be summarised as follows:

- emphasis on the expansion of cultivation area rather than increase of labour input;
- attention to the sowing action only, without subsequent crop management;
- relying on soil fertility and natural recovery, with few external inputs;
- product fluctuation with climatic conditions.

Related to the abundance of land resources and low population, historically, the FEA was implemented by a 'rotational cultivation system', in which land slopes were cultivated and intensively utilised for 3–5 years, with few external inputs, until the soil became exhausted. The land was then exposed to a natural process of revegetation for about twenty years before the next cycle of cultivation. As the population grew and available land declined, the period of revegetation reduced until the 1970s, when no surplus land was available for rotation (ZARO 1985).

With the disappearance of the rotational cultivation, the demands of grain growth in the FEA could not be satisfied except by the expansion of cultivated areas on the steep slopes, resulting in increasing over-cultivation. These has resulted in a vicious circle of the rising demand for grain, over-cultivation and ecological degradation. Unless new elements are introduced, growth in grain demand leads to over-cultivation, which accelerates the decline of soil fertility and deforestation. Deforestation not only exacerbates soil erosion and ecological risk, but also leads to a decline in animal carrying capacity, which, in turn, reduces organic fertiliser supply, resulting in increasing conflict between grain demand and supply.

Possible innovation elements to break down the vicious circle are thus included:

- *Technical push* to promote grain growth and erosion control. Introduction and extension of new farming systems and terrace construction falls into this category.

- *Market pull* to promote product structural adjustment from reliance on a single crop to a diverse cropping system (e.g. commercial forestry, fruit orchard and cash crops) leading to the growth of both forestry and fertiliser inputs.
- *Administrative intervention* to promote new technology and product element adoption on the one hand, and to prohibit over-cultivation on the other.
- *Land system reform* to strengthen the linkage between farmers and their land for a long-term utilisation and investment.

The term *innovation strategy* here refers narrowly to the first two categories above, which are differentiated from the institutional/organisational dimension in the last two categories. Needless to say, innovation strategy and institutional intervention are not separate, but are interconnected and interacted. The rest of this section focuses on innovation strategy, leaving institutional intervention to the next section.

5.3.2 Innovation strategy in the collective commune system

As distinct from the traditional farming system, the innovation strategy in the CCS gave the priority to mobilisation and utilisation of local labour to improve farmland quality. The emphasis was on 'conquering nature'. In particular, irrigation was listed as the top priority in the 1970s, leading to a rapid growth in the amount of irrigated land in Zhidan (ZCEG 1997: 209).

By utilising limited mechanical methods, large-scale construction of the irrigation system, which consisted of seven reservoirs, a number of dams and 30,000 mu of irrigated land, was completed in the mid-1970s and about 9 per cent of the total water resources was used for agricultural production (ZARO 1985: 289–290). The turning point in irrigated agriculture happened in 1977 when a terrible flood destroyed many of the irrigation facilities. The decline of the irrigation system was further accelerated in the period of rural reform, and reached its bottom in 1990.

Many lessons can be learnt from the period of focus on irrigation agriculture, in particular, the extent to which the capacity of water control was overstated and the impacts of soil erosion neglected, leading to inappropriate technology choice. For instance, the Shigo reservoir, the largest in Zhidan, was completed in 1976 without vegetation protection in its up-stream areas. Three years later, one-third of the reservoir's capacity (total 4 million m^3) was lost due to sedimentation, and only one-fifth of the intended area could be irrigated (ZARO 1985: 284).

Whereas there was little fertiliser input in the FEA, organic fertilisers were featured and intensively utilised in the CCS. As key measures for grain growth, manure collection and rational utilisation were viewed as political tasks, which were planned, mobilised, monitored and assessed by the government from county to township. The average input of organic fertilisers was said to be as high as 4–5,000 kg/mu in highly productive land in the 1970s in contrast to only 1–2,000 kg/mu in the 1990s (ZCEG 1997: 156–157).

It seems that before rural reform, the central focus of technological strategy in Zhidan was on intensive use of labour resources. Without the CCS, it would be very difficult to imagine that so large a volume of rural labour could be organised to participate in innovation projects over a long period (1972–6). Following county government planning, for instance, thousands of labourers from three townships were organised to participate in the Shigo Reservoir project in the early 1970s. The majority of them received nothing from the project besides their working scores and the welfare of their own 'production teams', whilst their communities did not directly benefit from the project either.

In contrast to the FEA, the innovation strategy in the CCS may be called labour-intensive agriculture (LIA). This was not limited within Zhidan county, but was popular nation-wide, closely related to Mao's regime and the specific environment of the 'cultural revolution' (1966–76). During this period, technological innovation was treated as a political activity that followed a common regulation: 'national objectives (or interests) are superior to collective ones and so are collective to individual ones', which left little room for farmers' individual decision-making and economic return.

5.3.3 Innovation strategy in the household responsibility system

Compared with the CCS, many technological changes have occurred in the HRS since the 1980s. The ambitious objective of runoff control and irrigated agriculture has been abandoned to be represented by terrace building, which has led to a high growth rate in terraced areas in the last decade (ZCEG 1997). Moreover, in contrast to the organic fertilisers favoured in the CCS, the consumption of inorganic fertilisers has continuously accelerated since the mid-1980s, and reached 8,800 tonnes in 1995 (Table 5.3).

Compared with the change of production inputs, however, the more important innovation in the HRS is related to product structure. Accordingly, an innovation programme, namely the LPI programme, was initiated by the county government in the late 1980s. Its characteristics include:

- *Market profit orientation.* In contrast with low profits in grain production, all products listed in the programme have a comparative profit in the market.
- *Local resource utilisation.* With a view to commercialisation of agriculture, it seeks to promote the development and utilisation of land resources.
- *Intermediate technology.* Rather than complex and expensive technology, it emphasises technology interface and operability within the present farming system.
- *Administrative intervention.* Similar to grain cropping, administrative measures are frequently used to ensure technology adoption, production scale and extension speed.

In contrast to the LIA in the CCS, the innovation strategy in the HRS is called the HEA, and is characterised by high capital and external-energy inputs, high outputs of both grain and cash crops and high economic return for households.

Table 5.3 Average utilisation of chemical fertilisers in Zhidan (1966–95)

	1966–70	*1976–80*	*1981–5*	*1986–90*	*1995*
Fertilisers ('000 tonnes/year)	0.4	1.7	2.8	4.1	8.8
Sharing (kg/person)	6.4	21.8	33.1	45.7	85.9
Inputs (kg/mu)	0.5	1.7	1.7	2.3	5.9

Sources: ZARO (1985), ZCAD (1990) and ZCEG (1997).

Notes
(1) The amount of fertilisers is selling weights.
(2) The sharing and inputs result from the re-calculation based upon official data.
(3) The area of farmland before the 1980s is estimated.

The emergence of the HEA strategy cannot be separated from decentralisation, the market economy and the HRS, in which individual households have become independent producers and decision-makers. Reflecting market signals, commodity production has provided a new basis or dynamic for rural innovation compared with tight political mobilisation and administrative control in the CCS.

Aimed at both grain and income growth, however, the HEA does not necessarily lead to the alleviation of over-cultivation and environmental improvement. While high-quality farmland and external inputs are utilised to develop cash crops or economic fruit plantations, sloping land continues to be over-cultivated or cropped at the same time to secure a subsistence grain supply. Moreover, in the absence of organic fertiliser inputs, the marginal utility of chemical fertilisers has continuously declined. According to farmers' own estimates, constant production of grain in recent years required the growth of chemical fertiliser inputs at a rate of no less than 20 per cent yearly.

It is not seldom in marginal areas that government projects are inappropriate in terms of technology choice and intervention styles, which cause economic loss to farmers rather than the government. This raises questions: who chooses technology and to whom is a technology appropriate? These issues will be addressed in Chapter 7.

5.3.4 *Concluding remarks: comparison of innovation strategy*

Reviewing the evolution of Zhidan's agricultural system in the last half-century, three types of innovation strategies can be recognised, namely: farmland extensive agriculture, labour-intensive agriculture and high-efficiency agriculture. The FEA, popularised in history through the 'rotational cultivation system', is a subsistence agriculture characterised by little external input, few products for the market and poor food security. In contrast, the LIA, focusing on irrigated agriculture, was characterised by labour-intensive inputs, organic fertilisers and experienced management, and many modern elements (e.g. electricity, chemical fertilisers) were introduced. The HEA, aimed at both grain and income growth, tries to facilitate GR technologies through intensive utilisation of external capital, and targeting urban markets.

Various agricultural strategies have different environmental impacts. As the rate of population increases, the destructive impacts of the FEA have gradually increased, leading to a vicious circle between grain growth, over-cultivation and devegetation. Highlighting the need to prevent runoff and improve farmland quality, the LIA had positive impacts on alleviating the pressure from over-cultivation, but suffered from technological inappropriateness due to an imbalance between farmland construction and afforestation. Compared with the LIA, the HEA has had complex environmental impacts because of the conflict between technological push and market pull, and between grain and income growth, which is beyond the technological system itself.

Furthermore, technology strategy cannot be separated from the prevailing rural institutions, which have experienced two fundamental changes. The CCS provided a sound basis upon which the FEA was replaced by the LIA through large-scale labour mobilisation and a centralised planning system, with little space for farmers' decision-making and economic return. When substituted for the CCS, the HRS returned production decision-making to households, stimulating commodity production and labour migration to non-farm areas. As a result, while the HEA was employed to promote capital input and household income growth, it has led to something of a recovery of the FEA for the purposes of grain security, resulting in a rapid expansion of cultivated areas.

5.4 Institutional dilemmas and innovation organisation

The variety of innovation strategies cannot be isolated from the prevailing rural institution, which determines the relations between farmers and their land. Institutional change, furthermore, influences not only farmers' attitude to land use and management, but also the relationship between farmers and professionals, resulting in different innovation organisation processes and mechanisms. Focusing on the HRS, this section attempts briefly to identify institutional barriers to the technological innovation, and to examine various types of innovation organisational practices adopted by government and urban professionals in particular. The above aims are addressed through a combination of field observation, secondary information and, in particular, key informant interviews. The section consists of seven parts. Section 5.4.1 outlines institutional dilemmas related to land utilisation and management at village level. This is followed by a case study on governmental innovation intervention. Section 5.4.3 concerns the county's agricultural extension system, which is contrasted with the case of a commercialised county seed company in Section 5.4.4. In contrast to the top-down intervention approach, Section 5.4.5 draws attention to 'property reform', illustrated by a case of waste land auction, whilst Section 5.4.6 concerns the variety of roles played in innovation by community organisations. Summarising the field findings, the final section provides concluding remarks.

5.4.1 Land resource management and institutional dilemmas

Land resources are both the core of rural institution and the base of agricultural innovation. In Zhidan county, exploitable land is ample in quantity (about 30 mu/capita) but very variable in quality, as illustrated in Table 5.4.

Based on topographic and vegetation conditions, agricultural production should be limited to Zone 1 (about one-sixth of the total exploitable land), whilst Zone 2 (about half of the total) would be used for forestry and pasture, and Zone 3 for natural revegetation until development capacity is reached. According to a survey by the Zhidan Land Management Office, however, less than 30 per cent of the present cultivated land is located in Zone 1, which produces about half of the county's grain product. This means that over 70 per cent of farmland is actually located in Zone 2, which is responsible for another half of the county's grain. Of the farmland in Zone 2, about 40 per cent on the slopes (15–25°) needs to be transformed to terraces if its use for grain production is to continue, while the 60 per cent that is on steep (>25°) areas should be stopped as soon as possible, and the area given over to forest or pasture instead. Due to agricultural utilisation and over-cultivation, according to field observation, Zone 2 has little forestry and pasture, while sheep breeding has actually been forced to move to Zone 3, the so-called 'waste land', with the features of poor vegetation, infertility and steep, eroded land.

The unsustainable utilisation of land resources in Zhidan, however, cannot be blamed on the traditional technology itself, but is also related to the rural institution of the HRS. Before collectivisation, the rural land was utilised and managed through a private-ownership and household-farm system, in which the owner, user and manager were actually the same. Due to the plentiful land resources and small number of rural population, understandably, the FEA dominated the rural economy and resource management (ZCAD 1990).

Since the collectivism from the late 1950s, all land in rural China has come under collective ownership but is utilised and managed through different institutions. Under the CCS, management responsibility for most of the land was taken by collective organisations that could mobilise rural labour to participate in innovation practices, such as irrigation systems and organic fertiliser utilisation.

Table 5.4 Division of village land grade and utilisation

Zone/grade	*I*	*II*	*III*
Category	Basic farmland	Slope cropland	Waste land
Typical features	Irrigated, terraces, plain or gentle (<15°)	Slope (>15°), fertile, distant	Steep (>35°), remote, eroded
% of land area	20	40	40
Ideal pattern	Grain	Animal/forestry	Reveget./forestry
Present utilisation	Grain	Grain	Animal

Note
Based upon the field observation and Figure 5.2.

Under the HRS, in contrast, the majority of collective land (Zones 1 and 2) has been distributed equally among all members of the community for household utilisation for a limited period (e.g. 5–15 years), whilst the remainder (mainly Zone 3), is 'public land' for sheep husbandry. The major issues facing the HRS can be summarised as follows:

- *Unclear land ownership.* Without a clear definition of property relationship between farmers and their land, the conflicts between long-term development of collective land and short-term household utilisation cannot be solved in the HRS because no one knows when and how land utilisation will be adjusted amongst community members.
- *Sharing duty of land management.* Households involved in the HEA in Zone 1 and afforestation in Zone 2 cannot be viewed as managers of the land, nor can they be viewed as collective organisations. Rather, management responsibility is best seen as sharing between local government and collective organisations.
- *Small scale and scattered distribution.* To ensure equality, all land in Zones 1 and 2 is distributed equally among community members, which has led to many small-sized plots around a hill (the so-called 'needle land').
- *Frequent adjustment.* In contrast to the permanent utilisation and management in the CCS and before, land utilisation in the HRS is subject to frequent adjustment (every 3–5 years) so as to reflect population change amongst community members and to secure equal access to collective land.

Because of the uncertain relationship between ownership, usage and management of collective land, the HRS itself seems to provide no stimulus for land users to consider long-term utilisation and investment. This constrains the sustainable utilisation and management of land resources.

5.4.2 Administrative intervention: the case of mechanical terracing

Because it involves complex institutional issues, over-cultivation in Zone 2 is difficult to solve merely by technological change itself. With the aim of achieving sustainable land utilisation and management, two approaches have been employed by the government: administrative intervention to promote new technology adoption; and property reform to stimulate innovation demand. The following case will address the reasons for and results from strengthening administrative intervention by tracing the process of mechanical terracing, while Section 5.4.5 will consider the 'property reform' for improving land resource management.

Terracing has been introduced to Zhidan since the late 1950s. In relation to institutional change from the CCS to the HRS, at least three changes have occurred in terracing. First, labour-intensive methods have been replaced by machinery-intensive ones (mainly tractors), increasing terrace width to 8–14 m compared with 4–5 m under the manual system. This has significantly improved terrace quality in terms of water conservation, duration, suitability for mechanical seeding. Second, instead of mass mobilisation and farmers' participation in the CCS, terracing projects are implemented mainly through a special tax, called 'farmland construction and maintenance fees', levied by the government. Finally, the organisation of terracing has been transferred from the community (administrative village) level to the township government, in order to concentrate the limited funding available for machinery.

Besides considerations of the scale effect, the administrative intervention is actually related to rural institutional contradictions in the present HRS. Without the security of long-term access to land, it is difficult for individual households to invest in farmland improvement and construction. Without a collective economic basis, community organisations are unable to mobilise rural labour to participate in rural infrastructure and collective land construction. To cope with the serious degradation of agricultural infrastructure, a national policy has been issued and implemented since the late 1980s (Liu 1994: 228–229), which requires all farmers to contribute their labour to rural infrastructure and collective farmland improvement for at least 1 month/year. This compulsory labour system services the national objectives of grain growth and security, offering local government rights of administrative intervention in rural labour mobilisation and organisations to achieve national objectives (Zhu and Jiang 1996).

Mechanical terracing has not only improved farmland quality, but also solved the dilemma of labour mobilisation and organisation. Instead of the compulsory contribution of labour, however, machinery terracing relies on intensive capital inputs, which cannot be taken from other channels but depends on a new tax paid by farmers. As a result, mechanical terracing is heavily dependent on government engagement and administrative intervention, which raises many issues.

First, compared with manual terracing in the CCS, the adoption of machinery has actually led to farmers being excluded from participation in project decision-making and implementation. As a result, not only is the tax burden on farmers and rural poor, in particular, increased, but also the tense relationship between government and farmers is exacerbated. To ensure tax collection and family population control, for instance, all ad-villages have an officer, which is one of the reasons for the expansion of township government staff from less than ten in the CCS to around fifty in the 1990s.

Second, the emphasis on terrace growth in Zone 2 neglects a more important issue, the need to improve the utilisation of the present farmland in Zone 1. Without a fundamental change in farming systems, mechanical terracing will not necessarily alleviate over-cultivation. Because of the neglect of rural heterogeneity, according to field observation, the potential of considerable areas of the terraces remains unrealised due to lack of enough production inputs (both organic manure and chemical fertilisers).

Third, influenced by 'road biases', unavoidably, terracing is often located neither in urgent demand villages nor in serious soil erosion areas. As a result, terracing was less helpful for the rural poor to improve their livelihoods and environments as expected.

The case of terrace building is not exceptional, but actually indicates a pattern of innovation organisation in the HRS, in which the government is not only the initiator and catalyst for innovation, but is also the direct organiser and controller of the innovation process. Since it excludes farmer participation, unfortunately, administrative intervention can hardly be responsive to the diverse demands of farmers, nor strengthen their responsibility for resource utilisation and management. Without farmers' participation, therefore, administrative intervention itself is unable to eradicate the FEA and initiate sustainable innovation practices.

The roles of government suggest that rural innovation in marginal areas of the Loess Plateau cannot be separated from macro-economic and political reform to deal with conflicts between the market economic system and the traditional political system generally, and between national interest and local development demand in particular. As a government governor pointed out:

> Without political pressure, in my opinion, Zhidan might have become a county specialised in animal breeding through large scale pastoral planting. In transition to a market economic system, unfortunately, the administrative system in China is still governed by an out-dated regime characterised by too many compulsory administrative commands from superior government such as grain growth, added area of terracing, extension projects. As a result, county government actually has little choice but to implement these commands.

5.4.3 Broken network of agricultural extension: various stories

With the dissolution of the CCS, the agricultural extension network in marginal areas has been subject to adjustment and reorganisation. With rural and urban institutional change unavoidable, many kinds of operative mechanisms and conflicts of interests exist in the system. To uncover the complexity and diversity of the extension networks, the following paragraphs will present and compare three cases: the agricultural extension station, an official veterinarian and an indigenous veterinarian.

In the 1970s, the agricultural extension system was proud of its well-organised four-tier network from county to sub-village. Since the HRS, the network has been broken down and its branches at township level exist in name only. Box 5.1 shows the impacts of rural reform on agricultural extension.

Compared with the broken network of agricultural extension, the township veterinary station was luckily recovered by 1996, due partly to sheep being listed as the county's pillar industry, and partly to sufficient demand from sheep breeding households who were able to pay the service charge. Field observation indicates, however, that a considerable number of farmers are not satisfied with these stations, for many reasons, such as inflexible service, bureaucratic attitude and high charges, etc. In particular, a case of conflict between a formal station and an indigenous veterinarian occurred during the fieldwork. Box 5.2 shows what kinds

> ***Box 5.1* Case of county agricultural extension station**
>
> Outside the county town, station A shares a basketball-sized yard and an out-of-date cave-building (made in the 1950s) with another station B. In the absence of any overhead budget, the telephone line has been cut down, while the yard is rented by a private garage. Unlike his colleagues in the county government, Director H in the station does not have either a car for extension service or a modern house for his family, but two poor caves for both his office and accommodation in the noisy yard. Before the rural reforms, according to him, the station had enough budget for experimentation, extension and farmer training. In contrast, now they have nothing but a basic salary (for their food security).
>
> Without the necessary working conditions and welfare security, not surprisingly, qualified extension staff can hardly concentrate on agricultural extension but 'jump out' to the administrative sectors. In contrast, more and more non-skilled employees have entered the extension stations arranged by the county government. As a result, qualified staff are only one-third of the total staff. These qualified professionals, furthermore, spend only 30–80 days a year in rural areas, less than 30 per cent of the normal 250 days/year extension activities. The total effective utilisation rate of human resources in the station is thus only 15 per cent.
>
> In rural areas, the central task of the station, according to Mr H and his colleagues, is to establish several demonstration zones for highly efficient agriculture countywide. These projects are, not surprisingly, located in areas with good facilities and farmland, and so have little impact on remote and high mountain villages. Due to the lack of market profit and economic compensation, few farmers are interested in participation. The success of the projects, thus, relies largely on administrative support from the township government, which is, in turn, dependent on personal relationships between extension staff and township leaders.

of technological services farmers need and how an 'underground network' exists in rural society, and competes with formal organisation.

Concerning the agricultural extension, veterinary stations and indigenous veterinarian, some conclusions emerge. First, related to rural institutional change, conventional agricultural extension suffers from structural breakdown and functional degradation. To cope with the challenges, the administrative means have become an important condition for technology extension. In view of the lack of professionals in the township or below, and bearing in mind that all affairs of agricultural extension are actually delivered and implemented through the township government, 'all staff in the township government are agricultural extensionists' whether or not they are qualified for this role.

Second, different mechanisms are employed in the agricultural extension system. In the absence of profit stimulation, many extension and service

Box 5.2 Conflicts between township veterinary station and indigenous veterinarian

In one of the sampled townships, the conflict between the township veterinary station and an unauthorised indigenous veterinarian attracted the local people's attention. According to Mr W, the head of the veterinary station:

> The indigenous veterinarian, about 58 years old, came to this region three years ago from outside Zhidan without official permission. Utilising expired chemicals and non-scientific methods, a number of sheep in the area have died. According to relevant regulations, we have asked the county government to stop all the activities of the indigenous veterinarian.

Interestingly, the effort from the county government failed because local people surrounded the official car and rejected the government's decision. Meanwhile, many local cadres seemed to stand on the side of the indigenous veterinarian. Summarising the farmers' statements, a comparison between the indigenous veterinarian and the veterinary station emerges:

- *Friendliness*. The indigenous veterinarian views all villagers as his friends and always does his best for them, which is in contrast to the arrogant and imperious attitude of the veterinary station.
- *Immediacy*. Due to constraints in transportation facilities, it is not easy for farmers to see the veterinary surgeon in the township, while the indigenous veterinarian can provide his services to a client's home quickly because the local people are able to pass the request for help to him.
- *Lower charge*. Compared with the veterinary station, the charge of the indigenous veterinarian is much cheaper while rural poor can get his service first and pay later.
- *Reliable*. Despite his lack of professional training, the indigenous veterinarian's techniques and experience were even better than those of professionals. Regarding the high death rate of sheep, it was argued that without the indigenous veterinarian, it would have been worse, due to a serious drought in 1997.

activities have to utilise administrative channels and top-down measures, in which government dominates the technological choice and process. In contrast, many innovation areas (e.g. sheep, tobacco) close to market demand and profit are actually dominated by farmers themselves.

Finally, the broken network of county agricultural extension has provided opportunities for the emergence of informal organisational networks. The plural tendency of the agricultural extension system unavoidably leads to conflicts and competition, in which market demand and farmer selection have gradually strengthened whilst administrative intervention is facing challenges.

5.4.4 Combination of agribusiness and farmers: the case of a seed company

In contrast to agricultural extension organisations, agribusiness agencies pay more attention to market change, farmers' demands and product profits. Representing a new direction, the case of the Zhidan Seed Company provides a good example of co-operation between an urban agency and farmers.

Originating twenty years ago, the company is responsible for raising and disseminating various hybrid seeds. At first, few farmers wanted to join the project and administrative measures had to be employed in three selected villages for demonstration. Realising the value of the hybrid seeds, according to Ms L, a staff of the company, now 90 per cent of farmers county-wide have adopted hybrid seeds, and more and more farmers want to join in hybrid seed raising. Due to its success in technology innovation and market exploration, in particular, the company has become a leading enterprise in provincial seed supply since 1994, which has led to a rapid expansion of hybrid seed use, rising from 400 mu and 50 tonnes in the early 1990s to a peak of 5,400 mu and 1,250 tonnes in 1996.

As a special cash crop, hybrid seed raising relies on the conditions of soil fertility and irrigation, which are available only in the valley region. In addition, it requires strict ecological isolation; no other crop can be planted in the nearby area, to avoid corn-fertilisation. For a community, to adopt the hybrid seed raising technology, therefore, it is a necessary condition that all households are prepared to join in the project.

According to Mr W, the manager of the company, the success of the hybrid seeds in Zhidan is mainly due to the new mechanism employed by the company:

- *Cash generation security.* Unlike from the governmental agricultural extension, the company can ensure participants' income through signing a purchase contract in Spring whereby it promises to collect all seeds in the Autumn at no lower than a protection price (about three times the current market price of grain).
- *Comprehensive services.* Different from the county agricultural extension stations, which focus merely on the production process, the company provides a comprehensive service including: delivery production elements (including seeds, fertilisers and plastic sheets) to farmers in Spring (pre-production) without deposit and interest charges; technology consultation and services in farmer plots or villages in Summer (in-production); and finally collection of all product at a reasonable price in Autumn (post-production).
- *Community participation and co-operation.* Related to the eco-segregated zone of hybrid seed raising, the project is implemented neither in administrative villages nor in individual households, but at the sub-village level, which promotes farmer co-operation and secures extension results. In other words, individual farmers cannot participate in the project unless all members in the village agree to join.

The process and mechanism used by the seed company are widely described as a new pattern of 'company + farmers', which focuses on a reciprocal partnership between an urban company and rural household, instead of administrative intervention. Scattered households are expected to reorganise and join specialised and commercialised production through urban companies.

Reviewing the case, however, the experience of the seed company should not be overstated. First, the company plays a double role: agricultural extension and business company. At the time of the survey, the government was paying the salary of all staff in the company, which reduced the cost of their business greatly. Second, seeds as special goods were monopolised by the government, so the profit of the company was more secure, due to a lack of competition. Finally, hybrid seed raising is confined to the valley, the best location in Zhidan; the scheme cannot be copied by mountain villages. Despite the above limitations, however, this case indicates a novel approach to agricultural extension in the market era.

5.4.5 Can property reform promote innovation? The case of afforestation

The objective of sustainable resource utilisation and management, as suggested in relation to mechanical terracing, is difficult to achieve merely through administrative intervention. As an alternative, property system reform has increasingly been emphasised as a solution for institutional dilemmas since the 1990s. Utilising the example of afforestation in Zone 2, this case attempts to illustrate the background and limitations of the new approach.

Compared with farmland construction, afforestation (pasture plantation as well) in Zone 2 is much slower and less fruitful. The poor survival rate of young trees may be best described by a local popular saying: 'Forest plantation is organised (by government) every year but it always occurs in the same plot'. Reading the main reasons for the poor record of forestation, less than 20 per cent of interviewees pointed out the demand for grain production, and a few people complained of natural factors (e.g. weather or soil). Instead, the majority (more than 70 per cent) believed that management institutions or systems should be changed because activities damaging collective forest cannot be efficiently prohibited and penalised. It seems clear that agricultural innovation does not necessarily lead to the decline of over-cultivation.

With regard to institutional contradictions, poor forest management is linked to two factors. One is a lack of long-term expectation regarding land utilisation, which leads to a few farmers being prepared to consider long-term investment in forests. Another is that the segments of collective land are too small for management responsibility to be shared. As a result, young trees are actually exposed to hungry sheep from over-grazed land in Zone 3.

To overcome the above barriers, 'property relationship reform', a new system of land management emerging since the mid-1990s, seeks to stimulate and secure production inputs in afforestation for the long term. Without changing the collective nature of land resources, it emphasises three transitions: from equal distribution of land amongst village members to efficient utilisation by innovators in the community; from short-term utilisation to long-term investment; and from community utilisation alone to encouraging outside investment. In particular, it includes the following new policies (ZRPO 1996):

- In contrast to the oral agreements on land utilisation between farmers and collective organisations that were common in the past, the new policy has clarified the division of land utilisation through legislation and farmers are asked to sign a land contract with collective organisations in which Zone 1 has been clearly defined for agriculture utilisation, whilst Zone 2 is for forestation, orchards or pasture plantations only.
- Land responsibility in Zone 1 has been prolonged from 15 to 30 years and a guarantee has been given that no land adjustment will be made, whatever household population change takes place in the period.
- Average utilisation in Zone 2 was to be broken down through 'auction' or rent within the community first and then to the public, for long-term investment, 30–60 years or longer.

Focusing on clarifying the property relationship between the collective ownership of land resources and the utilisation rights of individual households, the new policy has tried to achieve a balance between agriculture in Zone 1, animal breeding and 'forestry' in Zone 2, and between social equality in Zone 1 (equal distribution for food security), economic efficiency in Zone 2 and gradual ecological sustainability in all the zones. Meanwhile, it was expected that the reforms would create opportunities for outsiders to contribute their capital, technology and management experience to local economic development and environmental improvement.

These expectations, in practice, have not been achieved due to many factors. First, it is difficult for farmers to give up cultivated land in Zone 2 and return it to collective organisations for redistribution without any compensation. Second, it seems difficult for some households to take others' cultivated land if it will lead to neighbourhood tensions. Third, the auction and rental of Zone 2 involves many complex issues such as value assessment, price acceptation and rental utilisation, etc., which are particularly related to the uncertain roles of collective economic system.

While the 'wasteland auction' was highlighted in official documents as a successful reform with a bright future (ZRPO 1996), according to the field observation and survey, the average area of village forested land (including collective and household-owned forest) in 1997 was only 1.8 mu/capita, just over 10 per cent of land area in Zone 2. Of the total sampled households, 37 per cent did not have any wooded land and another 37 per cent had less than 1 mu of forest land.

One lesson can be learnt from the fruitless reform: the hypothesis of 'rational economic man' is called into question in addressing sustainable resource management in the Loess Plateau because it neglects the impacts of rural social relationships and cultural traditions. Focusing on individual economic motivation, the neo-liberal approach actually misses the role of neighbourhood and inter-household co-operation. One conclusion emerges in this cases: neither re-collectivisation nor privatisation can provide a sound solution for the institutional dilemmas of the HRS.

5.4.6 Roles of community organisations

Located in the intermediate position between government and farmers, village collective organisations often find it difficult to mobilise farmers to participate in government projects or to initiate their own projects without government support.

From the perspective of organisation structure, the community organisations can be divided into three parts, namely: Administrative Village Branch of the Communist Party for political control, Villagers' Autonomous Committee for administrative management and Village Co-operative Economic Organisation for managing collective property (i.e. land), enterprises and economy. In reality, they can be viewed as the same organisation with different titles. In the marginal areas there is little collective economy except land (the so-called 'empty shell village'). Without the basis of collective economy, all working subsidies of community cadres are actually paid through the township government. Due to heavy political pressure from the top, unavoidably, the township government needs to control the community organisations well to ensure the implementation of various administrative commands.

It would be a mistake to suppose that the community organisations do nothing but follow the government. According to the village surveys, the roles of the community organisations in community development and innovation vary greatly. They can be distinguished as follows:

- *Village unity and co-operation.* It is particularly important for the community organisations to solve land disputes, an important base for agricultural innovation.
- *Sustainable resource management.* Field observation indicates that the adoption of household orchards in villages is closely related to the survival rate of wood plantations in the past, which is, in turn, dependent on whether the community organisation is able to penalise those who have broken the regulations.
- *Access to government projects.* There are a number of government projects that are often accompanied by capital investments, comprehensive technology services and consultants without any charge. Competition is neither equal nor open; the winners are often those communities whose community organisations are powerful, united and reliable. Some communities, for example, are able to pay the cost of the electricity power connection because the leaders of the community organisations have been successful in gaining external funding through personal relationships.
- *Innovation opportunities for villagers.* Beside government projects and funding, according to the field surveys, many new technologies and projects

(e.g. potato processing, apple orchards, green houses) shared by villagers were actually generated from village cadres who have wide social contacts and a good reputation with outsiders (discussed in Section 6.3.6).

These functions, however, may be explained neither by the HRS institution itself nor by the top-down administrative control system. Rather, social and cultural dimensions are essential to understanding the exceptions above, which will be re-addressed in Chapter 6.

5.4.7 Concluding remarks: system transition and conflicts

Resulting from rural and urban institutional transition, the urban-based innovation system has changed in terms of both structure and mechanism. From the perspective of organisation structure, three changes can be recognised as follows:

1 a four-tier network of agricultural extension established in the period of the CCS has broken down and its function has partly been taken by administrative organisations, especially the township government;
2 in contrast to the extension network, the independence of agribusiness agencies has been strengthened through commercial linkage with rural customers, especially sub-villages;
3 without the basis of a collective economy, village collective organisations lack the ability to mobilise and organise farmer innovation, although there are exceptions.

From the perspective of organisation mechanism, the top-down extension model is still dominant in the rural innovation process due to the control from the traditional political and administrative system, which leaves little space for information feedback and farmers' participation in decision-making. Related to the HRS and market mechanisms, however, the following changes have occurred that influenced the innovation process:

- Household decision-making is in close response to market signals and profits, which often conflict with government objectives.
- Related to capability and response to market change, agricultural extension is increasingly dependent on the government whilst the agribusiness agencies are moving towards independence and profit orientation.
- Adapting to the market economy, the local government has paid increasing attention to market profit and appropriate technology. Due to rural complexity and diversity, however, it is often difficult to satisfy diverse demands, especially for the rural people in remote villages.

Besides the urban-based innovation systems and top-down extension mechanisms, informal technological diffusion networks and farmer innovation groups have emerged, which are characterised by common neighbour mutual aid, group learning and innovation. These informal innovation organisations are not necessarily in conflict or incompatible with the present institutional framework, but offer new elements or opportunities to improve the present innovation systems. This is the theme of Chapters 6 and 7.

5.5 Conclusions: institutional contradiction and rural innovation

Before initiating a rural enquiry on farmer innovation potential and self-organisation pattern, this chapter has tried to answer two questions: what challenges are facing rural sustainability in the sampled Zhidan county? What institutional and organisational barriers have impeded agricultural innovation? The above questions were addressed by a combination of secondary information, field observation and informant interviews. To end this chapter, the following paragraphs intend to summarise the field findings and discussion briefly, and to clarify research questions and foci. Accordingly, many conclusions can be drawn out.

First, despite impressive achievements in rural development and agricultural innovation since rural reform, Zhidan is not free from challenges of ecological degradation and marginalisation. Of many barriers against rural sustainability, the traditional farming system, the FEA, is an important one, which is incompatible with ecological and livelihood sustainability. Overcoming the FEA is thus a precondition for ecological improvement and capacity enhancement of the rural poor in the market economic era.

Second, the existence and persistence of traditional agriculture (FEA) cannot be understood without a historical view of the interaction between technology and institution. Whilst rural reform and the HRS have successfully promoted the transfer of modern agriculture (or HEA) and diversity of household production, it has also led to a turn of the FEA, resulting in a rapid expansion of cultivated areas and over-cultivation. In this sense, the achievements of the HRS cannot be overstated because much progress has resulted from the HRS system, whilst negative impacts on rural disorganisation should not be underestimated.

Third, the co-existence and conflict with traditional and modern agriculture reflect the institutional dilemmas in the HRS, which involves a complex and uncertain relationship between ownership, utilisation and management of collective land. The case studies of mechanical terracing and 'waste land auction' seem to suggest that two coping strategies, administrative intervention on TT and 'property reform' to break down equal access to collective land, can hardly take account of the complexity of geographic environment and farmer demands, resulting in very limited progress in dealing with the FEA.

However, many new innovation patterns and organisation mechanisms have been developing. Whilst a new co-operation and interaction relationship between farmers and urban professionals can be found from the case of the county's seed company, informal technological extension and service networks have been developed to fill the gaps left by the broken agricultural extension networks.

One common conclusion that can be drawn from above findings is that rural innovation in marginal areas of China cannot be achieved and sustained without farmer participation and self-organisation. In this regard, many questions arise: How can rural innovation be organised by farmers themselves without outside intervention or involvement? What are the functions of farmer innovation and self-organisation in sustainable livelihood security? What variation can be recognised among farmers in terms of organisation patterns and innovative capacity? What is the interface between the informal and formal networks? Chapters 6 and 7 will consider the above issues.

6 Farmer innovative capacity and communication networks

Taking into account the market economy and marginalisation process in rural China, enhancing innovative capacity is vital for the rural poor to cope with various challenges to their livelihood security. Since government interventions and PRPs have suffered from location biases and inappropriate technology, the question is raised, whether and how the poor in the marginal areas can learn new technologies by themselves. From the perspective of innovation organisation, this general question can be further discomposed: by what kinds of information networks and organisational patterns do they learn and share new technologies? Are organisational patterns related to the variety of household innovative capacity (HIC)? What factors influence farmers' innovative capacity and organisation pattern?

The above issues were investigated in a tailored survey in rural Zhidan, which involved a combination of a village investigation (fifty villages), a household questionnaire survey (150 randomly selected respondents) and case studies. The results are presented in two chapters. Relying mainly on quantitative analysis, this chapter attempts to map out a general picture of the village environment, HIC and the social networks. By contrast, Chapter 7 uses qualitative information to gain a deeper understanding of the organisation process and co-operative mechanisms.

This chapter, which is based on field observations and the household questionnaire survey, consists of four sections. To begin, it outlines the differences among sample villages and the diversity of household livelihood systems. Section 6.2 discusses HIC and relevant factors. Focusing on the role of social capital in farmer innovation, Section 6.3 explores the relationship between farmer communication networks (FCN) and the HIC. The final section summarises the research findings and poses further questions, which will be explored through case studies in Chapter 7.

6.1 Village environment and livelihood systems: overview of samples

Based upon participatory observation, village investigation and household questionnaire survey, this section attempts to outline baseline information on the sampled townships, villages and households, and to establish a classification system for distinguishing village environments and household livelihood systems in particular. It consists of four sections. Section 6.1.1 introduces the sampled townships and administrative villages (ad-villages), while the next describes village divisions (sub-villages). Combing the elements of village environment and human capital, Section 6.1.3 explores the distribution of household livelihoods. The section ends with a summary of field findings on the complexity of village environment and the diversity of household livelihoods.

6.1.1 Baseline information of sampled townships and administrative villages

To understand farmer innovative capacity and demand, three out of a total twelve townships in Zhidan county were selected as samples for village and household surveys. Table 6.1 summarises some baseline information.

The three townships listed in Table 6.1 are representative of the different regions (zones) defined in Table 5.1. Located in the east of Zhidan, Zhouhe township is featured by relatively low altitudes and gently sloping land, high population density and grain product per capita and a rural net income 60 per cent above the county's average. By contrast, its 'poor neighbour', Zhifang township, is located in the highland of the north of Zhidan, with features of high altitude and cultivation rate, low forest cover and poor soil fertility.

Turning to organisation structure and population distribution, each township is composed of a number of ad-villages, each of which, in turn, can be further divided into a number of villages (sub-villages or villager groups). Differences

Table 6.1 Comparison of sampled townships (1995)

Category	*Indicator*	*Zhouhe*	*Zhifang*	*Jindin*	*County total*[a]
Land	% of county	6.3	7.0	10.4	100
	Cultivation rate (%)	33	27	35	26
	Forest covering (%)	12	5	16	26
Village	No. of ad-villages	15	14	19	189
	No. of sub-villages	99	87	145	1,092
	Total households	1,736	1,277	2,386	20,474
	Total population	8,455	6,656	12,518	100,698
	Road length (km)[b]	135	39	89	278
Livelihood	Net income (yuan/person)	1,300	480	760	816
	Grain product (kg/person)	465	311	395	393

Sources: All information from ZPSO (1996) except road information, which is from Zhidan Agricultural Survey Office.

Notes

a In country total column, urban population is taken out from number of households, population and grain product.

b It is incomparable for road length between selected township and county total, because the latter considers the main road (county-level road) that can be used in almost all seasons (including rainy or iced condition) whilst the former includes the sample (countryside) road for small vehicles (e.g. jeep or small tractor), which cannot be used in wet or iced weather.

among the sample townships can be distinguished by three indicators: area of village land, size of village households and total length of vehicle road. Regarding the interaction between farmers and outside, Table 6.1 shows the uneven distribution of rural road facilities: the total length of road in Zhouhe township is more than three times that in Zhifang although in terms of land area, the former is smaller than the latter.

Related to differences in environment and conditions, not surprisingly, household livelihoods varied greatly among the sampled townships. Table 6.1 shows that the variation in household net income is larger than that in grain production. In particular, Zhifang, the poorest township in Zhidan, has grain product and net income per capita 20 and 40 per cent lower than the county's average, respectively.

The aggregated picture above, however, is not enough to reflect genuine differences existing in rural societies, because each township itself cannot be viewed as a homogenous whole. To gain insight into the diversity of rural environments and development, three ad-villages of each sampling township were selected for further surveys. Turning to the ad-village level, field observation shows: first, despite great variation among these sampled ad-villages, there was less difference in grain product per capita than in household net cash income; second, it confirms that uneven distribution of rural income exists at the ad-village level; finally, grain product per capita is neither linked with household income nor a major issue of concern to farmers, even in these poverty villages. In this sense, the priority for farmer innovation may be related to cash cropping rather than grain production.

6.1.2 Types and features of sampling villages

Taking into account the complexity of geographic environment and rural development in the marginal areas like Zhidan county, even the ad-village is too big to be used as a basic unit of geographic observation and development planning. Instead, local people use the sub-village (or 'production term' as it was called in Mao's era) to distinguish the differences in local environment and development. To take into account local people's perspectives, all villages within the selected ad-villages were treated as unit of both village observation and the sample frame of the household questionnaire survey.

Using local terminology, village location can be divided into three types: *Chuan-dao Dui*, referring to these villages in valley areas; *Gou-dao Dui*, in downstream or low mountain areas where the slope is relatively gentle; and *Shan-ling Dui* in upstream or high mountainous locations. By integrating topographic, road accessibility and distance factors together, all fifty villages of the nine selected ad-villages can be distinguished into three types: valley, middle and remote. Table 6.2 lists some different characteristics among the sample villages.

Table 6.2 shows the significant difference among sampling villages not only in terms of geographic and resource environments, but also in terms of economic and social development. For instance, five of the fifty sample villages are located in the valley. They lie along the main road and are characterised by flat topography,

Table 6.2 Typology and features of sample villages

Village division	*Valley*	*Middle*	*Remote*
Topographic features	Valley	Low mountain	High mountain
Average altitude (m)	1,260	1,370	1,500
High productive land (mu)	5 (irrigated)	3 (terraces)	2 (terraces)
Road accessibility	main road	simple road	no road likely
Distance to main road (km)	0	4	8
Distance to market (km)	5	8	18
No. of sampled villages	5	18	27
No. of sampled households	22	64	63
Size of village households	29	20	14
Illiterate rate (%)	5	38	38
Net income (yuan/person)	1,318	740	578

Source: Author's household questionnaire survey.

Notes
Illiterate rate defined as percentage of household heads who received no or little (not more than 1 year) formal education. Child school enrolling rate defined as percentage of boys or girls whose ages were between 7 and 15 without enrolling in a school.

irrigated land, large village population and short distance to local market. By contrast, 60 per cent of the samples are remote villages located in the high mountains. They are difficult to access, a long way from the main road and local market and have comparatively small households. Intermediate between these two groups, middle villages account for 36 per cent of the samples, and share some characteristics with the other two types. If the valley villages are viewed as core zone, middle and remote villages can be seen as the marginal areas of Zhidan.

The difference between core and marginal zones is not confined to geographic environment but also includes human capital, which can be illustrated by the fact that nearly 40 per cent of household heads in marginal areas are illiterate, compared to only 5 per cent in valley villages. Regarding the accumulation of human capital for future development, 90 per cent of children in the valley are enrolled in schools, compared to only three-fourths in the marginal areas (in some villages, only 50 per cent).

Similar to Table 6.1, Table 6.2 confirms the uneven distribution of rural income at the village level. Three conclusions can be drawn. First, the distribution of household income coincides with the distribution of village geographic, resource and human capital. Therefore, a rural survey at the village level offers an efficient means to understand the complexity and diversity of the rural environment and development.

Second, the difference between valley and remote villages raises the question of comparability, unless environmental differences between them are clarified. It suggests that a conventional rural survey methodology, based upon administrative division, may underestimate the complexity of the environment and development in marginal areas.

Finally, compared with the difference between valley and remote villages, there is no absolute division between middle and remote villages in either physical environment or human capital. The similarity of the two locations allows a statistical analysis, regardless of the geographic differences between them in some respects.

6.1.3 Household livelihood system

The 'environmental analysis' in the previous sections has provided a basis to explore rural livelihood systems at the household level. These can be examined with reference to many factors such as household demography, production inputs and output structure.

From the point of demographic features, the mean size of the household in the samples was 5.1, with 14 per cent having up to three persons, 47 per cent having between four and five persons and nearly 40 per cent having six or more persons. The size of households seems to be related not to geographic location but to family structure pattern. Of a total of 149 sampled households, for instance, about three-fourths were two-generation (or core) families, whilst the traditional pattern, three- or four-generation households accounted for just over 20 per cent, leaving a marginal 3.4 per cent of one-generation households, the latter were mainly old people whose children had married and set up their own households.

The size of household scale is particularly related to labour supply. On average, small households (less than or equal to three) have 1.8 workers,[1] middle sized (four to five) have 2.3 workers and large households (greater than or equal to six) have 2.7 workers. A matter closely related to household size and security of livelihood is the age of the household head, which ranged widely from 25 to 68 years. Fifty-two per cent of household heads were in the middle age, defined as between 36 and 50 years, whilst 28 per cent were young, 35 years or below, while the remaining 20 per cent were elderly, above 50 years.

Regarding the distribution of production elements, the household survey revealed that one-fourth of the sample had no production cattle or only one donkey and over three-fourths had no seeding machine. These households might not be able to complete an agricultural production process without other households being involved.

To reveal the impacts of the above factors on household livelihood systems, many indicators need to be taken into account, including cash income, grain production and animal breeding. Concerning household cash income, all sources of household cash income fall into one of four categories: grain, animal breeding (mainly sheep/goat selling), cash crops (including forest product and fruit orchard income) and non-farm. The results from the household questionnaire survey shown that, generally, the first income source was non-farm, accounting for one-third of household cash income, followed by grain, 29 per cent, leaving the reminding 38 per cent shared between cash crops and livestock. Regarding the impacts of geographic factors, Figure 6.1 shows the great variation among the sample in terms of both income level and production structure.

A sharp contrast can be seen in the increase in household animal income and decline of non-farm income from valley to remote villages. Whilst valley villages enjoy opportunities for non-farm employment, the comparative advantage in

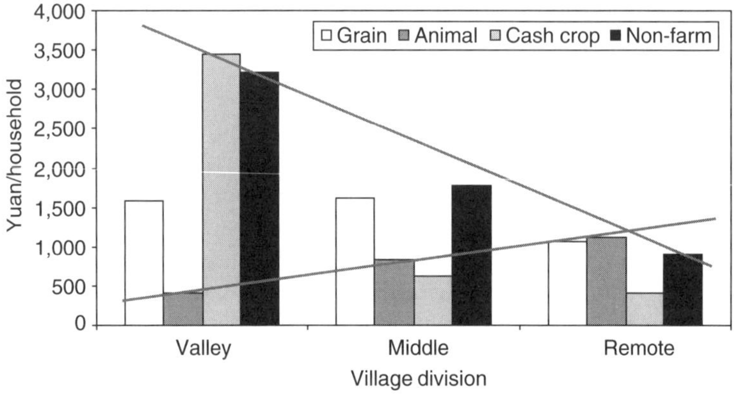

Figure 6.1 Household income source by village division (1996 yuan).

Source: Author's household questionnaire survey 1997.

remote villages seems to be in animal breeding, as a result of their larger areas of land. Particularly, Figure 6.1 shows that remote villages suffered from the deficiency in grain income, which was only two-thirds the average for the other regions. Viewed in conjunction with the official statistical data indicated in Figure 5.6, these data support the view that the poor areas are poor in grain production in general, and emphasise that the deficiency of grain production should be viewed at the village level rather than township or ad-village levels.

Geographic factors, however, are not enough to reflect the complexity and diversity of household livelihood distribution. For instance, although income from sheep and goats was important for household in the marginal areas of Zhidan, the household survey revealed that two-thirds of the sample in the middle village and over a half in the remote villages did not have sheep at all. Regarding causes for the above difference, the survey indicated that the number of household workers was an important factor. This can be illustrated by the mean household animal income that was 218 yuan/household in households with fewer than 2 workers, 787 yuan in those with between 2 and 2.5 workers and 1,264 yuan in the group with 3 or more workers.

To gain an overall picture about the distribution of the household livelihood system and relevant factors, Table 6.3 takes household net income as a key variable that is examined in relation to geographic and other factors, including grain production, sheep/goat flock and household demographic factors.

Focusing on marginal areas, many conclusions can be drawn from Table 6.3. First, it shows a strong correlation between grain product per capita and household net income. It is particularly serious for those households in remote villages whose grain product was below 350kg/capita whilst their household income is likely less than 60 per cent of the mean income for the whole sample. The importance of sheep/goat breeding for remote areas is also confirmed by Table 6.3, in

Table 6.3 Distribution of sample household income in marginal areas of Zhidan

Category	*Division*	*Net income (all samples)*	*Middle zone*		*Remote zone*	
			Samples	*Income*	*Samples*	*Income*
Grain division (kg/person)	<250	668	17	616	15	369
	250–350	744	19	757	23	448
	>350	830	28	805	25	823
Sheep	No	759	43	780	33	453
	Yes	753	21	659	30	716
Household size	⩽3	881	7	945	13	810
	4–5	779	32	761	25	559
	⩾6	686	25	657	25	476
Household head's age	⩽35	690	15	788	20	523
	36–50	729	36	689	29	528
	⩾51	923	13	829	14	758
Total		757	64	740	63	578

which significant difference can be found between household net income by sheep/goat flock.

Second, the distribution of household income is negatively associated with household size: the bigger the household size, the poorer the household income. Linked with Figure 6.1, this suggests that unequal distribution of rural livelihood is closely related to distribution or access to collective farmland resources.

Finally, it is surprising that the distribution of household income is skewed towards elderly farmers rather than young or middle age households. This is particularly true for the remote villages where both young and middle age households had income below the mean rural income. Regarding reasons why the older household should hold a favourable position in rural income distribution, small households and less economic burden could be a factor, whilst their production experience and social networks could be other factors. These will be discussed in subsequent sections.

6.1.4 Conclusions: environmental impacts on household livelihood systems

In moving from official data to sampling information, this section has attempted to provide fresh information about the complexity of the rural environment in general, and the division of household livelihood systems in particular. In line with local people's knowledge system, all sample villages have been categorised into three types: valley, middle and remote. Taking into account geographic environment together with resource distribution and household demographic factors, several conclusions can be drawn regarding household livelihood systems.

First, Zhidan's rural environment is so complex that administrative division at either township or administrative level is not enough to reflect the environmental constraints and differences of resource endowment. Instead, the sub-village is a more appropriate basic unit of rural environment comparison and household sampling.

Second, household livelihood systems in marginal areas are particularly diverse, as a result of many factors, involving geographic environment, resource allocation and demographic factors. Whilst valley areas depend heavily on cash crops and non-farm income, the main sources of household income in the middle and remote villages are still traditional grain production and animals. The difference between middle and remote villages is that animal breeding is more important in the remote areas than in the middle areas, in terms of securing household livelihoods.

Finally, although Zhidan's grain production was not a major concern for farmers, it is an important factor influencing the distribution of rural income. This is particularly true for households in remote villages, where household income is significantly related to capacity of grain production. This suggests that the improvement of conditions for agricultural production could be more helpful for the rural poor in remote villages than in other areas. This is in contrast to the government approach, in which the tendency has been to give the priority for poverty-reduction funds to the middle villages.

6.2 Household innovative capacity

The previous section has provided a base upon which variation and contribution from farmer innovative capacity can be revealed and measured. The aims of this section are thus to develop a working definition for distinguishing HIC in general, and to explore the relevant factors influencing its distribution in particular. Consisting of five sections, this section starts by defining the HIC, followed by an examination on distribution of the HIC. Section 6.2.3 concerns the impacts from geographic environment, whilst Section 6.2.4 focuses on the contribution from human capital. The final section provides a short conclusion.

6.2.1 Household innovative capacity: definition and measures

The notion of 'capacity', according to Amartya Sen,[2] is related to 'being able to perform certain basic functions, to what a person is capable of doing and being'. The term *innovation capacity* is used here to refer to the ability of farmers to learn, adopt, improve or create a new technology, method or tool. Farmer innovative capacity can be measured at many levels: individual, household, village and above.

In the circumstances of marginal areas like Zhidan, farmer innovative capacity is closely related to the adoption of a new technological strategy or farming system that is different from the traditional farming system. Such a new technological or farming system consists of the following interconnected elements: *new knowledge* (experience or technique) for commodity production; *new and/or intensive production element* inputs in contrast to low or no production inputs in the past; and *new products* for market profit.

In the context of the rural institutional transition from collective commune organisations to a household production system, however, the term *new* (knowledge, production elements or products) is not absolute. For example, many technologies (e.g. traditional crafts) might have existed for hundreds of years in that region, as the case of apple grafting has been adopted by collective organisations in Mao's era, but may still be new to individual households. The notion of HIC thus emphasises a process of household learning and adapting to these 'new technological elements', as distinct from the predominance of the traditional farming system.

The three innovative elements (i.e. new knowledge, production elements and products), however, cannot be separated from each other due to the following reasons. First, under the market economy, farmer innovation tends to be more concerned with market value of labour or production element inputs, which is quite different from the government focus on grain product per unit of farmland. This is particularly true for rural Zhidan where the majority of the rural residents were found to be free from grain shortage, and were concerned about opportunities for earning cash for their children's education, marriage or housing demands. Second, constrained by limited production scale and organisation, small farmers can hardly secure their cash income merely through selling their physical labour or traditional agricultural products such as grain or animals. In this sense, new knowledge or techniques are vital for them to provide 'highly skilled' services (e.g. fruit tree grafting), to develop new products (e.g. cash crops) or to adopt new production elements (e.g. new pesticides) for the purpose of obtaining a high economic return. In other words, high income without innovative elements (e.g. labour migration or sheep husbandry), cannot be viewed as high HIC.

Relevant factors influencing the HIC would be a long list from personal to community, from physical to social factors, from farmers themselves to government policy intervention. Regarding measurement of the HIC, all relevant factors can be distinguished into several categories, such as indicators of the HIC; household's human capital, physical environment and social capital. Since it is outside the scope of this chapter, government intervention is not shown as an independent dimension, but is encompassed in other relevant factors (e.g. education, road, land). Accordingly, the next section considers the distribution and measure of the HIC, followed by geographic environment and human capital. Social capital will be examined in the section on 'Farmer communication networks'.

6.2.2 Differentiation in household innovative capacity

Differences in HIC, according to the definition in the previous section, can be revealed by both inputs and outputs of the household production. Inputs refer to the capacity of household adopting new production elements including chemical fertilisers, new or high-quality seeds, plastics and pesticides, and others (e.g. farming tools, electricity power expenditure). The term outputs here concerns new products, such as cash crops, or non-farm activities related to 'new techniques' (e.g. crafting, tractor driving).

Regarding the capacity of household production inputs, according to the household questionnaire surveys, the total production expenditure was 840 yuan/household, or 23 per cent of household total expenditure in the year in question, 10 per cent lower than living expenses (e.g. clothes, food, resources), the biggest part of household expense, but 8 per cent higher than spending on education. Focusing on household production expenditure, chemical fertilisers were the largest household production inputs, accounting for nearly 60 per cent of the total. Use of other inputs, however, varied greatly. For instance, about one-third of the sample did not buy seeds, whilst over 40 per cent did not apply pesticides to control the spread of serious pest diseases in 1996.

The variety in production input capacity among the sample can be distinguished by household production inputs per capita. Whilst the mean inputs of household production were 170 yuan/person, nearly 40 per cent of households spent under 100 yuan/person, one-third spent between 100 and 200 yuan/person, while less than 30 per cent were in the high-input group, spending over 200 yuan/person. Concerning the structure of household production inputs, near 60 per cent of household production expenditure were spent in purchasing chemical fertilisers, leaving the rest to these 'new' elements such as: plastic sheets, hybrid seeds and pesticides. The difference among sample households, according to this survey, was mainly caused by household production inputs other than fertilisers, which accounted for only 67 and 153 yuan/household in low- and middle-input groups, respectively, but jumped to 931 yuan in high-input groups, in sharp contrast to fertiliser inputs. Particularly, around half of the samples did not use the new production elements in 1996. A number of conclusions can be drawn from the data analysis. First, the low production input level (about one-fifth of household cash income annually) suggests that Zhidan was still dominated by subsistence agriculture. Second, the uneven distribution of production inputs amongst households indicates that differentiation in the innovative capacity amongst households was quite large. Finally, the differences among farmers mainly occurred in new production elements except fertilisers.

The difference of the HIC can be further recognised through output structure. Due to ecological risk, farmers usually adopted a balance strategy to ensure both grain and cash security. Regardless of the grain consumption of households themselves, grain crops and animal breeding contributed to almost a half (47 per cent) of household cash income, and non-farm income one-third, leaving the remaining 20 per cent to cash crops. Turning to the variety of household production structure, the survey confirmed the uneven distribution of household cash crops and non-farm among sample households. This is particularly true for low-income groups (below 700 yuan/person) in which nearly half of the households are absent in either or both of them. It is reasonable to assume that the difference in the innovative capacity among households mainly occurs in new production areas, that is, cash crops and non-farm.

Based upon the information provided above, the HIC can be seen as a result of the interaction of household production inputs and new production output. In this sense, both input and output structures can be viewed as a means to achieve households' innovation objective: increasing and securing income growth. Adopting a similar format to assess household production inputs and outputs, Table 6.4 offers scores to distinguish the households into three capacity grades.

Table 6.4 Capacity division of household production inputs and structure

Type	*Rank score*	*1*	*2*	*3*
Inputs	Other inputs (yuan/person)	< 100	100–199	100–199
	No. of households	63	30	59
	% of total samples	42	20	38
Outputs	New products share (%)	< 30	30–59	≥60
	No. of households	63	40	46
	% of total samples	42	27	31

Note
'Other inputs' means all household production expenditure except fertilisers.

Table 6.5 Division of HIC by score and income

Score	*<300*	*300–699*	*700–999*	*≥1,000*	*Total*
6	–	3	9	15	27
5	–	9	3	4	16
4	10	11	9	13	43
3	8	17	3	4	32
2	10	19	1	1	31

Combining household capacity score with net income, the HIC can be classified into three levels: weak, medium and strong. Table 6.5 shows the criteria for classifying the sample into three groups. As a result, 28 per cent (forty-one) of 149 sample households are recognised as 'strong' in the HIC, 30 per cent (forty-four) as medium, leaving the remaining 43 per cent (sixty-four) as weak. The distinction of the HIC provides a means by which the relevant natural and social causes of farmer innovation can be analysed and compared.

6.2.3 *Distribution of innovative capacity by geographic factors*

Of many factors related to the HIC, impacts from geographic location are in the forefront. Figure 6.2 shows the strong relationship between the HIC and the locations. For instance, over three-fourths of households in valley villages fell into the category of 'strong' HIC, whereas, in contrast, about 60 per cent of farmers in remote villages were 'weak'.

Village division, however, is not enough to explain the differences in the HIC within the same zone. In middle villages, for instance, 30 per cent of the sample were ranked as 'strong' in the HIC, 28 per cent as 'medium', leaving 42 per cent as 'weak'. To reveal the impacts of geographic environment, household location needs to be examined in detail. According to field observations, two factors are particularly important for the HIC. One is the remoteness of the household from local economic and social 'centres' such as the central village of an ad-village (centre of community information) and township headquarter (local market assembly and township government with agricultural extension facilities).

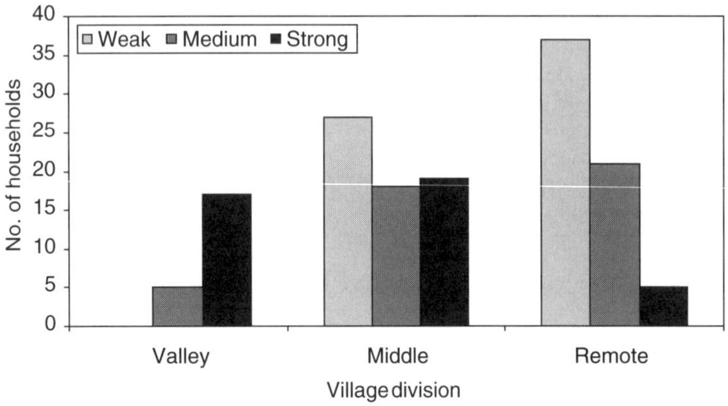

Figure 6.2 Distribution of HIC by village division.

Table 6.6 Average distance to main sites by HIC (km)

Capacity	*Strong*	*Medium*	*Weak*	*Total*
No. of households	24	39	64	127
To central village	1.9	2.8	2.0	2.3
To main road	3.9	7.5	5.6	5.9
To township	9.3	14.2	12.7	12.5

Note
The table excludes valley villages. Central village here means one of the sub-villages within an administrative village, usually the largest sub-village with facilities such as vehicle road, post office picking, retail shop and clinic.

Another is road accessibility because all sample households in marginal areas (except in the valley zone) were away from the main road (which gives entry to the public transport system), whilst about one-fourth of households lived in villages without vehicle-roads.

Table 6.6 shows that significant impacts of the geographic environment can be found from village location because compared with the 'medium' capacity group, the 'strong' group are more likely to live in or near a central village, or township, and near a main road. Distance to a main road, in particular, has stronger impacts on the distribution of HIC than other factors. In addition, Table 6.6 seems to suggest that there is no relationship between weak group and location. In other words, households with poor HIC are dispersed throughout the marginal areas, which can hardly be blamed on geographic factors.

Linked with the geographic background mentioned above, the HIC of the samples can be further distinguished by road accessibility. The data analysis indicated that 22 of twenty-four strong-capacity households were actually located in vehicle-road accessed villages, 15 per cent higher than the average of other

Table 6.7 Comparison of HIC by production field

HIC grade	*Non-farm* (yuan/hh)	*Cash crops* (yuan/hh)	*Trad. farm* (yuan/hh)	*Grain* (kg/person)	*Grain* (kg/mu)
Weak	236	224	2,061	342	55
Medium	1,406	507	2,727	372	57
Strong	4,218	1,307	2,386	373	54
Total	1,348	516	2,327	357	56

Note
hh Household.

groups. Taken in conjunction with the distance to main road in Table 6.6, this suggests that the simple roads in marginal areas have less impact on improving the majority of rural residents' innovative capacity. In other words, vehicle road accessibility is more important for a few strong HIC households than for the majority of rural poor, in improving their innovative capacity.

By contrast to household location, however, there is no significant relationship between the HIC and the distribution of land resources in terms of both quantity (area of farmland) and quality (availability of high-qualitative farmland). This phenomenon can be explained by the fact that the HIC in sampled Zhidan county is not directly related to grain production and animal breeding, which are more dependent upon the inputs of land resources than cash cropping and non-farm production. The above assumption is supported by Table 6.7, which shows the distribution of the HIC by production fields.

6.2.4 Impacts of household demographic factors and human capital

Whilst the impacts of geographic factors can clearly explain differences in the HIC across villages, it may be difficult to explain the variation within the village. Instead, it is reasonable to assume that human capital may play a crucial role in influencing the distribution of the HIC. To examine this hypothesis, the following paragraphs bring household demographic and education factors into account. As in the previous section, the valley zone is excluded in the following discussion.

It was surprising to find in the field observation that the village 'technological centre' was usually neither young nor middle age households, but their fathers or uncles. Of many possible interpretations, comprehensive farming experience accumulated over years of practice is one, whilst social capital is another that will be examined in the next section.

As an important component of human capital, the political status of households in the community organisation cannot be ignored. Accordingly, Table 6.8 contrasts ordinary farmers with cadres defined as households in which at least one of the members had responsibility for village affairs as a member of an administrative managerial board. Obviously, the distribution of HIC is significantly related to household political status, which can be illustrated by the slightly

Table 6.8 Contrast of innovation capacity by household's political status (%)

Political status	*Weak*	*Medium*	*Strong*	*No. of households*
Ordinary	55	28	17	87
Cadre	40	38	23	40
Total	50	31	19	127

Note
Cadre are all members of the administrative village managerial board (including village head).

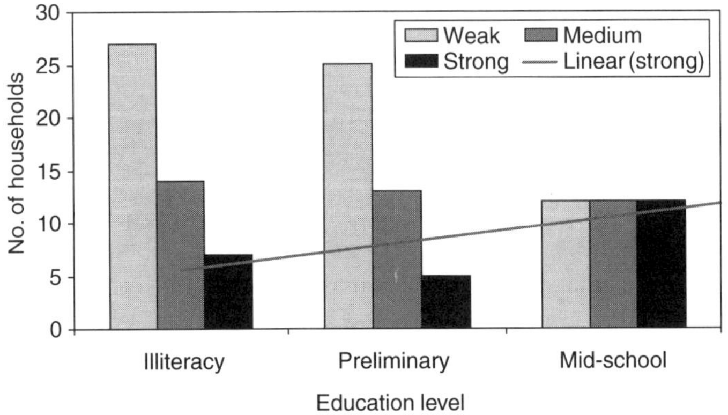

Figure 6.3 Impacts of education on HIC.

Source: Author's household questionnaire survey 1997.

higher percentage of the cadres in the category of the 'strong' group and lower percentage in 'weak' group compared with ordinary farmers. The difference of the HIC between cadres and others can be explained by three factors. The first is personality, because the cadres are more likely to be people considered strong. Regarding marginal areas, it is not less important that village cadres have more opportunities of access to public resources (including information, discount elements and government demonstration) compared with their neighbours. The third factor is related to social capital (see Section 6.3.6).

In addition to experience accumulation, indicated above, education provides another channel for households to enhance their capacity in technological learning and application. Regarding the educational background of household heads in middle and remote villages, according to this survey, 38 per cent of the sample were illiterate or semi-illiterate, defined as having had less than two years of formal education; 34 per cent were classed as preliminary level (2–6 years schooling), leaving 28 per cent as mid-school level. Figure 6.3 illustrates the distribution of the HIC by household head's education level. Three conclusions can be drawn from the schema. First, rural education has positive impacts on improving or enhancing HIC, which can be demonstrated by the decline of 'weak' households and increase of strong households response to improvement of education level. Second, education does not show a linear relationship with HIC, because it is one of many relevant factors. Finally, the similarity of household capacity distribution between illiterate household heads and those with preliminary schooling seems to suggest that preliminary education in marginal areas has little impact on improving the HIC. To promote sound agricultural innovation in these areas, the prevalence of middle education is necessary.

6.2.5 Concluding remarks

Among the many factors influencing the distribution of household livelihoods, this section aimed to reveal the existence and influence from HIC. A working definition has been developed in this section, which views the HIC as an integrative capacity of households to adopt new knowledge (skill), production inputs and outputs for the purposes of increasing market profit. Applying the above criteria, all households have been distinguished into three groups according to their positions in the HIC assessment panel (Table 6.5). Based on the analysis of the distribution of HIC by relevant factors, many conclusions can be drawn as follows:

1. Among all sample households, about 30 per cent were classed as 'strong' in the HIC, meaning those households had the capacity to seek, adopt or develop a new production technology (production, method) by themselves, without any outside aid or intervention. Another 30 per cent of the sample were 'medium' in HIC. Those were in the margin of the rural 'innovative army', depending upon the environment (both village and market environment), conditions (e.g. government subsidies) and risks. The remaining 40 per cent were 'weak', meaning that they would be unlikely to join an innovative team unless some barriers (e.g. information, credit or risk) could be removed. Despite the subjective factors involved, the HIC provides an efficient means to observe household production actions, and to seek the relevant factors behind the distribution of HIC.
2. The variety of the HIC is no doubted related to geographic environment, which can be further divided into many factors or levels, including village division: valley, middle and remote areas; road accessibility; village location, etc. Two conclusions can be drawn regarding the impacts from geographic factors. One is the comparability of the HIC between valley and marginal areas where resource bases, innovative environment and production patterns are so different from each other. Another is the relativity among marginal areas because HIC distribution seems to be sensitive to environmental impacts among 'strong' households, but less so for 'weak' households. In other words, the distribution of 'weak' HIC households is not related to geographic factors.
3. 'Blank areas' of the geographic environment can be partly filled by human capital involving household population, scale, labour, age profile, education

and political status, etc. Excluding valley villages, the evidence from this household survey showed that there is no strong (or linear) correlation between human capital and HIC, although the age, education level and political status of household heads do have certain impacts on the distribution of HIC. This suggests that the role of human capital might be over-estimated if the impacts from geographic factors (here valley villages) are not taken out.

4 The complexity of the HIC distribution and the relevant factors raises questions about government intervention: which areas should be given top priority regarding government innovative intervention: valley, middle or remote villages? Under the constraints of limited funds and diversity of innovative demands among rural residents, which groups should be targeted by government innovation programmes: 'strong', 'medium' or 'weak' in the HIC? By what kinds of procedure can government identify the innovative demands from different groups and achieve a balanced solution to satisfy their needs?

The limitation of geographic and human capital factors leaves considerable room for the influence of social capital, the theme of Section 6.3.

6.3 Farmer communication networks

The previous sections focusing on individual household performance may not be enough to cover all aspects of household production action and innovative practice. Alongside geographic and human capital factors, the role of social capital cannot be underestimated, as evidenced by the findings from the household questionnaire survey. When sample households were asked to indicate who was their primary source of advice on adopting a new technology or production technique, 60 per cent of interviewees identified their kin or relatives and one-fourth (27 per cent) highlighted their neighbours. Only 14 per cent attributed their technology acquisition to urban professionals or government officers. Accordingly, this section aims to reveal the role of social capital by defining and measuring the innovative function of the farmer communication networks (FCN), leaving development mechanisms of social capital to Chapter 7. Section 6.3.1 defines the FCN. Sections 6.3.2–6.3.4 examine the innovative function of its components, including kinship, relatives and neighbourhood, respectively. Section 6.3.5 provides an overall view on the relationship between the FCN and the HIC, whilst Section 6.3.6 discusses the impacts of community social structure and village cadres. Before concluding, Section 6.3.7 draws attention to the complexity of the FCN and impacts on the HIC.

6.3.1 What is the FCN?

The term FCN is used to encompass any kind of social interaction by which farmers can share and benefit from each other. In contrast to either exclusive competition, or complete independence from each other, it leads towards a more humanist style of life, including interdependence, mutual aid, co-operation and reciprocity.[3] The following aspects of the FCN are particularly important:

- *Inter-household communication*. As a manifestation of rural social interaction, the FCN can be viewed from various levels (individual, household, community or above). Consistent with the approach taken in discussing the HIC, the FCN will be discussed mainly at the household level.
- *Stable relationship*. Distinct from personal communication or community events (e.g. building a house, a wedding), the FCN is a relatively stable network, because all household members adopt a common strategy or harmonious activities to deal with inter-household affairs.
- *Functional network*. In the context of a household's strategy for survival and development, all members of the network have specific functions, for example, property safety, labour exchange, emergency aid. In other words, the FCN can be used to achieve specific objectives.
- *Reciprocal network*. It is very important that inter-household communication should give benefit to all parts, although not necessarily equal in economic terms; one-way giving or requirements would be difficult to sustain.

In short, the FCN can be seen as a stable relationship among households by which the demands of a household can be satisfied without compromising the others. According to the definition given above, some features of the FCN can be recognised, including:

- *A farmer network* that is totally established, controlled and managed entirely by farmers themselves without outside pressures or intervention.
- *A co-operation orientation* to overcome the limitations of a small-scale production, and to achieve those objectives that are beyond individual household capacity.
- *Informal organisation* as distinct from more rigidly formulated institutions, such as village committees or other formal organisations (e.g. FTAs, TVEs).
- *District links*. The FCN provides the possibility to break through geographic and administrative borders for technology and information diffusion.
- *Wide participation*. Rather than being a closed system, the FCN offers opportunities for outsiders' participation besides formal organisational channels.

As a social phenomenon, the FCN has many aspects and elements that are distinctive. From the perspective of its component elements, there are at least three categories: kinship, neighbourhood and friendship. Concerning the scope of the FCN, it can be characterised by a wide arrangement from village, through administrative village and township (sharing a district market) to urban town (county) level. In addition, it is possible to differentiate between rural members and urban participants. Thus, the 'members' of the FCN can be divided into the following categories:

- *Village kin* are male-line members of an extended family or 'clanlike structure' in the same or a nearby village, including brothers, father, father's brothers and sons. Generally, all kinship members are equal and independent in production and decision making.
- *Close relatives* regards the maternal side, including: mother's brothers and sisters, the main members of the wife's family. Unlike village kin, most of them live away from this village (usually $\leqslant$20 km, marriage distance) but keep in close contact.[4]
- *Close villagers*. Compared with traditional kinship linkages, communication between villagers is increasingly important in the HRS. Close villagers may be further divided into categories such as close neighbours within the community and friends in the district (township).

Rather than being separated from each other, these components are interconnected and interwoven for the purposes of livelihood security. Box 6.1 illustrates the structure and function of the FCN.

As a part of a farmer's daily life, the FCN plays an important role in helping households to cope with various challenges and uncertainty. Regarding rural

***Box 6.1* Farmer communication networks: scale and components**

In a remote mountain village N (20 km from the county town) with eighteen household residents and three extended families, Mr Zhang (37 years old) was a head of a household of five persons (his wife, two daughters and one son). He reported that he had four kin in his village including one parent (separated from his household), two married brothers and his father's brother's son (married as well). Of the other thirteen non-family residents in his village, five were identified by him as close villagers because they often joined together for labour (or farm tool) exchange. In addition, he had six close friends living in neighbouring villages, whom he met frequently either on his hill plots or in the township market, in order to discuss a range of issues concerned with production, technology, economy and other topics.

Ten of his 'close relatives' included parent in-law, two brothers in-law, one uncle (mother's brother), two of his father's sisters and three married sisters. Beside these rural relatives, he had three kin living in the county town, his father's brother and his two sons, one of whom is close to him.

As a result, a total of twenty-eight households listed above can be seen as members of his FCN for the purposes not only of information and technology exchange, but also of social support and security, although they are not all equal in terms of ability, expertise and closeness.

livelihood security, the FCN has many functions. According to local people, for instance, cash shortage was the most important and frequent constraint from household daily life. From the perspective of household cash balance, one-fourth of the sample suffered from a financial deficiency. Such a situation became even worse in cases of beginning of school term, severe illnesses or weddings, in which the FCN has the function of social support through provision of an interest-free loan or loan guarantee.

6.3.2 Innovative function of village kin

Concerning the innovative function of FCNs, village kin cannot be ignored, not only because it is an important dimension influencing the household's social contact, but also because nearly half of the village population in the sample villages had kinship ties. Reflecting the variety of the village social structure, the surveyed villages can be divided into three types: (i) *one-kin village*, defined as one where more than 80 per cent of residents belonged to an extended family or had the same grandfather; (ii) *mixed village*, where no more than three households shared kinship; (iii) *two-kin villages*, between the two extremes. Accordingly, Table 6.9 shows the distribution of village social pattern by location.

Table 6.9 shows that the social pattern of villages is closely related to geographic location. One-kin villages, for instance, are slightly common in remote areas. These are more likely to be headed by older men. This type of kin structure has some advantages in harmonising residents' activities (e.g. application of pesticide or forestation), but sometimes suffers from unresolved conflicts because outsiders to the clan may face difficulty in becoming involved in 'clan affairs'. The mixed pattern, by contrast, is more common in valley and middle villages.

To compare the impacts of kinship on HIC, all sample households in marginal areas (excluding those in valley villages) were regrouped by their capacity and social pattern. Figure 6.4 seems to suggest that the one-kin village is a poor innovative environment because few able households come from such villages, compared with two-kin and mixed villages.

Figure 6.4 is consistent with the field observations, during which many interviewees emphasised the complexity of one-kin villages, where many conflicts of interest were often difficult to sort out and had negative impacts on technological learning and co-operation. It is necessary, however, to be cautious about generation, because mixed villages do not necessarily enjoy collaboration among

Table 6.9 Social patterns by village location

Pattern	*One kin*	*Two kin*	*Mixed*	*Total*
Valley	1	2	2	5
Middle	7	2	10	19
Remote	9	9	8	26
Total	17	13	20	50

residents, and because many excellent innovation events were found to have occurred in one-kin villages. One such exception is illustrated by the story in Box 6.2.

As a part of traditional kinship organisations and culture, kinship alliance is neither limited within a village nor to cash crops. In fact, most rural migration and non-farm opportunities are related to kinship organisation, by which village kin and sometimes their neighbours are organised to participate in some projects outside their village. This suggests an important fact, that technology diffusion in

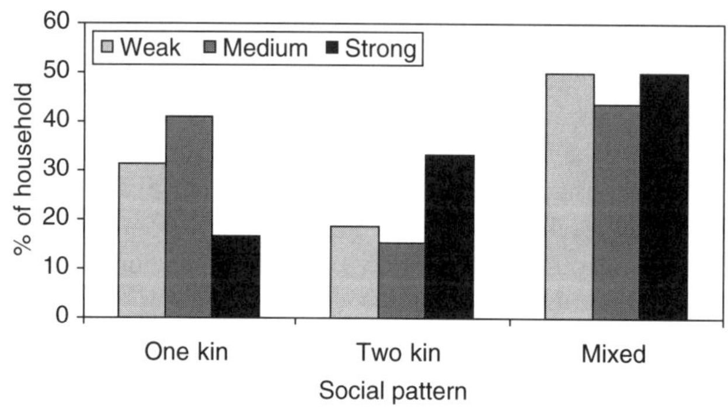

Figure 6.4 HIC by village social pattern.

Source: Author's household questionnaire survey, sample size 127, valley villages excluded.

Box 6.2 Role of kinship alliance in innovative co-operation

Two remote villages were close to each other (only 3 km apart) in the same administrative village. Village A had a strong advantage in apple orchards because all residents had established their own orchard to share benefits from an expert living in the same village. By contrast, its neighbour, village B, had just begun to develop orchards with three households when the survey took place in the villages. It was surprising, however, that the technical sources in village B were not related to the nearby village A, but to a distant village C in the next township (10 km away). The 'unusual technology transfer', according to an explanation by an initiator from village B, was mainly related to two interconnected factors. One was the scale demand of the village orchard. It is seldom that a graft technician would go to a village if the scale of the orchard is less than 5 mu, which needs at least three household participants. The other is discount service, because the normal price of 6 yuan/tree was too expensive for most of the farmers in village B. The orchard development might not have happened, had not his relative (brother in law) in village C offered a very cheap service (only 2 yuan/tree), and his father and brother in the same village joined in the orchard construction with him.

marginal areas is not always determined by the factor of 'physical distance' but sometimes by 'social distance'.

6.3.3 Importance of close relatives

Close relatives are often located far away from the household, and their impacts are weaker and uncertain, compared with those of village kin and neighbours. As an important channel to gain outside information and market opportunities, not surprisingly, the roles of close relatives vary greatly in 'utility' from one household to another, depending largely on the household's production orientation. According to the household surveys, the mean number of a household's close relatives differs significantly from nine households in valley villages, eleven in middle and thirteen in remote villages. It seems to suggest that households in marginal areas need various support from their relatives, more than do their counterparts in valley villages.

Turning to the contribution to the HIC, field observation showed that close relatives have a particularly strong impacts on innovative capacity in middle villages. It may be explained by the innovative function of rural marriage patterns, because 'close relatives' in local terms mainly meant the housewife's family and her kin. According to local people, the marriage distance was often no more than 20 km, so that families could keep in close contact and help each other. As a result, the large scale of relatives' interaction is very important for households in remote villages to secure their livelihoods, but is weak in innovation because all relatives are similar in the HIC. By contrast, close relatives have a positive impact on the HIC in middle villages because they provide an important channel for technology diffusion and production co-operation between valley and middle zones. The innovative function of close relatives can be illustrated by Box 6.3.

Box 6.3 **Role of a relative in technological diffusion**

The role of relatives in new technology adoption can be illustrated through a real story told by a housewife in a remote village, 20 km away from Zhifang Township:

> The wide furrow (a new sowing method with plastic sheet covering) has interested this village for many years, but we were uncertain of the details until a relative of mine from a low mountain area came to my plots for a demonstration last year. Seeing the good result, all the residents in the village have adopted it this spring.

In her opinion, farmers do not like to adopt a new technology until they have seen it in action. A lack of professional consultation meant her relatives' views were crucial for her family and neighbours in adopting the new method.

6.3.4 Impacts from villagers' co-operation

Compared with traditional kinship and relatives, neighbourhood co-operation and interaction among villagers seem to have been increasingly important in the marginal areas of China. One of the important factors leading to villager interaction and co-operation is that most households suffer from labour shortage in the busy farming seasons (e.g. seeding time). According to this survey, on average, each household had only 2.4 workers and 60 mu (4 ha) farmland, so it was not easy for them to complete the seeding process alone in a short period (e.g. 1–2 weeks). The labour shortage is even more serious, given that frequent spring droughts may reduce the window of opportunity to only a few days. To overcome these issues, a common strategy practised in this region is for several households to join together for labour exchange or collaborative sowing. However, it would be a mistake to suppose that all households in a village are prepared to exchange their labour (or farm tools) with others. While most households may benefit from their close co-operation in sowing and machine sharing (collaborative buying), others may find it difficult to complete the process without their relatives' help.

The importance of FCN for the HIC can be partly interpreted by the scale demand of some technological innovation in the terms of knowledge, information, labour and management cost. Apple growing, as a new technology, for example, often occurs in those villages where more than two households had joined together for technology learning and tree management (avoiding sheep damage and theft). Of those villages that had apple orchards, according to the household survey, 36 per cent had two orchards (i.e. two households' engagement) whilst 41 per cent had more than three. Similarly, Box 6.4 provides another example of village collaboration in technology adoption.

6.3.5 FCN pattern and household innovative capacity

The previous sections have considered individual elements of the FCN and their impacts on the HIC. Questions now arise: how do these elements join together to influence the HIC? What variety of the FCN pattern can be found related to innovative type, village location or household demographic factors? To address the above issues, the variety of the FCN's scale and structure needs to be examined first.

Reflecting the quantitative aspects of social capital, the FCN can be measured through the sum of a household's kinship, close relatives and villagers. Roughly, the mean size of the FCN is twenty-nine per household in all sample villages, of which kin account for one-fourth and close villagers for one-third, while close relatives constitute two-fifths. Regarding the distribution of the FCN, interestingly, there is a little difference existing in either the total FCN or kinship by village division. While about half of the household's FCN in valley households comes from close villagers, the figure in the remote villages is less than 30 per cent. However, the mean number of close relatives in the latter is thirteen per household, by contrast to nine in the former.

With respect to the impacts of the FCN, all sample households in marginal areas (i.e. middle and remote villages) are divided into three groups according to

Box 6.4 Neighbour mutual-aid and level plough seeding method

Level ploughing as a new seeding method was extended in Zhidan in the 1980s to replace traditional methods. Unlike the traditional seeding method, which can be done by one household without fertiliser or a seeding machine, the new method requires a furrow to be made along the horizontal line first, and then seed saw, mixed with fertiliser; finally, the seed is covered by a deep furrow. Such a process cannot be implemented without four labourers and four draft cattle together with sowing machine and chemical fertilisers. According to the household survey, however, only one-fifth of the sample had sowing machines, whilst one-fourth either did not have production draught cattle or experienced a cattle shortage. Neighbour mutual-aid was thus an important precondition for adopting these methods. One of the common strategies popularised in the Loess Plateau is that several neighbours co-operate to complete sowing based upon the principle of 'equal exchange' of labour or labour and farm tools (e.g. cattle or seeding machine). However, it is not true that all households are able to exchange their labour or tools with their neighbours. For those who suffer from difficult relationships with their neighbours, it would be difficult to join in co-operative processes. Instead, they would have to depend on their kin or relatives' assistance. The household questionnaire survey provides support for this statement: compared with the average adoption rate (60 per cent) in remote villages in those villages with a large extended family (e.g. one-kin village) or more friendly neighbours, use of the level plough was higher (>15 per cent) because they enabled farmers to overcome the constraint for insufficient household labour.

the grade of the HIC. Figure 6.5 confirms that significant impacts can be found in both total scale of the FCN and close villagers. Compared with neighbour or village-wide co-operation, the contribution from close relatives is relatively weak.

The results above seem to support a local popular statement: 'Able men are those who have more social links (called *menlu*)'. In the face of constraints from the geographic environment and the broken-down extension networks, a greater number of *social links* (i.e. larger-size FCN) in local people's view means more opportunities of access to scarce resources (including information, technology, financial capital and consultation) and provides an illustration in relationship between FCN elements, FCN total and HIC. Although individual elements of the FCN may not necessarily have an innovative function, all these elements together, however, are significantly related to the HIC.

6.3.6 Impacts of local community on innovative capacity

The correlation between the number of close villagers and the HIC leads to an assumption: community collaboration as an important element of the social

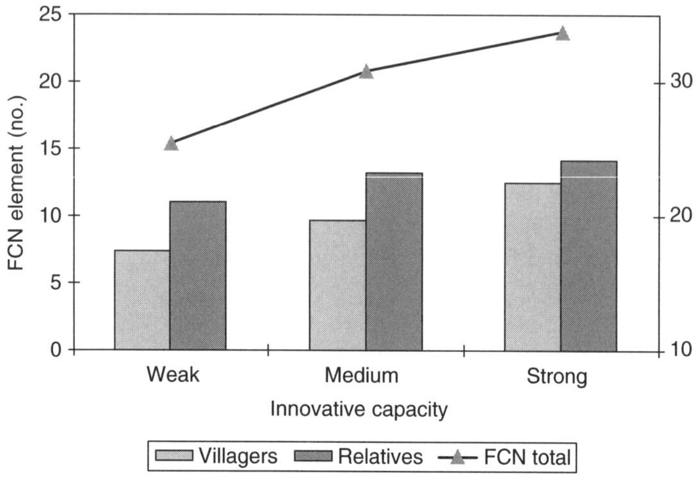

Figure 6.5 Distribution of the FCN by HIC.

Source: Author's household questionnaire survey 1997.

capital plays a vital role in influencing and enhancing the HIC. In other words, the FCN is not a private property of the household, separate from the local community, but an important part influenced and shaped by the latter.

The impacts of the local community on the HIC can be illustrated by a genuine story. In a valley village, 80 per cent of households specialised in tobacco plantation. According to the village survey, all these specialised households actually belonged to five competitive groups in terms of technological learning and information exchanges. All 'technical centres' or 'group leaders', however, were originally from the same group and learned the techniques from an urban kin member, who was a technician employed in a county tobacco company. It was group learning and the urban kin-member's contribution, according to interviewees, that provided a sound social basis for technological diffusion.

Whilst group learning and the roles of urban kin will be discussed in detail in Chapter 7, Figure 6.6 provides statistical evidence to support the correlation between HIC and village environment.

Regarding the distribution of the HIC in marginal areas, Figure 6.6 divides all 45 sample villages and 127 households into two parts according to the average income of the sample villages. It shows that a total of 42 households lived in 15 'high-income' villages (net income $\geq$800 yuan/person) and 85 households in 30 'low-income' villages ($<$800 yuan/person). These 42 households in 'high-income' villages, however, had different grades in the HIC on the one hand, and could be distributed among 15 villages in different ways on the other. Whilst the right bar shows the distribution of household's innovative capacity, the left bar indicates how many villages accommodate them. At one end, for instance, 18 of

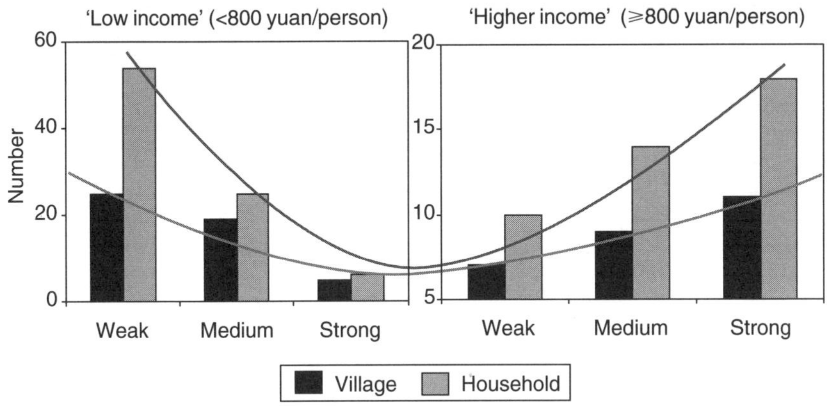

Figure 6.6 Distribution of innovative capacity by household and village.

the 42 households who were 'strong' in the HIC can be randomly spread among all 15 villages, suggesting that these 'strong' households had less relevance in terms of technology learning and exchange. At the other end, they may live within a few villages, meaning their skills are more likely related to each other. The larger the difference between the two bars, the fewer villages in which the 'strong' households lived, the more likely it is that these 'innovators' were related to each other. As a result, vertical distance between the two lines (two bars) provides a means to observe the correlation between village innovation performance. It should noted that the sum of all left bar values is more than virtue villages because many villages appeared more than once in the calculation, due to their being composed of various capacity households.

Figure 6.6 shows an increase of difference between village and household bars from both 'high-income' and 'low-income' villages with different direction. In the former, the gap grows as the household capacity group increases, and the reverse is true. Three conclusions can be drawn from Figure 6.6. First, it is confirmed that there is a correlation between village economic performance and HIC. Second, it indicates clearly that HIC is not merely a variable response to personal (or household) human capital factors, but also involves village social and innovation environments. In other words, the innovative capacity of one household is not totally independent from but is likely to be influenced by that of its neighbour. Finally, two different patterns of village environment can be distinguished from each other, which have opposite impacts on the HIC: a 'positive innovative environment' in 'high-income' villages where strong households have function as village 'innovative centres' for knowledge and information diffusion; and a 'negative innovative environment' in some 'low-income' villages where the strong and medium skill households are dispersed, and their knowledge and skill can with difficulty be shared around poor-capacity neighbours.

Table 6.10 Village innovative performance by cadres' HIC grade

Cadre's HIC	*No observation*	*Net income*	*New products*	*Village HIC score*
Weak	11	402	27.7	2.9
Medium	13	746	35.6	3.8
Strong	8	1,094	48.2	4.2
Total	32	715	36.0	3.6

Notes
Excluding valley areas. Household net income, yuan/person; new products of total products, per cent; village HIC score is mean score of sampling household HIC score as defined in Table 6.5.

Figure 6.6 provides a strong support for the field observations, which revealed a great variation among villages in terms of social environment, and skill levels, even within the similar geographical environment and resource endowments. For instance, some villages may be empty in the daytime during the agricultural business seasons, while in neighbouring villages many people might be seen joining together to play cards or enjoy the sunshine. Adopting local terminology, this can be explained by *Zhuangfeng* involving village tradition, social relationship and production co-operation.

Of many factors contributing to village innovative environment, village cadres play an important role, which can be shown by the correlation between the village cadres and distribution of HIC by village. Although rural cadres in our samples did not differ greatly, not obvious from ordinary households in terms of their HIC or FCN pattern, the impacts from the former cannot be underestimated. According to the field observation, if a village leader was strong in HIC, more households in that village were likely to be involved in enjoying innovation.

To prove this hypothesis, village innovative performance is measured by many indicators such as village net income, production structure and the average score of HIC. Table 6.10 shows a strong correlation between village innovative performance and village cadres' innovation rating. It seems clear that the overall innovative capacity of households in the marginal villages of Zhidan cannot be separated from, and is likely to be influenced by the capacity of village cadres. The stronger the village cadres' innovative capacity, the more the village residents benefit from innovation performance and vice versa.

6.3.7 Complexity of FCN and HIC

Rural societies do not necessarily consist only of peasants themselves but sometimes include urban residents whose permanent houses are still in rural areas or who maintain close contact with their home villages as if they were members of the villages. Many examples can be cited of these special participants, such as township officers who were promoted from village cadres; rural teachers who have just become formal employees of the education authority; and other urban employees. According to the village investigation, 'urban–rural households' (where one member of a household is formally employed in an urban institution) account for about 10 per cent of rural households.

As an important innovation source, these urban–rural links cannot be neglected because they may play major positive roles in rural social development and innovation practice, including:

- *Information centre.* Through frequent returns to the village home or visits by village kin, these urban persons can supply the latest information related to technology, market and policy, actively and deliberated collectively.
- *Experiment centre.* Not all, but a considerable number of them, according to field observation, were early adopters of new technologies, because of their good education, wide information and strong economic basis.
- *Organisational centre.* Taking advantage of both knowledge and social links, some of them were actually located at the centre position of village affairs although they may not have been awarded any formal titles.

Urban–rural links are a complex social phenomenon, and it would be a mistake to suppose that all urban–rural links have a strong impact on innovation or organisation, or have a positive role in community participation and co-operation. As an intermediary between mountain villages and outside resources and markets, however, such links provide an important informal and social channel for outsiders to promote community co-operation and an interface with external resources (see detailed case in Chapter 7).

Beyond the borders of the village, there are many informal organisations or assemblies available for villagers to exchange various information, and to initiate some kinds of co-operative actions, including technological innovation. Related to a liberal rural economic and social environment, farmers can develop their communication network through various public opportunities, such as regional trade assemblies (which usually take place in the township every 10 days), traditional cultural events (e.g. arts or opera) and even regional ceremonies. In this respect, the story in Box 6.5 may offer some clues to the diversity of the FCN and innovative organisation.

The story given in Box 6.5 is not unique to Zhidan because a considerable number of farmers have expertise in some areas, and are able to pass their techniques to more people if appropriate opportunities and encouragement are available. In addition, many 'organisations' like *Maohui* or other religious groups may have some positive functions to play in technological diffusion. One lesson that can be learnt from this case is that rather than lack of innovation resources (e.g. budget, professional staff, etc.), the neglect of indigenous talent and intrinsic potential is perhaps a more serious issue impeding rural innovation in marginal areas.

***Box 6.5* District technique centre**

In a market assembly, an expert in apple plantations was valued for both his good technique and voluntary service to many fruit planters in the township. As an important innovation source for the district's fruit plantation, the expert actually lived in a remote village, 20 km north of the township. Through a difficult period since his immigration from an outer region (about 200 km away), he had succeeded not only in surviving a village collective orchard but also in gaining acceptance from village residents.

Based on his 10-year experience of technical consultancy around the Loess Plateau before his residence here, the old man (nearly 60 years old) felt that Zhidan's people were very kind and honest but poor in innovation capacity due to their rich land resources and backward technological tradition. Inspired by his ideas, techniques and business success, many of his neighbours had established their own orchards, while their relatives came to the village to observe, question and book a graft service. In a period of three years, according to him, more than 100 households and twenty villages in the district had benefited from his services.

To diffuse his technique, he had hoped to take responsibility for a township orchard as a basis for training and demonstration, but the idea was not approved by the township government, partly because government priorities have changed from apples to domestic apricots; and partly because the role of the indigenous expert is often underestimated.

6.4 Conclusions: communication, networks and innovation

Using the data generated from field observations, household questionnaires and village surveys, this chapter has tried to address the social basis and organisational patterns of farmer innovation in Zhidan. Using the HIC as a device, it has identified contributions from the FCNs, an informal system of inter-household communication and co-operative linkages with the aim of securing livelihoods. Accordingly, special attention was paid to the following questions: what factors influence the HIC in the marginal areas of Zhidan? Can the impacts from the FCN be found or confirmed and, if so, how? How are the different FCN patterns related to the complexity and diversity of rural natural and social environment? Based on the field discoveries and the discussions in this chapter, the following conclusions can be drawn:

1. Empirical evidence displayed in this chapter has shown that household livelihood systems in marginal areas like Zhidan are shaped by the HIC, defined as a capacity to integrate new knowledge (techniques, skills, methods), intensive production inputs and new production structures. Based upon field observation and household questionnaire surveys, the HIC can be distinguished into three

levels: strong, medium and weak. The strong households are those that are more independent in initiating or introducing new technologies, methods or products. Medium-capacity households may join innovative projects, depending on many factors, such as technical maturity, market demand, production costs, etc. By contrast, weak households are unlikely to participate in innovative projects, unless many barriers, both external (e.g. infrastructure, access to land) and internal (e.g. labour, loan, attitude) can be removed. Distinction of the HIC is very important to understand the complexity and diversity of rural livelihood systems in marginal areas of China because it offers a sound base to reveal the spatial distribution of farmer innovative demands and structural barriers facing different types of households.

2. The HIC as an 'independent' factor impacting on the differences in rural livelihood systems, however, is not predetermined but is influenced by many factors that can be aggregated into four categories: geographic and resource environments, human capital, policy factors and social capital. Among them, geographic factors are perhaps the most influential, as shown by the uneven distribution of the HIC among sample villages. If we exclude the valley zone, the impacts of geographic environment can be identified from many indicators such as village location, elevation, distance to main road and market, etc. Based on adopting local knowledge and household survey information, all marginal villages can be further divided into two types according to geographical features: middle and remote villages. Significant difference can be found in the distribution of the HIC between them. The impact from geographic environment, however, is relative, being mediated by both household human capital features, and rural policy or institutional factors. In consequence, whereas the distribution of the 'strong' households is closely related to village division, the 'weak' households are actually dispersed throughout the marginal areas. This can be seen in impacts from unequal distribution of road facilities and farmland among households. One conclusion that arises regarding this complex situation is that there is neither a linear relationship between the HIC and the above factors, nor a universal solution to improve the HIC, because different households may have different difficulties and demands.

3. Alongside geographic and human capital factors, this chapter has argued that social capital is a vital factor in influencing the distribution of the HIC in marginal areas of China. Focusing on the FCN, a form of social capital, this chapter has revealed its components, structure patterns and impacts on the HIC. Many conclusions can be drawn from the empirical surveys. First, FCN is an important channel for farmers in marginal areas to enhance their innovative capacity. The larger the household FCN, the more likely the household is to have a higher HIC group. Second, no standard pattern of FCN for farmer innovation can be found, as it varies with geographic, historic, social and technical factors, and which is also highly dependent upon household strategy in using and developing the FCN. Third, in general, mutual aid and co-operation among villagers have strong impacts on the HIC. Finally, the village environment is more likely related to village cadres who play a key role in leading village co-operation and innovation.

4. The importance of the FCN in the HIC cannot be overstated. First, the FCN is one of many factors influencing the HIC. Further research may be needed to understand how the FCN is inter-related to other factors in determining the HIC. Second, the FCN is not new for rural people because it has existed for thousands of years, but why do some people enjoy while others do not? This question cannot be answered by a quantitative approach, but needs to be explored in more qualitative research. Finally, the FCN is not the whole of social capital, but only part of it. For instance, not all members attach importance to household capacity improvement, and not all households have equal demand for technological innovation and inter-household co-operation. This raises the questions, how is FCN used and developed for farmer innovation? What kinds of role division and organisational mechanism can be found in marginal areas? These issues are explored in Chapter 7.

7 Farmer self-organisation for innovation

Cases and model

In Chapter 6, it was argued that the FCN is one of the important factors contributing to HIC in marginal areas. The innovative function of the FCN, however, needs to be further explained: why are some people able to enjoy the FCN for livelihood growth and security while others are not? How can the FCN be developed to meet household innovative objectives or 'community project' targets? Corresponding with various village environment and technology types, what kinds of collaborative mechanisms or roles amongst participants can be recognised? What evolutionary process and development phases can be recognised regarding farmer innovative collaboration? Bearing in mind that the FCN is a form of social capital, the above issues can be encompassed in one question: how can social capital be accumulated or created for the purposes of farmer innovation and self-organisation?

Based upon detailed case studies, this chapter aims to outline the process of social capital accumulation and creation in general, and to explore its contribution to farmer innovation organisation process and mechanisms in particular. With respect to the organisational aspect of 'appropriate technology', the first case, 'greenhouse' adoption, indicates the process and roles of group learning in technology adaptation. Concerning the innovative potential of marginal people, the second case will describe a revolutionary technological invention concerning rainfall collection and storage, which was created by a group of farmers in a high mountain village. In the light of the release of farmer innovative potential, the last case uncovers a wonderful story of sustainable development and innovation in a remote village, in which urban participation is highlighted. Summarising these field discoveries and the results reported in Chapter 6, a farmer innovation system and self-organisation model will be defined and explained in the last section.

7.1 Technology appropriateness: the case of greenhouse adoption

The FCN, as suggested in Chapter 6, provides a social base for scattered farmers to participate in innovative practice and to share co-operative achievements. As a complex social phenomenon, however, household innovation actually involves two interwoven processes: the interaction between technology and organisation on the one hand, and the integration between the interests of participants on the other. The former relates to technological choice, while the latter is related to the role relationship between participants. Many questions are raised while addressing the relationship between appropriate technology (AT) and innovative organisation: What are the social and organisational dimensions of AT? How can technical change lead to organisational innovation? Through what kinds of role division and integration mechanisms can households with differentiated innovative capacity join together for technological learning and innovative co-operation? Before introducing the story of greenhouse adoption, the issues of technological choice and appropriateness in marginal areas will be briefly introduced, while the section will be completed with a discussion and conclusions on the organisational dimension of AT.

7.1.1 Appropriateness of technology: lessons from extension practice

Because administrative intervention dominates China's agricultural extension (Delman 1991), 'appropriateness' is actually a crucial issue influencing rural development and innovation in marginal areas. Setting aside the organisational dimension, according to field observations and surveys, a considerable number of projects were questionable as regards technological choice and project decision-making.

For example, when it was seen that apple plantations had mushroomed in middle Shaanxi with great success, several townships in Zhidan were selected as 'apple bases' in the early 1990s, and all residents in targeted townships, without exception, were asked to establish household orchards. Accordingly, an 'expert' from Shandong province was invited by the county government to take charge of raising young trees, grafting, supply and consultation, and all households in the district had to buy his trees. Due to virus infection of the saplings, in addition to a lack of technical preparation, unfortunately, few participants succeeded while the 'expert' disappeared as soon as he had sold all his trees.

Such cases, unfortunately, are not uncommon in the Loess Plateau, and reflect the deficiency of the conventional innovation model. From the perspectives of technology choice, many lessons can be learnt from the failure of the apple extension case. First, the top-down procedure of technological decision-making does not adequately reflect either the need of the rural people, or the opinions of local cadres. Second, due to heavy political and economic pressures, in addition to the short-term view of the administrative system, 'technical leapfrogging' is a common issue in marginal areas, which suffer from the weak interface with farmers' needs and capacity. Third, due to constraints of financial resources, qualified staff and experimental bases, the lack of necessary experiment and demonstration is also responsible for some failures of extension projects. Finally, utilising traditional styles of political mobilisation and implementation, administrative-oriented extension takes no account of the heterogeneity of household innovative capacity and demands.

However, it would be unfair to say that administrative intervention has always made mistakes in technological choice and project decision. Actually, many new technologies adopted in Zhidan in the last decade, such as tobacco, hybrid corn and the level plough, were also introduced through similar procedures to the apple plantations: they began with strong administrative intervention to overcome resistance from below and gradually became farmers' own practice.

The complexity of innovation practice in marginal areas suggests that the appropriateness of technology is more than simply a matter of technical and economic choice, but also involves political and organisational dimensions. In relation to the HRS, many questions arise to address the organisational dimension of 'appropriate technology': To whom is a technology appropriate? By what kinds of organisational conditions may the nature of technology be changed from inappropriateness to appropriateness? The following case may provide some clues to address these issues.

7.1.2 Greenhouses for vegetables in WG: history

Owing to the short period of warmer frost-free weather and the small size of the urban population, there were few vegetables grown in Zhidan. With urban enlargement and income growth since the 1980s, the external vegetable supply from far away Zhidan (around 400 km) could not meet the expanding demands of the urban market, which left considerable space for local vegetable production.

Because it is dependent on many conditions such as irrigation, cropping technique and transport, etc., commercial vegetable production was concentrated in valley areas. A market survey suggested, however, that the majority of local vegetables were not from nearby villages surrounding the town, but from WG, a distant village (8 km away), due to its technical advantage.

As an administrative village, WG is located on the valley of the *Zhouhe* River with main road access to town. Of a total of 150 households, 130 were distributed in five valley villages, leaving the remaining 20 households in two middle villages. In the early days of the rural reform, only four households were involved in vegetable production with a few seeds (e.g. potato, Chinese cabbage, radish, etc.) for the urban market in summer. It was a common pattern at that period that irrigated land (1 mu/capita) was used for grain planting, while surplus labour flowed into non-farm areas such as urban construction, stone mining, transportation and rural industry (a brick factory). Until the late 1980s, according to villagers' recollection, the urban vegetable market was actually dominated by farmers from nearby villages, and a few from WG.

The turning point of vegetable development in WG was the introduction of green house farming in 1993, when the county government decided to develop a winter house for vegetable production (W-house) in several villages in valley areas including WG. As the new technology was transferred from a county in East China, the W-house needed a large amount of investment, and thus faced high risk, both technologically and economically. Poor responses from farmers meant that the government had to combine administrative measures with a low-rate interest loan to ensure project implementation. Because of the neglect of climatic constraints (cold winters) and the technical gap between traditional farming and capital-intensive agriculture, not surprisingly, such a radical and large-scale extension intervention seemed to be unsuccessful, and a considerable number of participants destroyed their W-houses due to poor economic returns. The exception is WG, where the majority of W-houses have survived, and many more households have joined in vegetable production. By summer 1997, the number of households specialising in vegetables had reached fifty, representing about 70 per cent of the county's vegetable producers. Meanwhile, another twenty households in WG were involved indirectly with service activities, for example, delivery of organic manure from the urban area to the vegetable fields.

7.1.3 System innovation: technical and economic features

The success of technology adoption in WG was related to its innovative effort, because the original W-house was not at first appropriate to Zhidan. As a greenhouse, the W-house, like a permanent house, can be continuously used throughout the year, but needs regular maintenance (e.g. re-covering with new plastic sheets yearly). To keep vegetable production up in cold winters requires heating facilities inside, and an anti-freeze sheet covering outside. Due to the cold winters (usually below $-10\,^{\circ}C$) plus technical complexity (e.g. many infectious diseases), the economic return from the W-house was poor at first, and many farmers suffered severe losses.

Between W-house and non-greenhouse (N-house) cropping, however, an intermediate technology, called the 'summer house' (S-house), had been set up in WG before the introduction of the W-house. As a simple greenhouse was made to be utilised between late Spring and early Autumn only, the S-house offered WG technological preparedness prior to adopting the W-house. In addition, it was WG that developed and utilised the W-house function of raising seed to supply S-house and non-house producers, which benefited both sides. The users of W-house seeds gained profit, not only by being able to sell their products 1–2 months earlier, but also by achieving one more harvest than the previous schedule. For the W-house owners, raising and supplying seeds enabled them to share the cost of W-house utilisation with those needing seeds. In addition, during the period of a long winter, the users of vegetable seeds came to the W-house to contribute their labour for seed raising on the one hand, and exchange cropping techniques and experience on the other. As a functional expansion, more S-houses and N-house plots were set up around W-houses, so as to share in the technological progress. By 1997, there were, in total, ten households engaging in W-house production, twenty using S-houses and another twenty using N-houses.

From the economic perspective, the difference in greenhouse type often reflects the differentiation of household techniques. Because the W-house represents an expensive investment, requiring much maintenance and entailing risks, the W-houses' owners were those who had more experience and better techniques and a better return on their income. Due to intensive inputs of both capital and labour, these households relied completely on vegetable production, having no other source of income. In contrast, N-house producers were generally late comers, with

Table 7.1 Technical–economic comparison of vegetable producers in WG

	Winter greenhouse	*Summer greenhouse*	*No greenhouse*
No. of households	10	20	20
Nature of greenhouse	Permanent	Yearly	No
Capital investment	5,000	1,000	No
Labour involved	12 months	8 months	6 months
Technical level	High	Middle	Low
Harvest times (no.)	4–5	3–4	2
Vegetable income	>10,000	6–8,000	4–5,000

Notes
All data are results from interviews while income is estimated by informants. S-house excludes the W-house holders who own one or two S-houses.

poor technical ability, lack of capital or labour, or involved in other business (e.g. seasonal migration). The main features of these households are summarised in Table 7.1.

7.1.4 The role of the innovation leader

In consideration of the reasons why WG had been successful in greenhouse adoption, the role of Mr Wang was highly valued by interviewees. As an innovator, he acquired a good reputation because of his record in Zhidan, as the first adopter of the S-house in the county, before the W-house came; the first supplier of vegetable seeds through his W-house; and so on. Equally important were his large scale of FCN (double his village average) and personal qualities such as kindness and lack of self-aggrandisement, which provided a sound social basis for technology learning and diffusion. It is due to his contribution that WG has successfully avoided or reduced technological risks and many poor were able to join in vegetable cropping. To understand the role of this indigenous talent, two in-depth interviews were arranged in Mr Wang's W-house and the urban market.

Aged 47, Mr Wang had a background of only 3 years of primary education. Due to his wisdom, innovative capacity and good personal relationships, he has been the head of a village for nearly 30 years. He began to plant commercial vegetables in 1981 and faced a number of technical difficulties, which could not be solved by urban professionals, because there were no extension staff in Zhidan with special technique or experiences in vegetable production. To overcome his difficulties, he adopted various coping strategies, including: seeking technical reference books; carrying out exploratory experiments in his plots; and exchanging experience and information with other producers. Not surprisingly, some of his neighbours did not feel free to discuss technological issues with him at first, because they feared market competition. As they came to realise the benefit of communication, however, more and more households joined in his group for information and technique exchange. By the end of the 1980s, the number of his co-operative partners had risen to ten, which was actually the basis for the introduction of W-house production and later seed supply.

According to him and his villagers, the roles of Mr Wang can be summarised as follows:

- *Research centre*. In the absence of a vegetable experimentation and extension station in Zhidan, for instance, most of the new seeds and chemicals were first utilised and given trials in his house and then adopted by his colleagues.
- *Training school*. Due to his openness and his wife's kindness, his house was viewed as a 'free training centre' for demonstration of new technology and a place where latecomers could learn.
- *Service centre*. Not surprisingly, his reputation and communication network were strongly attractive to outsiders who saw opportunities for providing various services (e.g. seeds, fertilisers, chemicals) or supplying information through his network. During the period of this survey, he was invited by a state oil-drilling company to act as a 'greenhouse consultant', which offered a good opportunity for his career development as well as his friends' outside employment.
- *Integration centre*. In addition to technological innovation and services, his house was often utilised for solving various social tensions and conflicts between his colleagues, which is very necessary for maintaining village unity and innovation.

7.1.5 Group innovation co-operation

The role of Mr Wang as a centre of innovation cannot be separated from his innovative group, which can be viewed as an improved and developed FCN. Without the latter, the innovation would be confined to the activities of individuals, few of whom would have benefited from his innovation achievements. Related to the supply–demand link of vegetable seeds, in particular, the W-house provided a unique opportunity for vegetable producers to join together in the long winter for collaborative seed raising and strengthening neighbourhood and friendship. As a result, these households had such close production co-operation and inter-household relationships that they called the W-house where they meet, *xiao tian di*, meaning a small but very convenient place like a warm family. As a stable and close co-operative group for greenhouse innovation, this kind of innovation group was not owned by Mr Wang and his colleagues. According to the field observations, in fact, three groups can be recognised in WG, among which there was a somewhat competitive relationship. Some functions of the group can be summarised as follows:

- *Technology sharing*. Due to close co-operation and communication in a W-house, the participants of an innovation group had more chances to exchange and share techniques with each other. According to Mr Wang, many technological issues had been solved in his house through group discussion and diagnosis, rather than by himself. Because of the traditional irrigation network that had no control system fitted, for instance, one of the common issues in vegetable cropping was over-irrigation, which causes low temperature and root decay. In the absence of a solution from an outside expert, a simple method was invented by a housewife in his group, by which the dust from the stove was spread on the plots, both to absorb surplus water and to increase potash fertilisers. It was so effective in a group experiment that all participants adopted the technology immediately.

- *Labour concentration.* Seasonal labour shortage is more serious in greenhouse production than in traditional agriculture. Due to the limited scale of production, however, few households employed external labourers. To overcome the constraint, an informal regulation was implemented in Mr Wang's group: if a household needed extra labour inputs in some circumstances (e.g. greenhouse construction, seeding, etc.), all members should contribute their voluntary service without any special announcement or request. This voluntary labour contribution, which went beyond the principle of 'equal labour exchange', according to Mr Wang, was a result of their long-term co-operation.
- *Scale of benefit.* Group labour concentration can be further understood if the scale of benefit is considered. Generally, all participants were responsible for daily selling in the urban market by individual households themselves. It often occurred, however, that demand information from a large purchaser (e.g. an oil exploitation team Zhidan-wide or nearby) was first circulated within the group. In addition, there were other benefits, such as joining together to purchase fertiliser or pesticide at a discount price; co-operative experiments on new seeds or pesticide to reduce and share the risk, etc.

Mr Wang's group was the largest in WG, with about 30 member households. Among them there were various ranks and roles: 5 W-house owners as core members were most closely allied with him in terms of new technology exploitation and co-operative selling, while 15 learners as outer members were benefiting from regular visits and seasonal demonstrations in his W-house. Midway between them were 12 close-member households, which were mainly S-house holders, who joined together frequently to exchange experience, seek solutions, co-operate in production (i.e. labour concentration) and sometimes sell co-operatively. The core members were actually his sons and close neighbours, and the close members were mainly his neighbours and some friends from near WG as well, while the outer members were mainly from outside villages, some of them being his relatives. The features of Wang's group are summarised in Table 7.2.

7.1.6 Conclusion: organisational dimension of appropriateness

More than pure technical or economic process, the successful adoption of greenhouse technology in WG suggests that the appropriateness of technology in the marginal areas cannot be properly defined and understood without identifying the organisational dimension of technological adoption and utilisation. In relation to

Table 7.2 Organisational structure of Wang's innovation group

Membership	*Core*	*Close*	*Outer*
No. of households	5	12	15
Technical nature	W-house	S-house	No-house
Position in group	Partners	Participants	Learners
Co-operative scope	New tech./market	Solution/production	Demo/inform
Living location	This village	This + nearby villages	Nearby villages
Meeting frequency	Daily	Weekly	Monthly

the case of WG, the organisational meaning of appropriateness can be clarified as follows.

Technical system and reciprocal co-operation Appropriateness cannot be isolated from the technical system, because the latter provides the necessary conditions or environment (e.g. knowledge, techniques, methods, etc.) for the application of new technology. The success of W-house adoption in WG, for instance, is closely related to a new production and technical relationship between W-house, S-house and N-house, referring to, seedling raising and demand. These relationships could not have been established and sustained without close co-operative relationships amongst participants. It is not doubted that economic reciprocity between the W-house and S-house (or N-house) producers is very important. Group co-operation in WG is actually based on more than pure economic activities (equal exchange) but has social and cultural implications, which can be understood from the reconstruction of rural social relation through three competitive groups in WG.

Technical continuity and group learning Appropriateness is not static but changeable, because it relies not only on the technical gap between the new and original technical system, but also on the learning or adaptive capacity of farmers. One of the important factors related to the success of WG is the fact that an S-house had existed before W-house was introduced, which provided a 'technical bridge' between the W-house and N-house production. Equally important is the mechanism of 'group learning', which had also existed there prior to W-house introduction. In contrast to formal technical training and extension service, 'group learning' is not merely a self-learning process, but a process of social communication and co-operation, which leads to a positive feedback from individual experience and then group wisdom, to group experiment and innovation. From the economic perspective, group learning and co-operation can easily achieve the scale of demand and benefit, which could further strengthen the competitive capacity of group members in the vegetable market. Similar stories were heard from other examples (e.g. tobacco, apple orchard) in the field.

Technical exploration and innovative organisation Constrained by rural disorganisation and the broken-down nature of the agricultural extension network, in particular, appropriateness is actually a 'variable' that is dependent on the FCN and organisation process. Although the FCN is shared and used by all farmers for technological exchange and production co-operation, it is often too loose, dispersed and private to produce effective innovation demand and dynamics. The key to strengthening household innovative capacity is for individual FCNs to be joined together and formed as a close group with clearly defined innovation objectives and role division. As a result, the innovative centre or leader becomes a crucial variable for innovation organisation and group development in marginal areas. It was Mr Wang's technique, communication networks and personality that were so strongly attractive and influential with his villagers that a group co-operation mechanism was able to emerge and be exploited for cash cropping in WG.

7.2 Innovation potential: invention of a rainfall collection system

As an interactive process between technology and organisation, according to the previous case, technological change (e.g. 'greenhouse' introduction and evolution) can produce external pressure or dynamics on farmers' co-operation so as to adapt technological change and strengthen their innovative capacity. A reverse process, from farmer co-operation to new technology generation, also exists, which will be examined through the case of a rainfall collection system (RCS), a 'technological revolution' popular in the Loess Plateau in the 1990s. Many have claimed to be the inventor of the RCS (Chao and Zhou 1999; Liu and Wu 2000). During this fieldwork, however, it was found that Zhidan county government and local people had heard nothing about the invention outside, but viewed a group of farmers in a high mountain village of Zhidan as inventors of the system. This section is not concerned with who was the first inventor of the RCS in rural China, but rather focuses on how farmers in a remote village of Zhidan were able to make such an important technological invention by themselves. What innovation/creative potential can be recognised among the rural people? By what kinds of organisational process and conditions may such potential be used and released? To address the above-mentioned issues, the notion of innovative potential and its relationship with farmer innovative capacity and FCNs will be outlined, before a detailed description of the case. At the end of this section, relevant lessons learnt from the case will be highlighted.

7.2.1 Innovative potential, capacity and organisation: an outline

Compared with valley areas, the innovative capacity of farmers in marginal areas is seriously constrained not only by the lack of sources of AT, but also by lack of innovators or innovative leaders. The latter impedes the formation and development of farmer innovation networks. To seek a proper strategy for strengthening the HIC, it is necessary to ask whether and how we can learn about farmers' innovative potential, and what kinds of organisational elements influence the innovative potential and release.

The term 'innovative potential' here refers to a state of innovation in which all available (accessible) innovative elements (knowledge, technique, tools, talent, etc.), can be utilised maximally, assembled optimally and shared widely. According to the definition, low HIC is not necessarily the same as low innovative potential, because the former focuses on present, individual and tangible innovative activities, while the latter emphasises future, collective and intangible aspects of innovation practice. For instance, the rural poor who are weak in the HIC are not necessarily low in innovative potential because they may have the chance to learn from their skilled neighbours or gain capital assistance from their relatives.

In addition, the definition suggests that the innovative potential is not determined by individual techniques but by the combination of various technological and organisational elements. It is, thus, significant that under the same conditions (e.g. geographic location, infrastructure, education, etc.), households with a large FCN have more innovative potential than those with a small FCN because the former have more chance to join innovative co-operation and to share techniques and experience. So do united villages more than conflicting communities, because the former can produce stronger innovation demand than the latter. In this sense, the innovative potential of farmers could vary greatly with their organisational pattern and level of co-operation.

These claims regarding the innovative potential of marginal people and the role of inter-household co-operation can be supported by the following case.

*7.2.2 **Water demand pressure and the traditional water cellar***

The problem of water supply is the most serious issue that constrains rural and agricultural development in the Loess Plateau. Frequent severe drought in recent decades, for instance, ranked first among the ecological issues listed by farmers in the household questionnaire surveys. According to the farmers' estimates, the average loss of grain production in the mountain area due to drought was as high as 40–50 per cent in the mid-1990s.

Compared with grain production constraints, insecurity of drinking water is an even more serious issue for both people and animals. Field observation suggests that more than half of the villages (56 per cent) in Zhidan suffered from the difficulties of water supply to various extents. In remote villages, for example, the average distance from village to water resources at the bottom of a hill is about 2 km, with a relative height difference of 100 m, and in some villages the figures are double. Owing to steep and narrow paths, water delivery was hard and dangerous, particularly in the icy winter season and during the summer floods. In addition, most of the water sources in marginal areas were actually dependent on small streams or trickles from overhanging rocks, with no storing facilities. As a result, the reliability and security of water supply was very poor.

Despite a serious shortage of water resources, unfortunately, scarce rainfall had little chance to be utilised. In particular, more than 60 per cent of rainfall is concentrated in the summer, and downpours of heavy rain lead to floods, soil erosion and breakdown of drinking-water delivery. To utilise rainfall resources, a traditional method of rainfall collection, called a 'water storage cellar' (WSC), was

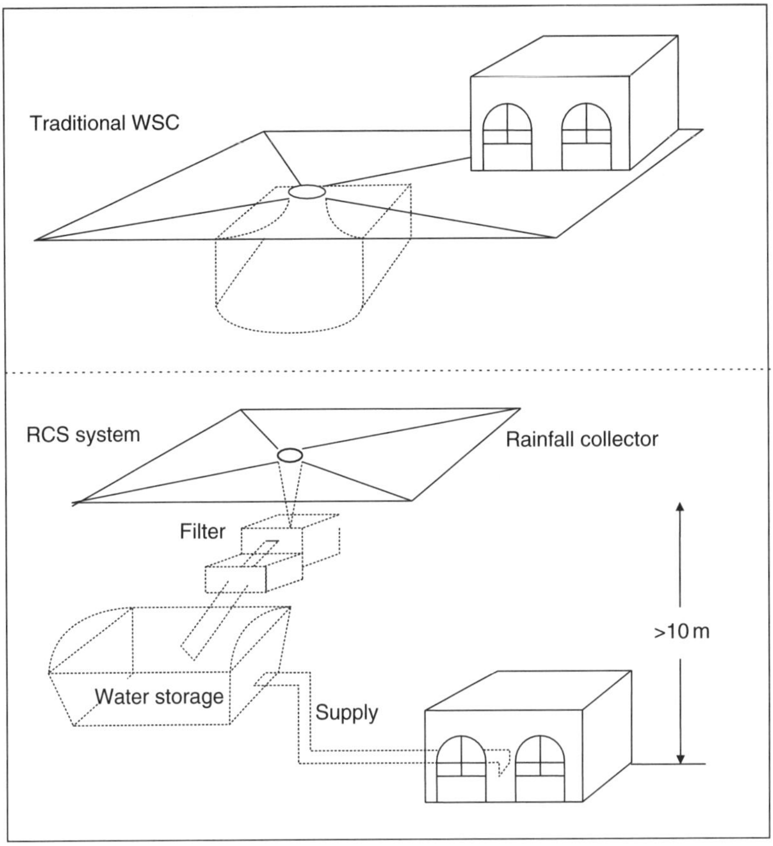

Figure 7.1 Comparison of traditional WSC and new RCS system.

popular in some places of the Loess Plateau. Located in the middle of a household courtyard or plot (Figure 7.1), it suffers from poor hygiene (related to pollution by animal dung) and contamination by earth (due to soil erosion). Efforts to improve the traditional water cellar for drinking water security had being tried for a long time but without success until 1996, when a new system of rainfall collection was made public in a remote village of Zhidan.

7.2.3 Technical characters of the RCS

The new system, called the RCS, is based on the following principles: rainfall collected from a higher surface of land near to the living accommodation passes through a twin filter and is then stored in a covered water pool, and finally passes down to household users through a plastic tube, controlled by a tap (Figure 7.1).

Compared with the traditional WSC, the RCS has undergone many modifications. First, rather than a mixed function as in the WSC, the whole system of the RCS is divided into four independent parts or sub-systems, including: rainfall collection, filtration, water storage, supply and control systems. The functional division in the RCS leads to great improvement of system efficiency and reliability. Second, the force of gravity is utilised to drive all systems through the raised position of the rain collector, which leads to a labour-free and convenient utilisation of water. Finally, modern materials, such as cement and plastic tubing, are applied in the new system, which increases its quality and reliability.

With full utilisation of local resources and mountain topography, according to field observation, the RCS has many advantages:

- *Security of water supply.* A 100-m^2 field can collect about 47 m^3 under the average rainfall of 500 mm/year, which is enough for a five person household.
- *Reliability of utilisation.* Like a stone cave, the RCS can be permanently utilised with no need for maintenance because the whole system is closed.
- *Hygiene of drinking.* Because it is free from pollution by both air and cattle dung, thanks to the filtration process and covering of the system, it was said that the quality of rain water from the RCS met the national hygiene standard for human drinking water.
- *Green technology.* Utilising natural resource (rainfall) and dynamics (earth gravity), it is a totally green technology, without energy inputs or waste outputs.
- *Lowest cost.* The cash cost of purchasing materials (e.g. bricks, cement, plastics, etc.) was about 2000 yuan/system, 20–30 per cent of household cash income or one-fifth of the cost of a new house.
- *Long chains of innovation.* In addition to drinking water security, it has great potential in its application for agricultural production and cash crops, which could produce multiple and long-term effects on rural development in the Loess Plateau.

In summary, it would not be an exaggeration to call the invention of the RCS a ‘technological revolution’ in the marginal areas of the Loess Plateau, because its function consists of more than the satisfaction of drinking water, the basic demands of marginal people. As an intermediate technology between irrigated and rainfed agriculture, the RCS actually provides a new agricultural technological basis, ‘rainfall collected agriculture’, instead of traditional agriculture. In addition, it is unique in that the RCS is both an appropriate and green form of technology.

7.2.4 Innovation process

Without information and outside financial assistance, the RCS originated in an unknown remote village, called Maogou (1,600 m in elevation), in north Zhidan.

In the past, water sources were far away from the village (3 km and 250 m respectively). To satisfy daily consumption, it took a labourer and two cattle about 3 h to deliver water. In rainy and icy seasons, it often occurred that no water supply came for 1 or 2 weeks. As a result, water was so scarce that one bowl of water was shared by the whole family for washing, while consumption by cattle was also strictly controlled by a 'quota system'.

The village was far away from the main road and town (8 and 30 km, respectively), and all twenty-four household residents were actually related by either kinship or marriage among four extended families. Confronted with a harsh living environment, it was said that the village had maintained friendly and close relationships for a long time.

The main advocate and designer of the RCS was Mr Zhou (37 years old), a high school graduate, with 5 years experience of being a 'peasant teacher' before he came back to the village. He had often discussed with villagers a coping strategy to overcome the difficulties of water supply. From an abandoned WSC in his village, he got the idea of the RCS, which was fully supported by his neighbours. After intensive discussions, a detailed plan of the RCS emerged in 1992, and three households, including a carpenter and bricklayer, became core members of the experimental group.

At the beginning, they utilised local stone and slaked lime as construction materials but it failed due to a serious leak. Then cobblestones, brick and cement were used instead, which required a lot of labour and capital for purchase and delivery. Having no other funding sources, Mr Zhou contributed 1,000 yuan from his household budget and borrowed 2,000 yuan from friends outside the project. Because a great deal of labour was needed to deliver construction materials (e.g. sand, cobblestone, bricks, etc.), all of the villagers volunteered to contribute their labour to various degrees, because they fully understood the potential value of the experiment's success. Inevitably, many technological issues and difficulties arose during the period of experimentation, such as collector location, filter design, consolidation of storing, guarding against leaks, etc. Through group wisdom, fortunately, all were finally overcome, and the first RCS was successfully set up on 12 October 1994.

It was long way to go, however, from the success of the RCS invention to adoption by all participants because of constraints of capital. To diffuse the new technology, Mr Zhou spent two years seeking financial assistance, but met with no response from either the township or county government until the summer of 1996, when a county governor came to know about the RCS and visited the village to verify the report. Since then, the RCS had rapidly expanded countywide, due to government encouragement and financial subsidy.

7.2.5 Conclusions: rethinking farmer's innovation potential

Making possible the satisfaction of the basic need of drinking water in mountain areas, not surprisingly, the RCS system was warmly welcomed by the local people who viewed the RCS as a long-term property investment, similar to housing.

In relation to the environmental and development dilemmas in marginal areas of the Loess Plateau, the RCS can be viewed as a 'technology revolution' due to its multi-functions: security of drinking water, saving labour, a green technological system and unexpected potential for innovation in the areas of agricultural, afforestation and the ecological system. The invention of the RCS reflects the great potential of innovation existing in marginal people to cope with the challenges from a harsh environment. From this unique event, many lessons can be learnt as follows.

First, the innovative potential of farmers cannot be isolated from traditional technological systems because the latter becomes the base for launching the new system. Rather than complete adoption or refusal of traditional technology, the RCS case suggests that it would be a good idea to promote integrative utilisation of traditional and modern technological elements according to local resources and conditions. Rather than technological substitution, technological synthesis would be helpful for the release of innovative potential of farmers through their own selection and decisions.

Second, the innovative potential of farmers is closely related to innovators, a crucial element influencing marginal areas. While attention is paid to the poor innovative capacity of marginal people, a more important question is often missed: whether their innovative potential has been fully revealed and used, and what factors constrain its release. According to the field observations, many resources of innovation exist in marginal areas, such as various indigenous experts and specialised households, urban–rural households, high-school graduates, school teachers, etc. Rather than waiting for outside assistance and 'new professionals' emerging, the above resources and their potential should be fully developed and used at first.

Third, innovative potential is a variable of farmer communication, co-operation and self-organisation. Although the FCN has positive functions in improving farmer innovative capacity compared with separate households, it is far from releasing full innovative potential because the FCN as inter-household network seems too loose to cope with challenges from both physical environment and technological systems. Similar to the case of 'greenhouses' in the previous section, Mr Zhou's FCN was developed and improved into a co-operative group for technological experiment and development. Different from individual technological exploration, therefore, the invention of the RCS is a process of farmer collaboration and self-organisation in which all villagers have opportunities to participate in an innovation 'project' and to contribute their knowledge and labour.

Fourth, the astounding success of the RCS raises the questions: why has so important a technology been invented by a group of farmers in a remote village rather than professional staff in the urban town and research institutes (a total of ten national research centres in Loess Plateau)? According to field observation and interviews, a common issue is the considerable distance between farmers' demands and professional supply. Constrained by both strong administrative intervention and the conventional innovation model, unavoidably, professional researchers and extensionists pay little attention to technological demands from the bottom but focus on government support and project funding. As a result, the innovation potential of marginal people is seriously underestimated while barriers of communication between marginal people and urban professionals are neglected.

Finally, the case of thc RCS invention requires a reassessment and reorientation of government innovation policy. Compared with uncountable policies to encourage professional research and extension, unfortunately, there is a lack of suitable policy to recognise and encourage farmer invention and creativity. Turning to the case of the RCS, for instance, no government officer emphasised the farmer's role as inventor, but stressed the governmental role in its extension. Disagreeing with the government, the inventors were seeking access to a patent application at the time of the fieldwork.

7.3 Social capital and farmer innovation: case of the 'green village'

Farmer innovation and self-organisation in marginal areas cannot be fully understood unless social capital is taken into account. Whilst substantial evidences described in previous sections have shown the existence of farmer communication and co-operation, and their contribution to technological innovation, many questions arise regarding social capital itself: how can social capital be accumulated and created for the purpose of farmer innovation? What relation exists between development of social capital and the release of farmer innovative potential? Where is the real beginning or starting point to initiate the processes above? Who can initiate the processes if no leadship exists in a marginal village? The following case may offer insights into the above issues.

7.3.1 'Green village': background to Taoliwa

Related to the rural institutional contradictions between farmers and collective land (Chapter 5), deforestation is perhaps the first dilemma in the Loess Plateau. Although it is surrounded by immeasurable deforestation and bare mountains, there are, however, some 'green islands' covered by meadows of plants and grass surrounding the villages. Down in these villages, the residents' income level and their mental attitude make a deep impression on visitors. Why do these 'green islands' exist and how have they been developed? To unravel the puzzles, a green village was listed as a priority for case study during the fieldwork, which led to the wonderful story below.

Taoliwa (meaning a convenient place producing pear and peach in Chinese), is a mountainous village, 45 km northwest from the county town. Of seventeen households, all belong to descendants (eleventh to thirteenth generation) of the eighth Liu generation, since their ancestor moved into the village from a neighbouring province 400 years ago. Unlike most modern Chinese families, the Liu's clan has kept the tradition of respecting and recording the clan's history. Due to the social revolution and political movement since the Communist Party took power, few families in contemporary China have kept and renewed clan books, a rare exception being Taoliwa, whose record of the Liu Clan was revised in 1993. The main function of the clan records, according to the villagers, is to strengthen the links between rural and urban kin. Of a total of sixty-nine close kin and relatives listed in the book, the majority are actually urban residents nation-wide and some live in big cities such as Beijing, Xian and Lanzhou. What they are proud of is that one famous Kuomintang general in the 1920–30s, namely Liu Baotong, from the tenth generation of the Liu clan, was born and buried in this village. As a hero of the Liu clan, General Liu has left a spirit pillar to attract these residents to conserve the clan's tradition and kinship unity.

According to interviewees, the Liu clan in history had a tradition of planting trees surrounding the village. At the beginning of the twentieth century, it was said that as many as 300 mature cultivated trees tightly encircled the village. Similar to other places in Zhidan, two-thirds of the village land had been covered by forest, until the middle of the 1930s, when large-scale deforestation was undertaken by the Communist Army after the 'Long March'. Deforestation was further exacerbated during the period of collectivisation, the 'Great Leap Forward' in the late 1950s, and the 'cultural revolution' (1966–76) in particular, when the village was identified as an 'object of dictatorship' due to General Liu's Kuomintang history. In addition, the continuous growth of population and cultivation was an important factor contributing to deforestation. In particular, the rural reforms of the early 1980s provided a strong stimulus to over-cultivation when the area of cultivated land reached a peak of 1,100 mu in 1984, nearly 40 per cent more than that in 1980. By the middle of the 1980s, while the village food needs were met, forest resources in the Taoliwa had been exhausted and the shortage of firewood became an issue that most concerned farmers.

7.3.2 From co-operative afforestation to sustainable village

Suffering from a serious firewood shortage, all the villagers felt too embarrassed either to collect wood outside or to plant trees within the village. The former act was often punished and offenders humiliated by host villagers, while the latter option carried no guarantee of success, due to the likelihood of damage by both animals and neighbouring villagers. To cope with the challenge of firewood shortage, the collaborative afforestation idea was gradually shared by all villagers. As a result, a plan for tree plantation was discussed and implemented by all villagers in the mid-1980s.

Without changing the nature of the HRS, the plan was based upon a principle: if the village was to survive and develop, all residents should share responsibility for tree plantation and management. To be practicable, it included the following points:

- a forest land seeding schedule was planned, with all households' participation in decision-making so as to secure a balance of interests between households;

- each household was responsible for its own tree seed selection, plantation and management under the village plan;
- responsibility for woodland protection was shared by all residents because all their plots are actually interconnected with each other;
- a villager was appointed as a woodland security co-ordinator, whose job was to harmonise woodland management between households;
- strict punishment was enacted if any animal got out of control and entered the woodland.

Due to close unity and co-operation, tree damaging incidents, the first dilemma of forest management in the Loess Plateau, were detected and stopped quickly. According to the villagers, young trees cannot survive if the village's sheep cannot be prevented from entering the forested land, which would be followed by flocks of sheep from neighbouring villages. The tree management regulations were strictly enforced, and many sheep owners in Taoliwa have experienced fines (0.5–1 yuan/sheep that enter the forested land) without exception. This made a deep impression and was a strong deterrent to outside invaders and infringement. Strict and successful management, in turn, encouraged villagers to make continuous efforts in afforestation year by year. All four hills of the village had been covered by trees, and the area of forest had rapidly expanded to 1,000 mu or nearly 60 mu/household by 1997, more than ten times the average of the samples' woodland area. The benefits of tree planting went beyond firewood and included a source of construction timber and conservation trees. In addition, fruit-trees had become an important source of household income, which reached 1,000 yuan/household by 1996.

Besides the satisfaction of firewood demand, successful afforestation produced many other effects. First, over-cultivation was reduced by the villagers themselves rather than by administrative intervention, and more than 200 mu was transformed to firewood land or fruit orchards. Meanwhile, new seeding methods such as level plough and wide furrow were adopted, instead of the traditional methods. Indeed, the demand for agricultural innovation was so strong in Taoliwa that the village representatives often went to the county town to seek new technologies (e.g. new crop seeds, tree seedlings, pesticide, etc.), which surprised government officers and professionals because it seldom occurred in their experience.

Second, to resolve the conflict between afforestation and grazing of livestock, a strategy of grass planting was successfully introduced in the early 1990s, which led to a rapid expansion of grassland to 400 mu in 1997. Accordingly, most of the animals were enclosed with cut-grass feeding, instead of traditional nomadic grazing. After the expansion of grasslands, according to the plan, commercial breeding of pigs and oxen could be introduced for the purposes of both cash generation and organic manure supply. By the time the project was complete, a comprehensive system of sustainable agriculture would be established.

Third, benefiting from successful co-operation in the afforestation project, farmers expanded their co-operation to infrastructure areas. As a result, an ambitious blueprint emerged, including: a 4-km vehicle road connecting to the main road; access to the outside electricity network; a central system of water supply for domestic use and animal breeding; a reservoir for fish breeding, etc. By 1997, two of the proposed projects (electricity and water) had been achieved and one (road) was nearly completed.

7.3.3 Urban kin participation and contribution

The great achievements in Taoliwa cannot be understood without uncovering the organisational process. The idea of co-operative afforestation and development in Taoliwa was originated by an urban kin member, Mr Liu Guang, the son of former General Liu. As an engineer in a state oil company (about 200 km away from the village), he has contributed both his knowledge, love and even life to his home village.

Owing to his father's history, Mr Liu was persecuted and forced to return to the village for agricultural production in the period of the 'cultural revolution', which provided a unique opportunity for him to gain in-depth understanding of rural poverty and development. Although his political reputation and position recovered in 1979, he kept close contact with his kin, and visited the village every year. Particularly, he always stressed the following opinions to his rural kin:

> Village environmental and development issues (e.g. deforestation, inaccessibility to road) cannot wait for the government to solve them. Compared with development through external assistance, it would be of more value if it could be achieved through self-reliance. As the beginning of village development, a 'green account', afforestation and pasture plantation, should be given priority, whose success will largely depend on all villagers' participation, unity and co-operation. The significance of co-operative afforestation is not only to provide a sustainable treasure for our descendants, but, if it succeeds, to *offer a novel path for our neighbouring villages or even Zhidan county, i.e. close unity and co-operation rather than the present individualist development would lead to a sustainable future.*
>
> (emphasis added)

During the period of his short stay in the village, in particular, he spent a lot of time to persuade those who were suspicious or hesitated to join the co-operative plan. Gradually, his idea was shared and supported by all villagers, and the first plan for a firewood plantation emerged in a village meeting chaired by him. Based upon the success of afforestation, a long-term strategy of agricultural innovation and village development was suggested by him, and fully discussed and improved by all villagers in the early 1990s, which became the blueprint for village development in the 1990s.

Besides designing the plan, his particular contribution was the establishment and development of a co-operative mechanism, by which all issues related to inter-household relationships and village development were discussed and negotiated in public meetings in which all households participated. Following Mr Liu's idea, a leading core of villagers of three middle-aged farmers took charge of organising, co-ordinating and harmonising all households to achieve the blueprint, with great success. Meanwhile, two innovative groups were developed with different technical orientations. One was pursuing agricultural innovation within the village through technology introduction, experimentation and demonstration; another specialised in non-farm innovation outside the village.

Mr Liu returned to the village to design and initiate a 4-km long vehicle road, just after he retired in summer 1993. Having no external funding, he contributed 3,000 yuan from his family savings and wrote letters to all his urban kin nationwide, asking for donations. His hard work, however, caused an acute disease, and he died during the period of road construction that winter.

Mr Liu's death did not halt the progress of the proposed projects, but encouraged the villagers to strengthen their unity and co-operation. Learning from Mr Liu, more and more urban kin (including his son) participated in home village construction and development in various ways. 'Building an evergreen home village' had become a common objective shared by both villagers and their urban kin.

7.3.4 Conclusions: social capital, self-organisation and urban participation

Despite its uniqueness in some respects, such as the clan tradition, General Liu's story and Mr Liu's contribution, the path of Taoliwa does contain some common elements regarding social capital, farmer innovation and self-organisation towards sustainable future in marginal areas of the Loess Plateau. By way of conclusion, the following paragraphs will reveal the significance and general lessons from Taoliwa's successful practice.

Whose development and innovation? Farmer self-organisation A fundamental question that is often missed from development debate is the subject of rural development and innovation. Taking Zhidan as an example, there have actually been long-term disputes on Zhidan's innovation strategies. There was no agreement between *high-efficiency agriculture, economic tree plantation* and *animal husbandry*. Since they neglect the roles and contribution of farmers, none of the officially introduced strategies was able to solve Zhidan's environmental and developmental dilemmas, as outlined in Chapter 5. In contrast, the Taoliwa experience offers a novel development and innovation path, in which farmers design, determine, control and share their innovation practice. It is farmer self-organisation that offers a sound base for sustainable development and innovation in marginal areas of the Loess Plateau. In particular, farmer self-organisation's development and innovation in this case was characterised by the following features:

1 *Farmers' own choice* in the whole process, in contrast to top-down governance in most of the marginal areas in China.
2 *Satisfaction of urgent demands*. Innovation in Taoliwa began with the need for firewood, on which a co-operative agreement was easily reached.

3 *From simple to complex.* From the perspective of project order, the first innovation was located on a distant hill, which had less impact on household livelihoods. As experience accumulated and capacity improved, innovative projects were gradually moved nearer to the village, with intensive capital inputs.
4 *Technical graduation.* The success of Taoliwa is closely related to the gradual process from simple to complex and from low to high technique, which is quite different from the governmental 'technological jump/leapfrogging' approach.

Enhancement of social capital: from clan unity to co-operative system It is unimaginable that farmer innovation could have happened and been sustained in Taoliwa without using and enhancing social capital, involving a process from narrow clan unity to an institutionalised co-operation system. As a process of social capital accumulation and creation, particularly, the success of Taoliwa highlights some important points.

First, the unique clan history and tradition have provided a good basis for promoting household unity and co-operation. It is suggested that village history, tradition and kinship organisations as a form of social capital can be viewed as an important resource for rural development under some conditions. Rather than narrowly focusing on his clan's development and future, Mr Liu's ambition was to show the feasibility of unity and co-operation to Zhidan county. The success of Taoliwa requires a rethink of China's mainstream thought on social policy, which has rejected and excluded the traditional culture and kinship organisations, in particular, since the Communist Party took national power, half a century ago.

Second, traditional culture and organisations can be used for initiating co-operation, while its sustainability is largely dependent upon establishing and developing a sound co-operation system. In Taoliwa, the co-operative system includes the following points: democratic decision-making, participatory management, strict implementation and penalty, equality sharing, etc. In particular, regular meetings can solve various contradictions at an early stage, while the financial subsidies provided to the forest co-ordinator by all village residents indicates the maturity of the co-operation system.

Finally, the co-operative system in Taoliwa was further strengthened through an outward expansion of the networks. Sharing similar developmental ideas, many of Liu's kin and relatives in nearby villages frequently visited Taoliwa to learn and exchange experiences, which led to the diffusion of the Taoliwa pattern without government involvement. In addition, through the composition and spread of Liu's clan book and Mr Liu's story as well, urban communication and co-operative networks rapidly expanded, and became an important part of Taoliwa's development and innovation.

Starting point: home consciousness and urban participation Even if social capital and farmer self-organisation are widely acknowledged, a dilemma facing rural development in marginal areas is that for various reasons a considerable number of villages have no organisational centre for farmer self-organisation.

Whilst the mainstream of thought focuses on outside NGOs' participation or initiatives, the case of Taoliwa has offered an alternative approach: urban participatory development and innovation. Different from government-manipulated urban assistance, urban participation here is based upon using and enhancing existing urban–rural networks to satisfy farmers' demands, as can be demonstrated by the following points:

First, the case of Taoliwa suggests that 'home consciousness', as a part of traditional Chinese culture, can be utilised to mobilise and encourage urban participation in rural development without administrative intervention. In his last letter to his urban kin for donations for the road construction, for example, Mr Liu painted a beautiful word-picture of Taoliwa's future, and invited them to assemble in the village at the turn of the new century.

Second, the case of Taoliwa indicates the importance of 'opinion leaders' in marginal areas. Due to many constraints from the natural and social environment, a considerable number of villages suffer from a lack of a leadership centre to initiate co-operative projects and harmonise inter-household relationships. In such cases, the introduction of a suitable 'opinion leader' from outside (or inside) is more important than physical and financial assistance.

Finally, compared with neo-liberal property reform and 'land auction', urban participation may offer an alternative path to absorb urban capital, technology and talent for promoting rural economic and social development. Field evidence suggests that urban capital has begun to flow into some marginal areas for co-operative forestation through kinship.

7.4 Farmer innovation system: a self-organisation model

The three cases presented in this chapter attempt to reveal one issue: by what organisational mechanisms can marginal people join together to meet their innovative demands and strengthen their innovative capacity? Associated with the discussion in Chapter 6, this section intends to establish a conceptual model or framework, a *farmer innovation system*, to summarise the field discoveries and to explain self-organisational mechanisms. Accordingly, it consists of four sections. The first step is to identify the innovation organisational elements shared by all field cases, upon which, then, the notion of farmer innovation system will be defined and explained. Applying this model, the typology of farmer innovation will be distinguished, while the relevant issues related to farmer innovation co-operation will be highlighted at the end.

7.4.1 Organisational elements of farmer innovation

Although the cases described in the previous sections are varied in terms of production field, technology nature, geographic location and social environment, they share some common elements:

- *Scale demand.* The demand for innovation is a precondition for farmers to participate in and contribute to innovative practice. In a marginal environment, generally, household innovative demands are dispersed, weak and heterogeneous. The case of Taoliwa suggests that although most of the households in the remote villages were anxious for firewood, new innovative practice might not have occurred, had not the barriers of disorganisation been removed. It is crucial, therefore, whether dispersed and individual demands can be scaled-up and transformed into efficient demands.

- *Appropriate technology*. Related to the complexity and diversity of innovative demands, the case of WG suggests that the appropriateness of technology is relative, and varies with location, household skill, communication networks and co-operative mechanisms in particular. Beyond pure technological and economic boundaries, appropriateness should include an organisational dimension. The more communication and co-operation farmers have, the wider the range of technologies they can select and use. The case of the RCS indicates that farmers are not only receivers and users of new technology, but also positive or potential creators and inventors of appropriate technology.
- *Social capital*. Neither farmers' innovative demand nor the appropriateness of technology are independent, but vary with the extent of farmer mutual aid and co-operation. Social capital provides a sound base upon which individual households join together to overcome various difficulties related to small production scale, to share knowledge and information. Serviced for the purposes of farmer innovation, social capital can be distinguished as various types and phases: FCNs, innovative group (circle) and co-operative system. The FCN and innovative group are employed to address the social basis and organisational style of farmer innovation, respectively, while the co-operative system that emerged in the cases of WG and Taoliwa indicates an 'institutional' process in terms of comprehensive innovation strategy, strict management regulation and co-operative mechanisms.
- *Innovative leader*. All cases suggest that group co-operation and innovation depend on the existence and contribution of an innovative leader who plays a key role in initiating process, harmonising relations between participants and interfacing with outside resources. The leader need not be a technology expert, a community organisational head, or even a rural resident, but must have clear ideas for innovation, an organisational strategy and a charismatic ability to lead all network members toward a common future. The stronger the core, the greater the possibility of innovation sustainability.
- *Outside participation*. Rather than being isolated from outside impacts and participation, farmer innovation is a process of social interaction between insiders and outsiders and between rural and urban areas. The term 'outside' here widely refers to all urban organisations and people, including local government, extension or agribusiness agencies and urban kin, who are involved in rural and farmer innovation practices. The case of Taoliwa suggests that urban kin may become important resources in innovation to overcome shortages of capital, technologies and innovative leaders in particular.

7.4.2 Farmer innovation system and self-organising model

Related to the complexity of the marginal environment, the farmer innovation elements above can be interconnected by different styles or strategies in practice. In response to environmental pressure or market stimulation, for instance, an innovation process can begin from cither the innovation demands of farmers, which leads to a search for creation of appropriate technology (as in the case of rainfall collection), or government initiatives (as in the case of the WG), which stimulate the emergence and expansion of farmers' demands. As a social process, however, the demand and satisfaction of farmer innovation are closely related to the style and extent of social capital (farmer co-operation), which is, in turn, dependent on the existence and roles of an innovative leader to initiate innovation and harmonise internal and external relationships. The relations between innovative elements is illustrated in Figure 7.2.

According to Figure 7.2, farmer innovation in marginal areas can be viewed as a system in which the demands of farmer innovation can be scaled-up and satisfied through strengthening social capital and outside participation. Many conclusions can be drawn from the model.

First, farmer innovation in marginal areas is a self-organising system for the following reasons:

- the beginning and end of farmer innovation is to satisfy their own demands;
- farmers are the primary actors or innovators, while all outside professionals and change agencies join in the system merely as participants;
- rather than individual actions, farmer innovation involves various social relationships and inter-household interaction through their own networks;
- farmers' co-operation and self-organisation are largely dependent on their own innovative centre or leadership to control and harmonise various relationships;
- in contrast to one-way extension or short-duration projects, farmer innovation is a continuous and evolutionary process with the mechanisms of self-learning, feedback, adaptation and adjustment.

Second, farmer innovation is a process of social capital accumulation and enhancement, through a wide range of communication, internaction and co-operation from neighbour mutual aid, group co-operation to urban–rural integration. In other words, farmer innovation in marginal areas is based upon the farmers' mutual aid and co-operative network, which, in turn, influences both the demand scale of farmers and appropriateness. A close co-operative network would be of benefit to technological exchange, diffusion and adoption. The neglect or lack of farmer co-operation is thus one of the important reasons for failure in satisfying farmer demands in marginal areas.

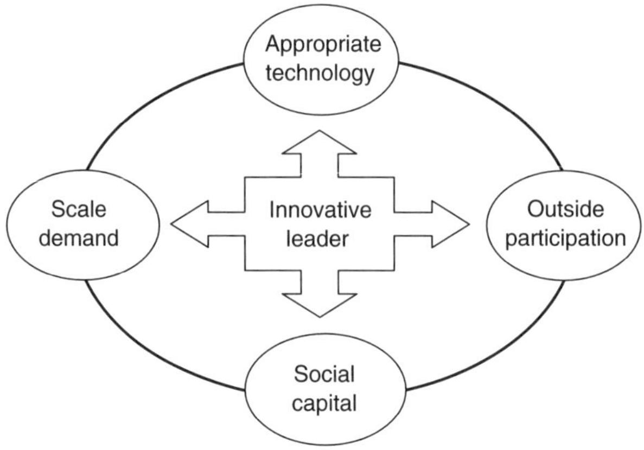

Figure 7.2 Self-organisation model for farmer innovation system.

Third, farmer innovation in marginal areas is a gradual system, because both demand scaling-up and capacity improvement are constrained by the factor of social capital accumulation and enhancement. It is indicated that:

- the appropriateness of technology is changeable, depending on both the technological system itself and the extent of farmer co-operation and organisation;
- the 'technological leapfrogging' strategy used by the government is often not appropriate in marginal areas;
- conventional administrative intervention, which neglects the complexity and diversity of farmer demands and capacity, is particularly questionable in innovation management in marginal areas.

Fourth, farmer innovation is an 'open' system. First, rather than focusing on the nature of technological elements (e.g. traditional or modern, low or high, labour intensive or capital intensive), farmer innovation emphasises on the technological relationship or compatibility between these elements. Second, in contrast to linear 'demand-pull' or 'technology-push', the system model emphasises plural dynamics from both inside and outside, rural and urban, formal and informal, family and non-family, etc. Finally, although it emphasises self-reliance and informal organisations, the model does not exclude external assistance and government intervention. Rather, it is suggested that external forces might not be able to satisfy the innovative demands of the rural poor unless their intrinsic innovative potential and a proper interface between farmer self-organisations and outside participation can be identified.

Finally, farmer innovation practices can be further distinguished into two kinds of processes. One is technological adaptation and demand satisfaction through the anti-clockwise circle in Figure 7.2, in which the government or professionals initiate the innovation process while farmers learn, adapt and adopt new technologies through strengthening their co-operative relationships. Another is system innovation and demand expansion through a clockwise process in which farmers' innovative demands and capacity are continuously driven and accelerated by social capital accumulation and enhancement and outside participation. While the case of WG (greenhouse) represents the former, the case of Taoliwa (green village) is related to the latter. To achieve sustainable development and innovation in marginal areas, therefore, the promotion of farmer co-operation should be put at the top of the development agenda in marginal areas of China.

7.4.3 Typology of farmer innovation practice

The farmer self-organisation model offers a new insight into rural innovation practice and organisational strategy. From the perspective of rural co-operation sharing, farmer innovation can be divided into two extremes. At one end, *collective innovation* requires all community members to participate in the innovation process and share innovation achievements, irrespective of the differentiation of household demands and capacity. At the other end, *individual innovation* assumes that farmer innovation is a totally individual activity, in which innovation in one household may not be learnt or shared by the neighbours. According to the difference of innovative capacity, farm households may be divided into two states: no technical difference (or homophile) within rural communities; great difference (or heterophile) between households due to different opportunities or no technological communication. Combining the two dimensions, four innovation types can be illustrated in Figure 7.3.

According to Figure 7.3, four types of farmer innovation can be described and explained:

- *Type I: no innovation* due to lack of both access to external innovation resources and lack of innovators within the community. Many marginal villages fall into this category.
- *Type II: individual innovation* which is limited to individual households, and few of their neighbours are able to learn and share knowledge with them. Due to lack of necessary communication and co-operation, the innovation demand and capacity of both sides is constrained.
- *Type III: collective adoption*. Technology originating from outside is adopted by all the community members. Lack of internal dynamics and differentiation means technological innovation is too dependent on exogenous sources to be sustained.
- *Type IV: collaborative innovation* which highlights a balance between individual innovation and community co-operation in order to release the creative potential of all the community members and generate a sustainable 'innovation circle' for village innovation and development.

Figure 7.3 shares a dimension with Rogers' image (Chapter 2): the high heterophile would promote or benefit farmer innovation. Disagreeing with both the neo-liberal model of individual innovation and the orthodox collective

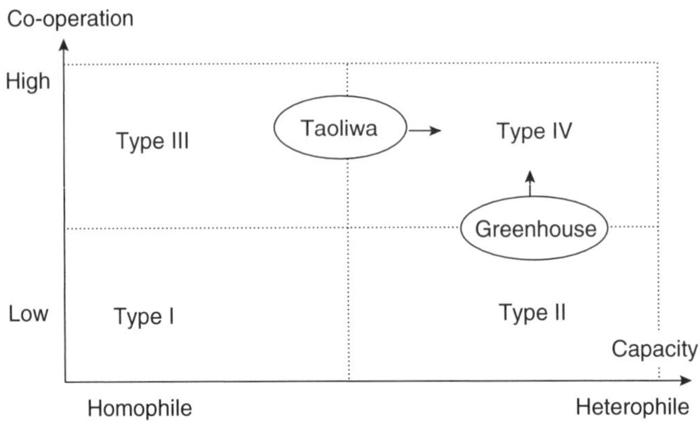

Figure 7.3 Typology of farmer innovation strategies.

pattern, the farmer self-organising model offers a 'middle' path, collaborative innovation, for marginal areas.

These are not mere theoretical constructs; all the types of innovation seen above exist in real rural society. According to the field surveys, for example, collective adoption emerged in the commune system, and is still employed by the government for agricultural extension and sometimes for commercialised agricultural programme initiatives. In contrast, individual innovation originated in non-farming areas, and is now dominant in the household responsibility institution. In consideration of post-Deng reform and development, particularly, co-operative innovation has offered a new direction, whose potential and advantages have been illustrated through the cases of Taoliwa and WG.

7.4.4 Enhancement of social capital: key issues for farmer innovation

The farmer self-organisation model emphasises the roles of social capital. Targeting the improvement of farmers' innovative capacity and the release of their innovative potential, social capital accumulation and creation have become a crucial condition for sustainable development and innovation in marginal areas of China. Accordingly, many issues need to be addressed.

Structural plurality: kinship, neighbourhood and membership Although rural mutual aid and co-operation is not new for farmers at all but has existed for thousands of years, social capital may not be static but continues to change and adjust in the both content and format in order to match with rural institutional and market economic environment. Focusing on farmer innovation in marginal areas, Chapters 6 and this chapter have shown that social capital cannot be reduced into a single pattern but rather takes multiple forms on the one hand, and varies greatly with environment, technology and economic development levels on the other. Many conclusions can be drawn regarding to the complexity of the components of social capital.

First, despite the decline of impacts in rural social life and household innovative capacity in particular, traditional kinship has functions to facilitate technology diffusions on the one hand, and influence household social community pattern on the other. This is particularly true for those remote villages where kinship plays a more important role than in other regions in influencing household social community pattern and innovative action.

Second, compared with traditional kinship, it is commonly acknowledged that neighbourhood plays a more positive role in terms of influencing household innovation action and village technological development. The importance of neighbour interaction and co-operation in social capital, however, cannot replace kinship, due to the complexity and plurality of rural society.

Third, close relatives and friends outside the village have become increasingly important for households, as a source of access to external information and developmental opportunities.

Finally, equal exchange and reciprocity have become a principle of farmer co-operation, leading to the emergence of 'formal memberships' in various 'innovation groups' instead of the traditional division between kinship and non-kinship. Although those 'innovation groups' or 'organisations' described in this chapter are not formal organisations at the moment, they have become an important basis to carry out farmer innovation.

Functional hierarchy: FCN, innovation circles and co-operative systems Plural components of social capital are not separate from each other, but have interwoven as a functional whole aimed to secure household livelihoods and innovative objectives. Whilst Chapter 6 showed evidence that the household innovative capacity is closely related to the scale of household communication networks, this chapter has examined the degree of closeness of household social interaction and co-operation and its impacts on innovative capacity. As a result, social networks and groups can be divided into three levels according to their functional hierarchy, ranging from loose FCN, through close innovation groups (circles) to institutionalised 'co-operative systems'. As a common social phenomenon, the FCN exists in all rural households allied to the function of livelihood security generally, and can be used and developed for innovation purposes in particular. The innovative function of the FCN can be achieved mainly through various kinds of innovative links/groups ranging widely from loose neighbour-centred mutual aid to close craft apprenticeship. Beyond the limitations of special techniques or seasonal co-operation in an innovation circle, more close co-operative relationships and organisations can be identified from the farmer co-operative system in the cases of Taoliwa and WG, in which co-operative principles and regulations have been developed into a strict system to ensure that all participate in decision-making and share in achievement. These forms of co-operation may be viewed as a process of organisational evolution from low to high levels.

Organisational centre: innovative leadership and its generation Social capital is not the private property of individual households, but is shared by all members of a group or community. Although there are many factors, channels or causes related to stock, growth or reduction of social capitals, it seems very clear that social capital is unlikely to be maintained and enhanced without a group or community 'centre' who is able to take 'responsibility' for 'organising' or 'harmonising' inter-household interaction. This is particularly true in rural reform as Chinese rural societies have suffered disorganisation on the one hand, and the privatisation orientation has undermined rural co-operation and the spirit of collectivism on the other. Whilst scattered households need charismatic and highly qualified people as 'leaders', the issue is not so much to select a leader for group innovation, but to recognise who is the real innovative leader or 'centre' (this may be different from the present administrative leader) and how to encourage his performance as a leader. Because of the complex geographic and social environment, however, a considerable number of villages are actually disorganised and no 'leader' exists in their societies. To promote farmer co-operation and innovation, according to the case of Taoliwa, 'opinion leaders' and urban participation play a crucial role in innovation initiative and social problem-solving.

Facilitating innovation: from innovative potential to real capacity Alongside other conditions or opportunities, such as technology, market and other capital, social capital provides a social basis and organisational 'bridge' by which farmers' innovative potential can be transmitted into real innovative capacity.

The importance of social capital can be illustrated through Figure 7.4, which suggests that the HIC can be simply divided into two parts: *individual capacity*, owned and utilised by individual households themselves; and *collective capacity*, which is generated from group co-operation and can be 'shared' by participants according to their positions or roles in the co-operation group.

According to Figure 7.4, variation in the HIC amongst farmers is thus related to: (i) whether a co-operative group exists (no co-operation, no group innovation return); (ii) to what scale and extent households participate in co-operation (the closer the co-operation, the higher the group innovation capacity); and (iii) what role the household plays in the co-operation group (the closer to the core, the more sharing of group capacity). The formula can be further explained through the case of 'greenhouses' (Section 7.1), in which the differences of innovative capacity of vegetable cropping farmers are reflected as their various positions in the innovation group.

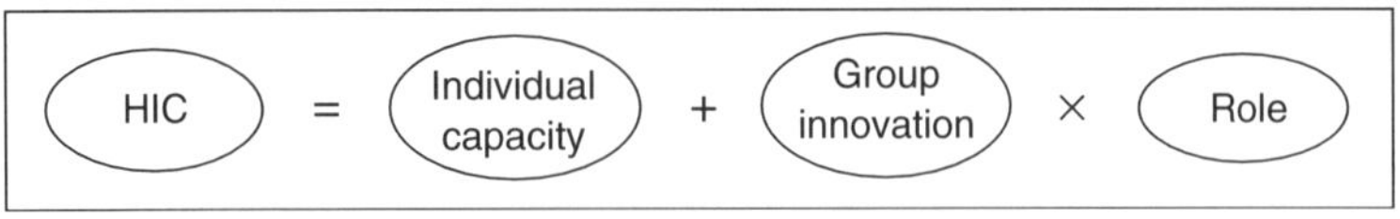

Figure 7.4 Composition of HIC.

Note
Role means position in group, for example, leader, core, close, outer (as in the case of 'green house').

Side-effects: social exclusion Farmer co-operation and urban participation do not always have positive functions in rural innovation and livelihood security. While the rural rich or innovators as organisational centres enjoy their wider communication network and larger scale of co-operation, their poor neighbours or other residents outside their clan may be excluded from the innovation process. In addition, it was found to be not uncommon in the field areas that through kinship linkages, public funding or projects were unfairly distributed or concentrated into some villages. These problems cannot be blamed on social capital itself but are rather related to deficiencies of political and administrative systems that lacked the public monitoring on the one hand, and favoured the rich and less marginal villages on the other.

8 Conclusion

Sustainability and farmer innovation in China

Chapters 1–7 have examined the background and organisational dimension related to farmer innovation in marginal areas of China. To conclude, this chapter attempts to summarise the research findings, and to indicate their theoretical and policy implications. It is divided into four sections, beginning with the challenges facing China's sustainable development. It is followed by a discussion on the roles of the rural poor in sustainable rural livelihoods. Section 8.3 focuses on farmer innovation and self-organisation model. This chapter ends with some policy implications.

8.1 What is the challenge? Unsustainability and marginalisation

China is facing the challenges of both ecological degradation and increasing socio-economic inequality at the run of the new century. This book has shown that the two processes above, environmental unsustainability and economic marginalisation, rather than being separate from each other, are actually interwoven. This is the biggest challenge against China's sustainable development.

The correlation between unsustainability and marginalisation in rural China has been confirmed by both secondary and fresh information collected from Shaanxi province. Empirical evidence shows that: from a time perspective, both ecological degradation and economic marginalisation have been accelerated since rural reform; in the spatial dimension, the two processes are particularly serious in the marginal areas. In addition, despite huge efforts made by the Chinese government, with impressive achievements in poverty reduction, environmental degradation and marginalisation are far from alleviation but have become increasingly serious. Furthermore, government intervention itself suffers from geographic, economic and social biases, which may exacerbate the sufferings of the rural poor.

The above facts seem to suggest that the barriers to China's sustainable development are not individual elements (e.g. its population, resources, technological, poverty or local economic growth), but the marginalisation process, whereby scarce resources are concentrated in core areas. As a result, the unstable ecological system in the marginal areas continuously deteriorates towards sterilisation, a trend in both the decline of environment carrying capacity and the increase of ecological risks. In this sense, China's sustainable development is unlikely to be achieved unless significant progress is made to break down the marginalisation process.

The correlation between unsustainability and marginalisation seems to challenge conventional assumptions that sustainable development can be achieved merely through meeting individual objectives, such as poverty reduction, local economic growth, green technology or tight administration/lcgal control. This is because all measures together are still not enough to address the deep cause or mechanisms of marginalisation itself, which involves reallocation of scarce resources and political power amongst different regions and groups.

The lessons from government intervention on poverty reduction in the past suggest a need for rethinking the current 'western China development' programme. First, western China is not a homogenous whole, and conventional regional division and economic analysis often underestimate its complexity. Second, economic growth in the West will not necessarily lead to ecological improvement, unless marginal areas at various levels are given top priority. Finally, sustainable development in the West can hardly be achieved without a novel approach to the demands, potential and innovative capacity of the rural poor in marginal areas.

Because marginalisation is so important for China's sustainable development, further researches and surveys are needed: why and how has marginalisation caused unsustainable development in the marginal areas? Can marginalisation be attributed to the economic transition from planned economy to the market economic system or other important factors? What are the impacts of globalisation on China's marginalisation? What lessons should be learnt from the marginalisation process and its effects?

8.2 Role of the poor: sustainable livelihoods and organisation

The challenge of marginalisation in rural China has also shown the limitations of mainstream development thinking, which has so far paid little attention to the intrinsic dynamics and development potential of the rural poor. In contrast to the popular 'development for people' paradigm (e.g. farmer participation in outsider-led projects), this book has attempted to explore a 'development by people' approach, which views rural development as a process of farmers' communication, interaction and co-operation to adapt to environmental changes, challenges and to secure their livelihoods. Using the theory of 'sustainable rural livelihoods' (SRL), rural sustainability requires at least a balance and harmony of natural, physical, human, social and financial assets; the role of the poor can be interpreted in terms of 'social capital', a crucial element of SRL system referred to trust, network and mechanism by which people can be able to work together. Whilst marginalisation leads to the outflow of 'tangible' capital (physical, financial and human resources) to core areas, social capital becomes a crucial element for farmers in marginal areas to maintain and even improve the SRL system by themselves.

Applying the above approach to sample areas of Shaanxi province, this book has aimed to address why social capital is important for sustainable development in marginal areas, and how it is used and developed by the rural poor to enhance their adaptation and coping capacity against various constraints, challenges and uncertainties. Focusing on the 'organisational dimension' of social capital, in particular, this book has developed an integrative approach to figure out its structural pattern and its functional effects on livelihood security. Summarising the field findings and discussion in previous chapters, many conclusions can be drawn:

1 Whilst rural reform and household responsibility systems (HRS) have successfully encouraged individual or private investments on property or human capital, unfortunately, the negative impacts on social capital have largely been neglected. Reflecting the costs of social capital decline, rural disorganisation in the marginal areas has returned as a result of lack of maintenance of rural infrastructure (e.g. irrigation, terraces, roads), increasing over-cultivation and the breakdown of agricultural extension networks. This suggests that sustainable development in the marginal areas cannot be achieved unless social capital can be greatly enhanced, resulting in a rural reorganisation. In this sense, rural sustainability does not exist outside of rural societies or among disorganised farmers, but is rooted in farmers' communication, co-operation and self-organisation.
2 Adapting to the HRS institution and market economic environment, an informal organisation network, the 'farmer communication network' (FCN) has been widely adopted by households for various purposes from information exchange and mutual production aid to social support and emergency aid. Despite great variety in components and structural pattern, Chapters 6 and 7 have shown that the FCN has positive functions in terms of securing household livelihoods in general, and is more important for households in marginal areas than in valley villages in particular.
3 Whilst the FCN provides a social base for inter-household communication and mutual aid, various types of co-operative groups have been established and developed by farmers themselves to achieve specific objectives related to agricultural production, technological exchange, market exploration and benefit/cost share. Compared with the former, the latter shares features of informality, diversity and reciprocation, and has a more clear 'organisational border' ('membership'), 'leadership', functional division, 'regulations' and so on. In spite of great variation, a hierarchy can be identified regarding the scale and extent of farmer self-organisation, including FCN (shared by all households), neighbourhood production groups (e.g. for seeding), village collective action (e.g. hybrid seeding project), trans-village group (e.g. WG greenhouse in Section 7.1) and rural–urban network (the 'green village' in Section 7.3).
4 Although the potential and contribution from social capital cannot be underestimated, it is merely one of many elements influencing the SRL. It would be a mistake to assume that social capital can be simplified as a standard pattern or that it is always good without negative impacts.

8.3 Innovation model for farmer self-organisation

Sustainable rural livelihoods in marginal areas of China rely largely upon enhancing farmer innovative capacity so as to cope with increasing challenges from both natural and market environments. Missing the dimensions of social capital, mainstream schools of innovation underestimate farmer innovative potential. By contrast, this book holds a 'social practice' approach, which views farmers as the 'first actors' of rural development and innovation. In particular, it emphasises that farmers are not merely participants or receivers of the benefit, but more importantly, explorers, experimenters, creators and final determiners of new technology and organisation (institutions). However, the release of farmer innovative potential is subject to constraints from both the external environment (referring to material, information and policy) and internal 'organisational conditions' (related to social capital and leadership). Linked with the difficulties of communication in marginal areas, 'organisational' scale and extent have become crucial factors in determining the distribution of farmer innovative capacity and its potential release.

The 'organisation hypotheses' above, however, need to be tested by empirical data. Based upon a tailored survey in Zhidan county, Chapter 6 examined the relation between distribution of household innovative capacity and farmer communication network, while Chapter 7 provided detailed case studies regarding the organisation process and mechanisms of farmer innovation. Many conclusions can be drawn from the survey results.

First, alongside geographic environment, resources endowment, infrastructure and human capital, social capital is important in influencing the distribution of household innovative capacity. In other words, social capital is an independent factor in reshaping the distribution of the HIC in the marginal areas. This suggests that by neglecting the dimension of the social capital, conventional innovation studies are likely to overestimate the role of other factors such as geographic environment, research and extension institution, government intervention or human capital.

Second, the innovative function of social capital may be served by various 'organisational' patterns, depending on geographic, technological, social and household demographic factors. The complexity and diversity of organisational patterns of farmer innovation have been revealed in terms of their components (kinship, neighbourhood and friendship), dimensions (family and non-family, within/outside community) and hierarchy (FCN, group, community, rural–urban). It seems to suggest that there is no linear relation between social capital and HIC, or a standard procedure or pattern that is suited to all villages or households. Instead, there are various 'start points' available to meet different 'organisational demands'.

Third, social capital cannot be viewed as either a static existence or simply utility for innovation purpose. Rather, the cases in Chapter 7 have shown that social capital can be accumulated and created step by step with the enhancement of the innovative capacity. As a result, an evolutionary image has emerged: individual technological innovation and inter-household co-operation attract more and more people, both neighbours and relatives outside, leading to positive feedback between social capital and innovative capacity. This positive feedback mechanism, therefore, provides the possibilities not only for new technological innovation organisation to emerge in marginal areas (institutionalisation), but also for technological and institutional interaction towards the creation of a new rural institution instead of the HRS. In this sense, farmer innovation in marginal areas is more than a narrow technological learning or project organisation process, but implies the potential, opportunities and possibilities of rural institutional innovation in which the core actors are not professionals or government, but ordinary people.

Finally, the crucial condition to initiate rural technological and organisational change is an 'innovation leader' who is able to mobilise and organise innovation process based upon the volunteering of participants. The case of the 'green village' (Section 7.3) has indicated that an innovation leader need not be a village resident but must have ability, will and charisma to get local people to join together for a 'common future'. In addition, village history, tradition and even regional ceremonies can be used to initiate innovative co-operation, although sustainable development and innovation are more dependent on the 'institutionalisation' of rural collaboration.

In summarising the research findings above, this book offers a farmer self-organising innovation (FSI) approach as an alternative to outside-led innovation. Regarding the marginal areas of China, FSI has a number of theoretical implications.

1 *Innovative capacity*. It is often the case that the variation in the innovative capacity of farmers is attributed to the geographic environment, access to public resources, education facilities, farmers' attitudes to innovation, etc. In contrast to these linear explanations, the FSI offers an organisational approach by which various relevant factors can be integrated into the farmer innovation system rather than separated from real social processes. The explanatory capacity of the FSI is based on the assumption that farmers are not totally independent individuals but group themselves into an interconnected and interactive whole, which is associated with technology learning and reciprocal co-operation. As a result, the innovative capacity of the rural poor is closely related to the styles and extent of their communication and co-operation.
2 *Technological appropriateness*. The concept of appropriateness is broader than technological or economic consideration, but should include an organisational dimension, because the adaptive and innovative capacity of farmers actually varies with the style and state of farmers' organisation. Many cases identified in the field suggest that the more that farmers communicate and collaborate with each other, the more easily they adopt and absorb a new technology.
3 *Innovative potential*. According to the FSI model, it is important to distinguish between innovative capacity and potential, because the former reflects

the real state of households' communication and co-operation in innovation, while the latter, defined as the sum of all innovation elements and resources, suggests a 'possibility space' for self-organisational development by which all potential innovation resources can be transformed into the real capacity of farmers. If the top-down technology transfer model underestimates farmer innovative capacity due to neglect of indigenous knowledge systems, farmer participation research may overestimate the innovative capacity of marginal people, without a distinction between innovative capacity and potential.

4. *Innovative system.* Farmer innovation practice in the FSI model was revealed through a system approach characterised by: (i) a functional system aimed at household income growth; (ii) a process system from simple information exchange to large-scale innovation networks; (iii) a plural system matching the complexity and diversity of both the natural and social environments; (iv) an open system for urban and professional participation.

As a model, the FSI leaves many questions to be explored: Why has farmer self-organisation been forgotten by development and innovation studies for such a long time? Can the FSI model be applied in central (developed) areas (e.g. east-coast China)? What kinds of institutional environment can be distinguished in terms of the impacts or constraints on the FSI? What kinds of evolutionary stages, development conditions and institutional change can be recognised for self-organising innovation, as a process of institutionalisation from informal to formal innovation organisation?

8.4 Policy implications: interface between insiders and outsiders

Emphasis on farmer self-organisations, however, does not mean that rural development can exclude external assistance. Rather, it is argued that effective development assistance and intervention must be based upon the full utilisation and release of the intrinsic dynamics and innovative potential existing in rural people. This needs a new dimension, to reveal farmers' own communication networks and interactive mechanisms. In this sense, rural sustainability can be viewed as a process of interaction and interface between farmer self-organisation and outside participation.

Based on the circumstances of north Shaanxi, particularly, relevant policy implications and suggestions can be outlined as follows:

- *Encouraging farmer innovation and co-operation.* Adopting a top-down approach, urban-based innovative systems can hardly recognise the value and potential of farmers' innovation (Tillmann 1995). It is also misleading to assume that all farmers are positive innovators. The release of farmers' innovative potential calls for a policy reorientation to encourage rural co-operative innovation.
- *Adjustment of research and extension policies.* With a view to improving the communication between urban professionals and marginalised people, a reform

of the urban-based innovation system needs to include the following points: (i) a procedure or system for farmers' participation in technological choice and innovation decisions related to their production (ICRA 1995); (ii) a stage of professional learning from rural people before they deliver new technologies to farmers or government (Pretty 1995; Scarborough 1996); (iii) a system of collaborative research, experimentation, demonstration and extension through a combination of urban professionals, local cadres and experienced farmers.

- *Promoting urban participation.* Besides the formal extension network and other innovation resources, it is argued that the role of informal urban–rural linkages in rural innovation cannot be underestimated. Similar to the phenomenon of *qiao xiang* on the eastcoast, the fieldwork in Zhidan suggests that 'home conscientiousness' can also be viewed as an important source of access to external technologies, information, markets and consultation for marginalised people. Compared to formal organisational channels, rural–urban networks have advantages in terms of the interface between farmers' demands and innovation organisations.
- *Improving innovative organisations.* Because of the great variety in marginal environments, farmers' innovation and organisation vary greatly. Unfortunately, present development policy can hardly reflect the complexity of marginal environments and farmers' demands because its minimum unit of operation and project implementation is the administrative village, which neglects the difference between sub-villages, and often suffers from road biases. To promote farmer and social participation, it seems necessary to redefine the unit of rural development by changing from the administrative village to the sub-village.

Notes

2 Substainability and farmer innovation in the developing world

1 Technology as a complex social phenomenon can be defined from various angles. Emphasising the nature of multiple dimensions, Jequier (1976) suggests that the term 'technology' consists of hardware (e.g. factories, machine, products or infrastructures) and software (knowledge, know-how, experience, education and organisational forms). Concerning the relation between 'hardware' and 'software', Galtung (1979) presented a formula: technology = technique (e.g. know-how, tools) + structure (social relations or 'mode of production' related to technique application). Furthermore, Marx (1887) saw technology as a social practice involving the interaction between human, nature and society, which leaves ample scope for the participation and performance of various actors, including ordinary workers and farmers. From the perspectives of social process, the terms technology and innovation are often interwoven and overlapped. In keeping with the theme of this book, technological innovation is broadly defined as a social practice related to improving and upgrading production processes, products or systems.

2 It is not easy to distinguish the terms organisation, institution and groups because there are considerable overlaps among them. Institutionalisation or organisational change of farmer participatory research can be used through different ways. Hagmann *et al.* (1998), for instance, attempts to shape the participatory approach into conventionally hierarchical structure, which can be viewed as an intermediate form between top-down technology transfer and bottom-up participatory development.

3 Neglecting the complexity of technology application, TT was first described as the *hypodermic needle model* (Rogers 1983: 272–274) by which TT is simply supposed to be a similar process to mass media, characterised by a direct, immediate and powerful effect on the mass audience (technology adopters), irrespective of the various conditions existing among them. Later, this give way to that of the transfer of complex messages between 'senders' and 'receivers', in which 'linkage catalysts' or 'linkage process facilitators' such as transformers and synthesisers, and extension agents play a crucial role to promote knowledge diffusion and adoption (Havelock 1969).

4 Alternative innovation paths have been explored and expressed in many terms such as: 'intermediate technology', 'farmer-back-farmer' (Rhoades and Booth 1982), 'people's science' (Richards 1985), 'participatory technology development' (ILEIA 1989), 'participatory rural appraisal' (Chambers 1997), and 'farmer-led extension' (Scarborough 1996).

3 Marginal areas and marginalisation in rural China

1 Despite the overlaps between them, marginalisation is differentiated from 'polarisation' in terms of both nature and extent. The former assumes that most people, if not all, can

receive the benefits from economic development to various extents, and gives emphasis to the contribution of geographic factors to regional inequality. The latter, differently, asserts that the development in some regions (or groups) is a result of the underdevelopment in others (regions or groups), and pays more attention to social and class conflict.

2 Many provincial governments might have funding sources for these 'poor counties', outside of central government lists. Compared with central government funding, the provincial funding sources were too small to take into account (World Bank 2001b).

4 Environment and innovation in rural Shaanxi

1 Of a total of 102 'agricultural related counties' in Shaanxi province, ten are actually semi- or urban-dominant counties (districts), which are not included the statistical analysis.

2 Definitions of the Loess Plateau varies. This is a narrow definition based on topography and agricultural climate. In a wider definition, however, the north border of the Loess Plateau is extended to the northeast of the Yellow River, making us an area of 627,000 km^2 (CAS 1991: vii).

6 Farmer innovative capacity and communication networks

1 Labour force in the survey defined as between 18 and 65 years for male and between 18 and 60 years for female. Beyond the scope are defined as 0.5 labour. Boys or girls between 15 and 18 years are viewed as half-labour if they did not enrol in school.

2 Quoted from Chambers and Conway (1992).

3 In Chinese philosophy and culture, according to Min (1992), 'the essential spirit is co-operation, unity, harmony and holism', which particularly considers 'the co-operation of opposites and that things which oppose each other are complementary'.

4 'Close relatives' in the household questionnaire surveys were defined as those relatives with whom this household keeps close contact (e.g. frequently visit each other on main festivals) and who are able to provide help in terms of technology, labour or financial assistance if required. A similar definition was applied to the term, 'close villagers'.

References

Administrative Centre for China Agenda 21 (ACCA) (1998) 'Prevention and control of soil erosion and land degradation in the middle and upper reaches of the Yangtze River'. Online: http://www.acca21.edu.cn/pp5-2.html

Agricultural Regional Planning Institute of Chinese Academy of Agricultural Sciences (ARPI) (1989) Distribution of Middle and Low Productive Farmland and Potential of Grain Growth in China, unpublished report (in Chinese).

——(1992) *Cultivated Land Resource Development and Utilisation in China*, Beijing: Chehui Press (in Chinese).

Anholt, C. and Zijp, W. (1995) 'Participation in agricultural extension', a contribution to the *Participation Sourcebook of World Bank*, Washington, DC: The World Bank.

Aziz, S. (1978) *Rural Development: Learning from China*, London: Macmillan.

Bebbington, A. and Farrington, J. (1992) 'NGO–government interaction in agricultural technology development', in: Edwards, M. and Hulme, D. (eds), *Making a Difference: NGOs and Development in a Changing World*, London: Earthscan.

——(1993) 'Governments, NGOs and agricultural development: perspectives on changing inter-organisational relationships', *Journal of Development Studies*, 29: 199–219.

Benjamin, D., Brandt, L. and Li, G. (2000) 'Markets, human capital, inequality: evidence from rural China', *William Davidson Institute Working Papers Series*, no. 298, Michigan: University of Michigan Business School. Online: http://ideas.uqam.ca/ideas/data/Papers/wdipapers2000-298.html

Bernstein, T.P. and Lu, X.B. (2000) 'Taxation without representation: peasants, the central and the local states in reform China', *The China Quarterly*, 163 (September): 742–763.

Bhalla, A.S. and James, D. (1988) *New Technologies and Development: Experiences in 'Technology Blending'*, Boulder/London: Lynne Rienner Publishers.

Biot, Y., Blaike, P.M., Jackson, C. and Palmer-Jones, R. (1995) 'Rethinking research on land degradation in developing countries', *World Bank Discussion Papers*, no. 289, Washington, DC: The World Bank.

Blackburn, J. and Holland, J. (eds) (1998) *Who Changes? Institutionalising Participation in Development*, London: Intermediate Technology Publications.

Blaikie, P. (1985) *The Political Economy of Soil Erosion in Developing Countries*, London: Longman.

Boyte, H. (1995) 'Beyond deliberation: citizenship as public work', paper delivered at PEGS Conference, 11–12 February 1995. Civic Practices Network. Online: http://www.cpn.org

Brohman, J. (1996) *Popular Development: Rethinking the Theory and Practice of Development*, Oxford: Blackwell Publishers.

Brown, L.R. (1995) *Who Will Feed China? Wake-Up Call for a Small Planet*, New York: W.W. Norton.

——(2001) 'Dust bowl threatening China's future', Earth Policy Institute, 23 May 2001. Online: http://www.earth-policy.org/Alerts/Alert13.htm

Burkey, S. (1993) *People First: A Guide to Self-reliant, Participatory Rural Development*, London: Zed.

Cannon, T. and Jenkins, A. (1990) *The Geography of Contemporary China*, London: Routledge.

Cao, J.Q. (2000) *China Along the Yellow River – A Scholar's Observations and Meditations on Chinese Rural Society*, Shanghai: Wenyi Press (in Chinese). English summary available Online: http://www.usembassy-china.org.cn/english/sandt/china-along-yellow-river.htm

Carney, D. (ed.) (1998) *Sustainable Rural Livelihoods: What Contribution can Make*? London: DFID.

Chao, Y.Z. and Zhou, L. (1999) 'Water storage cellar in the Loess Plateau: a system review' (in Chinese), posted in *Human & Nature in Harmony*. Online: http://home.enviroinfo.org.cn/FORUM/Zoulan/index.html

Chambers, R. (1983) *Rural Development: Putting the Last First*, New York: Longman S & T.

——(1988) *Sustainable Rural Livelihoods: A Strategy for People, Environment and Development*, Institute of Development Studies, University of Sussex.

——(1997) *Whose Reality Counts? Putting the First Last*, London: Intermediate Technology Publications.

——and Conway, G. (1992) 'Sustainable rural livelihoods: practical concepts for the 21st century', *Discussion Paper*, no. 296, Institute of Development Studies (IDS), University of Sussex, UK.

Chambers, R., Pacey, A. and Thrupp, L.A. (eds) (1989) *Farmer First: Farmer Innovation and Agricultural Research*, London: Intermediate Technology Publications.

Chen, Q.W. and Mu, X.M. (2000) 'State, causes and countermeasures of dry-up in Yellow River', *Journal of National Resources*, 15: 1 (in Chinese). Online: http://www.enviroinfo.org.cn/RESEARCH/Policies_and_Countermeasures/index.html

Chen, S.H. and Wang, Y. (2001) 'China's growth and poverty reduction: trends between 1990 and 1999', *Working Paper – Macroeconomics and Growth*, no. 2651, Washington, DC: The World Bank.

Chen, Y.S., Yao, Z.J. and He, X.W. (1999) 'Lessons learning from flood in 1998 and prevention strategy', *Journal of National Resources*, 14: 1 (in Chinese). Online: http://home.enviroinfo.org.cn/RESEARCH/Flood_and_Drought/index.html

Chenery, H., Ahluwalia, M.S., Bell, C.L.G., Duloy, J.H. and Jolly, R. (1974) *Redistribution with Growth*, London: Oxford University Press.

Cheng, X. (1992) 'Sustainable agricultural development in China', *World Development*, 8: 1127–1144.

China's Agricultural Scientific Networks (CASN) (2002) 'Policy issues transforming over-cultivation to forest and pasture use in upstream of Yangze River' (in Chinese). Online: http://www.9e.net.cn/ban/zhuanjialuntan/zhuanjia/zhuangjia.htm

China Daily (2001) 'Environment in west China keeps worsening', 30 December 2001.

China Internet Information Center (CIIC) (2002) *China in Brief*, Beijing: CIIC. Online: http://www.china.org.cn/e-china/administrative/administrative.htm (July).

China Population Information and Research Center (CPIRC) (2001) 'Population, top challenge in china's western development'. Online: http://www.cpric.org.cn/cpircint.htm

Chinese Academy of Sciences (CAS) (1991) *A Study on Rational Distribution and Harmony Development of Agriculture, Forest and Animal Breeding in the Loess Plateau, Survey Term for Loess Plateau Resources and Environment*, Beijing: Kexue Press (in Chinese).

Chinese Academy of Sciences (CAS) (1992) *Survival and Development: A Study of China's Long-term Development*, Beijing: Kexue Press (in Chinese).

Coleman, J. (1990) *Foundations of Social Theory*, Cambridge, MA: Harvard University Press.

Conway, G.R. and Barbier, E.B. (1990) *After the Green Revolution: Sustainable Agriculture for Development*, London: Earthscan.

Delman, J. (1991) *Agricultural Extension in Renshou County, China: A Case-Study of Bureaucratic Intervention for Agricultural Innovation and Change*, Aarhus, Denmark: Institute of East Asian Studies.

Edmonds, R.L. (1994) *Patterns of China's Lost Harmony: A Survey of the Country's Environmental Degradation and Protection*, London: Routledge.

——(ed.) (1999) *Managing the Chinese Environment* (in series of Studies on Contemporary China), Oxford: Oxford University Press.

Edwards, M. and Hulme, D. (eds) (1992) *Making a Difference: NGOs and Development in a Changing World*, London: Earthscan.

Ellis, F. (1992) *Agricultural Policies in Developing Countries*, Cambridge: Cambridge University Press.

——(1998) 'Livelihood diversification and sustainable rural livelihoods', in: Carney, D. (ed.), *Sustainable Rural Livelihoods: What Contribution can Make*? London: DFID.

Fan, C.C. (1997) 'Uneven development and beyond: regional development theory in post-Mao China', *International Journal of Urban and Regional Research*, 21, 4: 620–639.

Fan, S. and Pardey, P. (1997) 'Research, productivity, and output growth in Chinese agriculture', *Journal of Development Economics*, 53: 115–137.

Fang, J.Q. and Xie, Z.R. (1994) 'Deforestation in preindustrial China: the Loess Plateau region as an example', *Chemosphere*, 29, 5: 983–999.

Friberg, M. and Hettne, B. (1985) 'The greening of the World: towards a non-deterministic model of global progresses', in: Addo, H., Amin, S., Aseniero, G., Frank, A.G., Friberg, M., Forbel, F., Heinrich, J., Hettne, B., Kreye, O. and Seki, H. (eds), *Development as Social Transformation: Reflections on the Global Probematique*, London: Hodder & Stoughton, pp. 204–270.

Galtung, J. (1979) *Development, Environment, and Technology: Towards a Technology for Self-reliance*, quoted from Willoughby (1990), p. 15.

Gao, J.C. (2001), 'The peasants are suffering, the villages are very poor', English version posted online: http://www.usembassy-china.org.cn/english/sandt/peasantsuffering.html

Glaeser, B. (ed.) (1987) *Learning from China: Development and Environment in Third World Countries*, London: Allen & Unwin.

Glantz, M.H., Ye, Q. and Ge, Q.S. (2001) 'China's western region development strategy and the urgent need to address creeping environmental problems', *Arid Lands Newsletter*, 49, May/June.

Goodman, D.S.G. (ed.) (1989) *China's Regional Development*, London: Routledge for The Royal Institute of International Affairs.

Grootaert, C. (1998) 'Social capital: the missing link'. *World Bank Social Capital Initiative Working Paper*, no. 5, Washington, DC: The World Bank.

Gu, C., Shen, J., Wong, K.Y. and Zhen, F. (2001) 'Regional polarization under the socialist-market system since 1978: a case study of Guangdong province in south China', *Environment and Planning A*, 33, 1: 97–119.

Hagmann, J. *et al.* (1998) 'Scaling-up of participatory approaches through institutionalisation in government services: the case of agricultural extension in Masvingo Province, Zimbabwe', in: Blackburn, J. and Holland, J. (eds), *Who Changes? Institutionalising Participation in Development*, London: Intermediate Technology Publications, pp. 47–56.

Hamilton, N.A. (1995) Learning to learn with farmers. PhD thesis, Wageningen Agricultural University, Netherlands.

Han, N.Y. (2000) 'Policy issues of sustainable management on China's natural protection zones', *Journal of Natural Resources* (in Chinese), 15, 3.

Han, T. (2000) 'China: a shared poverty to uneven wealth'? Online: http://www.gwu.edu/~econ270/Taejoon.html

Hanstad, T. and Li, P. (1995) *Land Reform in China: Auctioning Rights to Wasteland*, Seattle: The Rural Development Institute.

Hao, H. (2000) 'Deep thoughts about dust sandstorm', *People's Daily* (in Chinese), 12 April 2000.

Hao, K.M. (2001) 'The dream of future sustainable development in China', *Science and Technology Daily* (Chinese), 8 August 2001. Online: http://www.enviroinfo.org.cn/Sustainable_Development/d080921_en.htm

Hardin, G. (1968) 'The tragedy of the commons', *Science*, 162: 1243–1248.

Harriss, J. (ed.) (1982) *Rural Development: Theories of Peasant Economy and Agrarian Change*, London: Hutchinson & Co. Ltd.

Havelock, R. (1969) *Planning for Innovation*, Ann Arbor, University of Michigan, Institute for Social Research.

Hayami, Y. and Rattan, V.W. (1985) *Agricultural Development: An International Perspective*, Baltimore: Johns Hopkins University Press.

He, D.F. (2001) 'Mission of Chinese NGOs in poverty alleviation of China,' keynote to the International Conference on NGO poverty reduction policy, 28–30 October 2001, Beijing (in Chinese). Online: http://www.fupin.org.cn/ngohy/zhutibaogao.htm

He, Q.L. (1998) *China and the Pitfalls of Modernization*, Beijing: Today's China Publishers (in Chinese).

Heilig, G.K. (1999) *Can China Feed Itself? A System for Evaluation of Policy Options*, International Institute for Applied System Analysis (IIASA), Laxenburg: IIASA. Online: http://www.iiasa.ac.at/Research/LUC/ChinaFood/index_m.htm

Hettne, B. (1990) *Development Theory and the Three Worlds*, Harlow: Longman Scientific & Technical.

Hoff, K., Braverman, A. and Stiglitz, J.E. (eds) (1993) *The Economics of Rural Organisation: Theory, Practice, and Policy*, Oxford: Oxford University Press.

Holland, J. and Blackburn, J. (eds) (1998) 'Whose voice?' *Participatory Research and Policy Change*, London: Intermediate Technology Publications.

Hossain, S.I. (1997) 'Making education in China equitable and efficient', *Policy Research Working Papers*, Washington, DC: The World Bank.

Huang, S.J. (2002) 'Why is continuous growth of China's desert areas despite non-stopped treatment' (in Chinese). Online: http://www.china.org.cn/chinese/OP-c/111735.htm (2 February 2002).

Information Centre for Low External Input and Sustainable Agriculture (ILEIA) (1989) *Participatory Technology Development in Sustainable Agriculture*, Leusden, The Netherlands: ILEIA.

International Centre for Development Oriented Research in Agriculture (ICRA) (1995) 'Farmer differentiation and participation in agricultural development planning in Longhui Watershed, Jiangxi, China', Working Document Series, no. 43, Wageningen, The Netherlands.

International Food Policy Research Institute (IFPRI) (2001) 'Education and agricultural research key to reducing rural poverty in China', research findings released at International Conference on Rural Investments, Growth and Poverty, 5 November 2001. Online: http://www.ifpri.cgiar.org/pressrel/2001/110501.htm

International Geographic Union (2001) *Commission Newsletter*, Commission on Evolving Issues of Geographical Marginality in the Early 21st Century World, March 2001. Online: http://www.swissgeography.ch/igucevol.htm

Jalan, J. and Ravallion, M. (1997) 'Spatial poverty traps?' *World Bank Working Paper Series*, no. 1862, Washington, DC: World Bank. Online: http://www.worldbank.org/html/dec/Publications/Workpapers/WPS1800series/wps1862/wps1862.pdf

Jequier, N. (1976) *Appropriate Technology: Problems and Promises*, Paris: OECD Development Centre.

Johnson, B.F. and Kilby, P. (1975) *Agriculture and Structural Transformation*, New York: Oxford University Press.

Johnston, F.M. (1999) 'Beyond regional analysis: manufacturing, urban employment and spatial inequality in China', *The China Quarterly*, no. 157, March.

Jussila, H., Leimgruber, W. and Majoral, R. (eds) (1998) *Perceptions of Marginality. Theoretical Issues and Regional Perceptions of Marginality in Geographical Space*. Aldershot: Ashgate.

——, Majoral, R. and Cravidao, F. (eds) (2000) *Globalisation and Marginalisation in Geographical Space. Political, Economic and Social Issues of Development at the Dawn of the New Millennium*. Aldershot: Ashgate.

Kanbur, R. and Zhang, X.B. (1999) 'Which regional inequality? The evolution of rural–urban and inland–coastal inequality in China from 1983–1995', *Journal of Comparative Economics*, 27, 4: 686–701.

Khan, A.R. (1998) 'Poverty in China in the period of globalization: new evidence on trend and pattern', Dicussion Paper, no. 22, *Issues in Development*, Geneva: International Labour Organisation. Online: http://www.ilo.org/public/english/employment/strat/publ/iddp22.htm#1

Kindopp, J. (2000) 'A new hope for rural China? – NGOs in China', Online: http://www.chinaonline.com/commentary_analysis/instreform/currentnews/secure/c00051949.asp

Krugman, P.R. (1996) *The Self-organisation Economy*, Cambridge, MA: Blackwell Publishers.

Lane, J. (1995) 'Non-governmental organisations and participatory development: the concept in theory versus the concept in practice', in: Nelson, N. and Wright, S. (eds), *Power and Participatory Development: Theory and Practice*, London: Intermediate Technology Publications.

Lea, D. and Chaudhri, P. (eds) (1983) *Rural Development and the State: Contradictions and Dilemmas in Developing Countries*, London: Methuen.

Leeming, F. (ed.) (1993) *The Changing Geography of China*, Oxford: Blackwell.

Lele, S.M. (1991) 'Sustainable development: a critical review', *World Development*, 19, 6: 607–621.

Li, T.Y. and Zhang, J.S. (1998) 'Returns to education under collective and household farming in China', *Journal of Development Economics*, 56, 2: 307–335.

Li, Z. (ed.) (2000) *Sustainable Development of Rural China in 21st Century*, Conference Collection. Beijing: Shike Wenxian Press (in Chinese).

Lin, Y.F. (1995) 'Endowments, technology, and factor markets: a natural experiment of induced institutional innovation from China's rural reform', *American Journal of Agricultural Economics*, 77, 2: 231–242.

—— and Li, Z. (1995) 'Current issues in China's rural areas', *Oxford Review of Economic Policy*, 11, 4: 85–97.

—— and Zhang, F. (1997) 'The effects of China's rural policies on the sustainable agriculture', paper for the *11th Biannual Workshop on Economy and Environment in SE Asia in Singapore*. Online: http://www.eepsea.org/publications/specialp2/ACF348.html

Liu, X.Y. and Wu, P.T. (2000) 'Review of research and application on rainwater catchment system', *Journal of Natural Resources*, 15, 2 (in Chinese). Online: http://home.enviroinfo.org.cn/RESEARCH/Regional_Planning_and_Development/index.html

Liu, Z.Y. (1994) *About China's Path of Agricultural Development*, Beijing: Fazhan Press (in Chinese).

Lipton, M. (1977) *Why Poor People Stay Poor: Urban Bias in World Development*, London: Temple Smith.

Long, N. and Villarreal, M. (1993) 'Exploring development interfaces: from the transfer of knowledge to the transformation of meaning' in: Schuurman, J. (ed.), *Beyond the Impasse: New Directions in Development Theory*, London & New Jersey: Zed Books.

Lyons, T.P. (1998) 'Intraprovincial disparities in China: Fujian province, 1978–1995', *Economic Geography*, 74, 4: 405–425.

Marx, K. (1887) 'Capital, a critique of political economy' (Vol. I), Quoted from Willoughby, K.W. (1990). *Technology Choice: A Critique of the Appropriate Technology Movement*, London: Westview Press.

Min, J.Y. (1992) 'Ideas of co-operation and struggle in Chinese philosophy, and its worldwide significance', in: Combs, A. (ed.), *Co-operation: Beyond the Age of Competition*, Philadelphia: Gordon and Breach, pp. 86–95.

Ministry of Agriculture of China (MOA) (1999) *Achievements of China's Rural Development in the Past Half Century* (in Chinese), internet version, Beijing: MOA. Online: http://www.agri.gov.cn/Agri50/ncjj50/

Moore, W.E. (1963) *Social Change*, Englewood, N.J.: Prentice Hall.

Morduch, J. and Sicuklar, T. (1998) 'Politics, growth, and inequality in rural China: does it pay to join the Party'? Online: http://www.wws.princeton.edu/~rpds/macarthur/downloads/politi~1.pdf

Muldavin, S.S. (1996) 'Impacts of reform on environmental sustainability in rural China', *Journal of Contemporary Asia*, 26, 3: 289–322.

Mullen, J. (2000) 'Support for very poor and marginalized individuals through appropriate social protection', *SD SCOPE Paper,* no. 3. Social Development Department, London: DFID.

Mundy, P.A. and Compton, J.L. (1995) 'Indigenous communication and indigenous knowledge', in: Warren, M.D., Slikkerveer, L.J. and Brokensha, D. (eds), *The Cultural Dimension of Development: Indigenous Knowledge System*, London: Intermediate Technology Publications.

Natural Bureau of Statistics of China (NBS) (2000) *Statistical Tables of Regional Development*, Beijing: NBS (in Chinese).

Natural Bureau of Statistics of China (NBS) (2001) *Statistical Tables of National Agricultural Census*, Beijing: NBS (in Chinese).

National Resource Development Institute in National Planning Committee (NRDI) (1996) *China's Environment Report in 1995* (in Chinese).

Narayan, D., Patel, R., Schafft, K., Rademacher, A. and Koch-Schulte, S. (2000) *Voices of the Poor: Can Anyone Hear Us*? New York: Oxford University Press, published for the World Bank.

Nicolis, G. and Prigogine, I. (1977) *Self-organisation in Non-equilibrium Systems*, New York: Wiley Interscience.

Oi, J.C. (1993) 'Reform and urban bias in China', *Journal of Development Studies*, 29, 4: 129–149.

Ostrom, E. (1998) *Social Capital: A Fad or Fundamental Concept*? Center for the Study of Institutions, Population and Environmental Change, Indiana University, USA.

Park, A., Rozelle, S., Wong, C. and Ren, C. (1996) 'Distributional consequences of reforming local public finance in China', *The China Quarterly*, 147: 751–778.

Pottier, J. (ed.) (1993) *Practising Development: Social Science Perspectives*, London and New York: Routledge.

Pretty, J. (1995) *Regenerating Agriculture: Policies and Practice for Sustainability and Self-reliance*, London: Earthscan.

Pretty, J. and Hine, R. (1999) 'Participatory appraisal for community assessment: principles and methods', Centre for Environment and Society, University of Essex. Online: http://www2.essex.ac.uk/ces/

——(2001) *Reducing Food Poverty with Sustainable Agriculture: A Summary of New Evidence*, Final report from the 'SAFT_World' (The Potential of Sustainable Agriculture to Feed the World) Research Project, February 2001, Centre for Environment and Society, University of Essex, Online: http://www2.essex.ac.uk/ces/ResearchProgrammes/CESOccasionalPapers/

Pretty, J. and Ward, H. (2001) 'Social capital and the environment', *World Development,* 29, 2: 209–227.

Prigogine, I. and Stengers, I. (1985) *Order Out of Chaos*, New York: Bantam.

Piazza, A. and Liang, E.H. (1998) 'Reducing absolute poverty in China: current status and issues', *Journal of International Affairs*, 52, 1: 253–273.

Putnam, R.D., Leonardi, R. and Nanetti, R.Y. (1993) *Making Democracy Work: Civic Traditions in Modern Italy*, Princeton, NJ: Princeton University Press.

Ravallion, M. and Jalan, J. (1999) 'China's lagging poor areas', *The American Economic Review*, 89, 2: 301–305.

Redclift, M. (1990) 'The role of agricultural technology in sustainable development,' in: Lowe, P. (ed.), *Technological Change and the Rural Environment*, London: David Fulton, pp. 81–103.

Research Centre for the Rural Economy (RCRE) (1996) *Farmer's Technical Associations in China's Agricultural Development: Putting Farmers First*, prepared for ODI 'Research and Farmers' Organisations', London: ODI (December 1996).

Rhoades, R.E. and Boot, R.H. (1982) 'Farmer-back-to-farmer: a model for generating acceptable agricultural technology', *Agricultural Administration*, 11: 127–137.

Richards, P. (1985) *Indigenous Agricultural Revolution*, London: Routledge.

Riskin, C. (1994) 'Chinese rural poverty: marginalized or dispersed?' *American Economic Review*, 84, 2: 281–284.

——, Zhao, R. and Li, S. (eds) (2001) *China's Retreat from Equality: Income Distribution and Economic Transition*, Armonk and London: M.E. Sharpe, Inc.

Rivera, W. (1997) 'China on the road to unsustainability: agriculture and natural resources in the northwest', *American Journal of Chinese Studies*, 4 (October): 198–208.

Robb, C. (1998) 'PRAs: a review of the World Bank's experience', in: Holland, J. and Blackburn, J. (eds), *Participations Research and Policy Change*, London: Intermediate. Technology Publications, pp. 131–142.

Robinson, M. (1992) 'NGOs and rural poverty alleviation: implications for scale-up', in: Edwards, M. and Hulme, D. (eds), *Making a Difference: NGOs and Development in a Changing World*, London: Earthscan.

Rogers, E. (1983) *Diffusion of Innovations*, New York: Free Press.

Roling, N. and Engel, P. (1989) 'IKS and knowledge management: utilising indigenous knowledge in institutional knowledge system', in: Warren, D.M., Slikkerveer, L.J. and Titilola, S.O. (eds), *Indigenous Knowledge System: Implication for Agriculture and International Development*, Iowa: Iowa University Press, pp. 101–111.

Röling, N.R. and Wagemakers, M.A. (eds) (1997) *Social Learning for Sustainable Agriculture*, Cambridge: Cambridge University Press.

Rozelle, S., Huang, J.K. and Zhang, L.X. (1997) 'Poverty, population and environmental degradation in China', *Food Policy*, 22, 3: 229–251.

Ruddle, K. and Rondinelli, D.A. (1983) *Transforming Natural Resources for Human Development: a Resource Systems Framework for Development Policy*, Resource Systems Theory and Methodology Series, Shibuya-ku: United Nations University Press.

Rycroft, R.W. and Kash, D.E. (1999) *The Complexity Challenges: Technological Innovation for the 21st Century*, London and New York: Pinter.

Qu, G.P. and Li, J.C. (1994) *Population and Environment in China*, London: Paul Chapman.

Scarborough, V. (ed.) (1996) 'Farmer-led approaches to extension', papers presented at a Workshop in the Philippines, July 1995, *AgRen Network Papers*, no. 59, London: ODI.

Schieve, W.C. and Allen, P.M. (eds) (1982) *Self-organisation and Dissipative Structures: Applications in the Physical and Social Sciences*, Austin: University of Texas Press.

Schultz, T.W. (1964) *Transforming Traditional Agriculture*, New Haven, CT: Yale University Press.

Schumacher, E.F. (1974) *Small is Beautiful: A Study of Economics as if People Mattered*, London: Abacus.

Schumpeter, J. (1934) *The Theory of Economic Development*, Cambridge, MA: Harvard University Press.

Scoones, I. and Thompson, J. (eds) (1994) *Beyond Farmer First: Rural People's Knowledge, Agricultural Research and Extension Practice*, London: Intermediate Technology Publication.

Selden, M. (1997) 'China's rural welfare systems: crisis and transformation', *Hong Kong Journal of Social Sciences*, 10, Autumn.

Shaanxi's Agricultural Department of Provincial Government (SAD) (1996) *Abstract of 1995 Shaanxi Agricultural Statistics*, internal document in Chinese, unpublished.

——(1997) *Statistical Book of Shaanxi Agricultural Extension*, internal document, unpublished.

Shaanxi's Agricultural Regionalisation Office (SARO) (1989) *Agricultural Regionalisation of Shaanxi Province*, Xian: Xian Ditu Press (in Chinese).

Shaanxi's Bureau of Statistical (SBS) (1990) *Statistical Yearbook of Shaanxi 1990*, Beijing: China Statistical Press (in Chinese).

Shaanxi Poverty Reduction Office (SPRO) (1997) *Statistical Table of Rural Poverty Population in National and Provincial Assigned Poor Counties*, internal document in Chinese, unpublished.

Shaanxi Water Resource Department (SWRD) (1997a) *Statistics of Shaanxi Drought (1949–1997)*, internal document in Chinese, unpublished.

——(1997b) *Sediment Statistics on Shaanxi Reservoirs*, internal document in Chinese, unpublished.

Shan, L. and Chen, G.L. (1993) *Theory and Practice of Dryland Farming in Loess Plateau*, Beijing: Kexue Press (in Chinese).

Shen, H., Zhou, L.A. and Chen, S.L. (1992) *Peasants in Marginal Areas of China: a Study of Poverty Generation Mechanisms*, Beijing: Renming Press (in Chinese).

Shen, X.P. (1999) 'Spatial inequality of rural industrial development in China, 1989–1994', *Journal of Rural Studies*, 15, 12: 179–200.

Silverberg, G., Dosi, G. and Orsenigo, L. (1988) 'Innovation, diversity, and diffusion: a self-organisation model', *Economic Journal*, 98: 1032–1054.

Smil, V. (1993) *China's Environmental Crisis: An Inquiry into the Limits of National Development*, Armonk, NY: M.E. Sharpe.

——(1997) *Environmental Problems in China: Estimates of Economic Costs*, Honolulu: East-West Center.

Sun, H., Shen, L.Q., Shi, Y.L., Zhang, Q.J. and Zhang, Q.L. (eds) (1994) *Agricultural Natural Resources and Regional Development of China*, Nanjing: Jangshu Keji Press (in Chinese).

Sundobo, J. (1998) *The Theory of Innovation: Entrepreneurs, Technology and Strategy*, Cheltenham and Northampton: Edward Elgar.

Tillmann, H.J. (1995) 'The role of Chinese rural people's knowledge in sustainable agriculture and rural development', presented to *European Conference on Agricultural and Rural Development in China*, Vol. IV, 10–12 November 1995, Manchester, UK.

Trupp, L.A. (1989) 'Legitimizing local knowledge: scientized packages or enpowerment for third world people', in: Warren, D.M., Slikkerveer, L.J. and Titilola, S.O. (eds), *Indigenous Knowledge System: Implication For Agriculture and International Development*, Iowa: Iowa University Press, pp. 138–150.

Xu, W. and Tan, K.C. (1995) *Chinese Agroecosystem: Health and Sustainability*, Armonk, NY: M.E. Sharpe.

Vivian, J.M. (1992) 'Foundations for sustainable development: participation, empowerment and local resource management', in: Ghai, D. and Vivian, J.M. (eds), *Grassroots Environmental Action: People's Participation in Sustainable Development*, London and New York: Routledge.

Walker, D.H., Sinclair, F.L. and Thapa, B. (1995) 'Incorporation of indigenous knowledge and perspectives in agroforestry development: review of methods and their application', *Agroforestry System*, 30, 1–2: 235–248.

Wang, G.H. (1994) *Rural Modernisation and Peasants in China*, Guiyang: Guizhou Renming Press (in Chinese).

Wang, S.G. (1995) 'The diffusion of agricultural technology in poor areas of south-west China: the role of farmer's organisation and village government', *China Information*, 10, 3/4: 141–155.

——and Hu, A.G. (1999) *The Political Economy of Uneven Development: The Case of China*, Armont, NY: M.E. Sharpe.

West, L.A. and Wong, P.W. (1995) 'Fiscal decentralisation and growing regional disparities in rural China', *Oxford Review of Economic Policy*, 11, 4: 70–85.

Willoughby, K.W. (1990) *Technology Choice: A Critique of the Appropriate Technology Movement*, London: Westview Press, Intermediate Technology Publications.

World Bank (1975) 'Rural Development' *Sector Policy Paper*, Washington, DC: The World Bank.

——(1990) *Nepal: Development Performance and Prospects*, Washington, DC: The World Bank.

——(1999) *Accelerating China's Rural Transformation*, Washington, DC: The World Bank.

——(2001a) *China: Air, Land and Water – Environmental Priorities for a New Millennium*, Washington, DC: The World Bank.

——(2001b) *China: Overcoming Rural Poverty*, Washington, DC: The World Bank.

World Commission on Environment and Development (WCED) (1987) *Our Common Future*, Oxford: Oxford University Press.

World Resource Institute (WRI) (1999) *World Resources 1998–99: China's Helath and Environment*, Washington, DC: World Resources Institute.

Xinhua News Agency (XNA) (2000) 'China stress overall economic protection', 23 August 2000, Beijing: Xinhua New Agency.

Yao, J.F., Yang, L.M., Fang, Y., Zhuang, P.Z., Ye, J.Y. and Xiu, H. (1996) *Rural Non-governmental Organisations in China: A Study on Rural Specialised Technology Associations*, Beijing: Nongye Keji Press (in Chinese).

Yao, S.J. (2000) 'Economic development and poverty reduction in China over 20 years of reforms', *Economic Development and Cultural Change*, 48, 4: 447–474.

——and Liu, J.R. (1998) 'Economic reforms and regional segmentation in rural China', *Regional Studies*, Cambridge, November 1998.

Ye, Q.C., Wu, X.D., Yang, Q.Y., Tang, K.L., Qian, Y.Y., Zeng, Q.H. and Xong, G.Q. (eds) (1995) *Researches on Environmental Changes of the Yellow River Basin and Laws of Water and Sediment Transportation*, Jinan: Shandong Keji Press (in Chinese).

Yin, R.S. (1998) 'Forestry and the environment in China: the current situation and strategic choices', *World Development*, 26, 12: 2153–2167.

Yonggong, L. (1998) 'Institutional and policy reform of rural extension in China during the transition towards a market economy', in: *Training for Agricultural and Rural Development 1997–98*, Rome: FAO. Online: http://www.fao.org/docrep/W9699E/w9699e09.htm

Zhang, X.B. and Fan, S.G. (2000) 'Public investment and regional inequality in rural China', *EPTD Discussion Paper*, no. 71, Washington, DC: International Food Policy Research Institute.

Zhang, X.S. and Chui, Z.H. (2002) 'Adjustment of national income structure: the key for farmer income growth' (in Chinese), posted in website of *China's Agricultural Scientific Networks* (CASN). Online: http://www.9e.net.cn/ban/zhuanjialuntan/zhuanjia/article/nongminzhengshou.htm

Zheng, Y.S. and Qian, Y.H. (1998) *Grave Concerns – Problems of Sustainable Development for China*, Beijing: Dangdai Zhongguo Press (in Chinese).

Zhidan's Agricultural Regionalisation Office (ZARO) (1985) *Agricultural Resources and Regional Planning of Zhidan County*, internal document in Chinese, unpublished.

Zhidan Chronicle Edition Group (ZCEG) (1997) *Annals of Zhidan County*, Xian: Shaanxi Renmin Press (in Chinese).

Zhidan County Agricultural Department (ZCAD) (1990) *Zhidan County's Agricultural Annals*, internal document in Chinese, unpublished.

Zhidan Planning and Statistical Office (ZPSO) (1996) *Statistical Yearbook of Zhidan in 1995*, internal document in Chinese, unpublished.

Zhidan Rural Policy Office (ZRPO) (1996) *A Summary Report on Zhidan's Property Reform*, internal document in Chinese, unpublished.

Zhong, Z.R. (1999) 'Natural resources planning, management, and sustainable use in China', *Resources Policy*, 25: 211–220.

Zhu, L. and Jiang, Z.Y. (1996) *Public Works and Poverty Alleviation in Rural China*, Commack, NY: Nova Science.

Zhu, Z. and Wang, T. (1993) 'Trends in desertification and its rehabilitation in China', *Desertification Control Bulletin*, 22: 27–30.

Index